DEEP DIGS!

Cartoons of the Miners' Strike

D1806528

A benefit book for
Women against Pit Closures

Pluto Press

First published in 1985 by Pluto Press Limited,
The Works, 105a Torriano Avenue, London NW5 2RX
and Pluto Press Australia Limited, PO Box 199, Leichhardt,
New South Wales 2040, Australia

7 6 5 4 3 2 1

89 88 87 86 85

Cover designed by James Beveridge

Printed in Great Britain by Photobooks (Bristol) Limited
Bound by W.H. Ware & Sons Limited, Clevedon, Avon

ISBN 0 7453 0088 X

Publisher's Note

Thanks to Jeremy Banx whose idea this book was, and
to the many cartoonists who generously donated their
humour. Most of the cartoons in *Deep Digs* are original.
We would like to thank The *Guardian*, *New Society*,
Labour Weekly and *City Limits* for allowing us to
reproduce those cartoons that first appeared in their
publications. All royalties from the book are going to
Women Against Pit Closures – whose essential work
continues.

'I've got a letter from my Dad saying no corporal punishment'

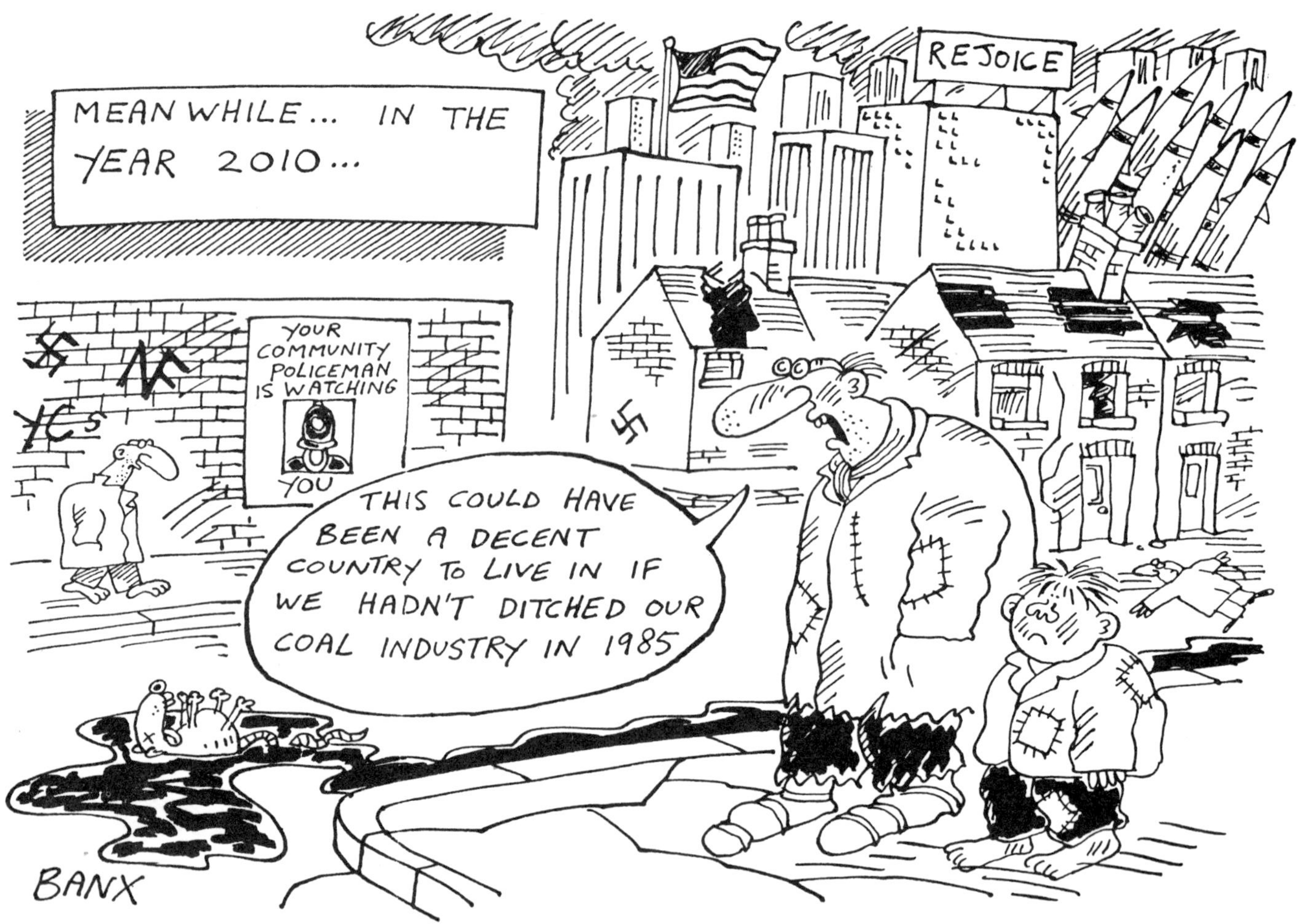
MEANWHILE... IN THE YEAR 2010...
REJOICE
YOUR COMMUNITY POLICEMAN IS WATCHING YOU
THIS COULD HAVE BEEN A DECENT COUNTRY TO LIVE IN IF WE HADN'T DITCHED OUR COAL INDUSTRY IN 1985
BANX

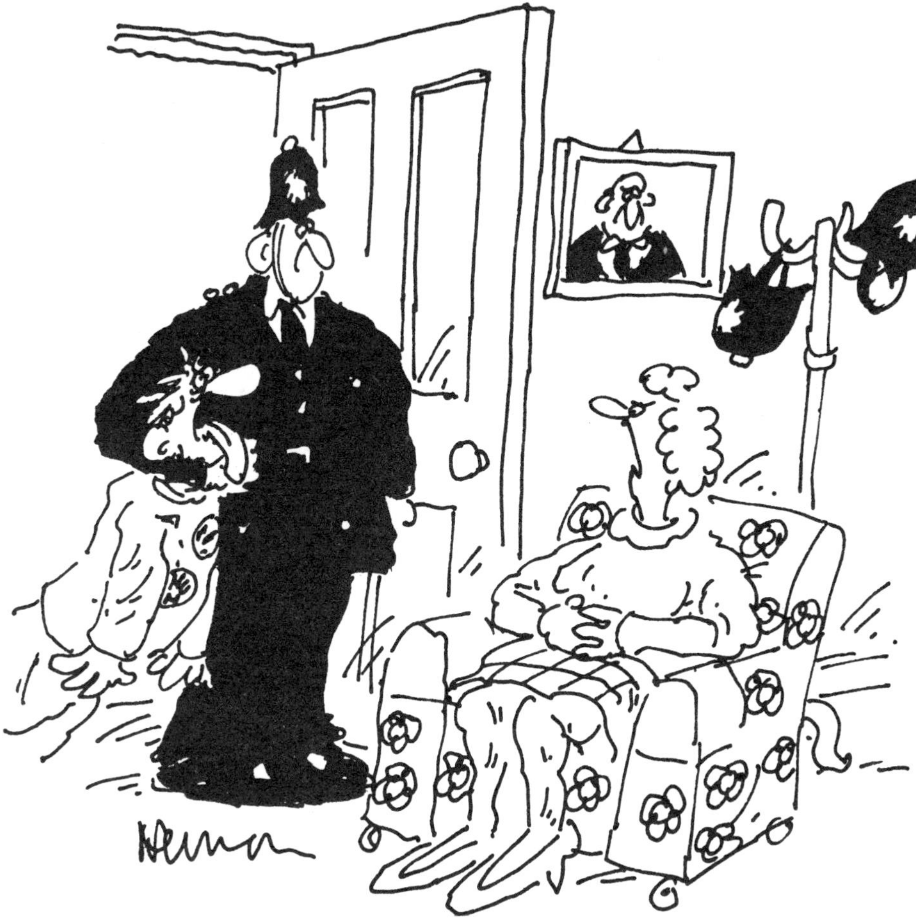

'I just wish you'd stop bringing your work home with you'

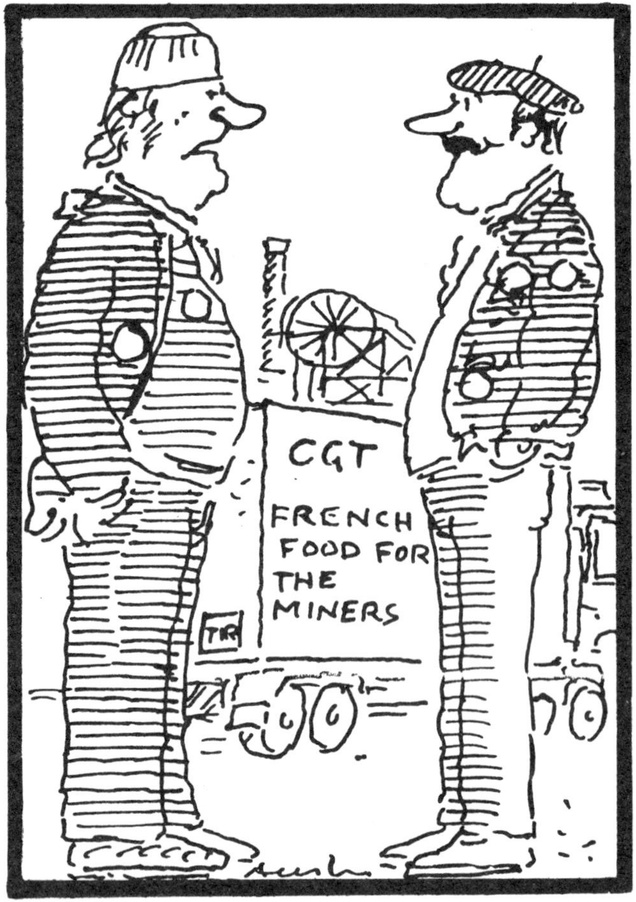
CGT
FRENCH
FOOD FOR
THE
MINERS
TIR

‘I thought *Cordon Bleu* meant a line of policemen’

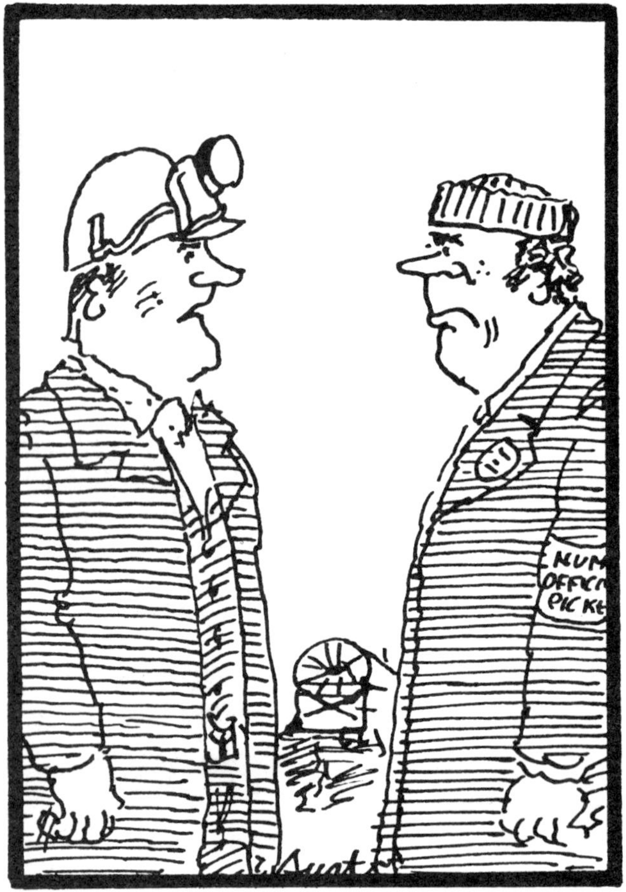
NUM

‘I’m going back to work, but I’ll withhold that portion of my income tax that goes to the police’

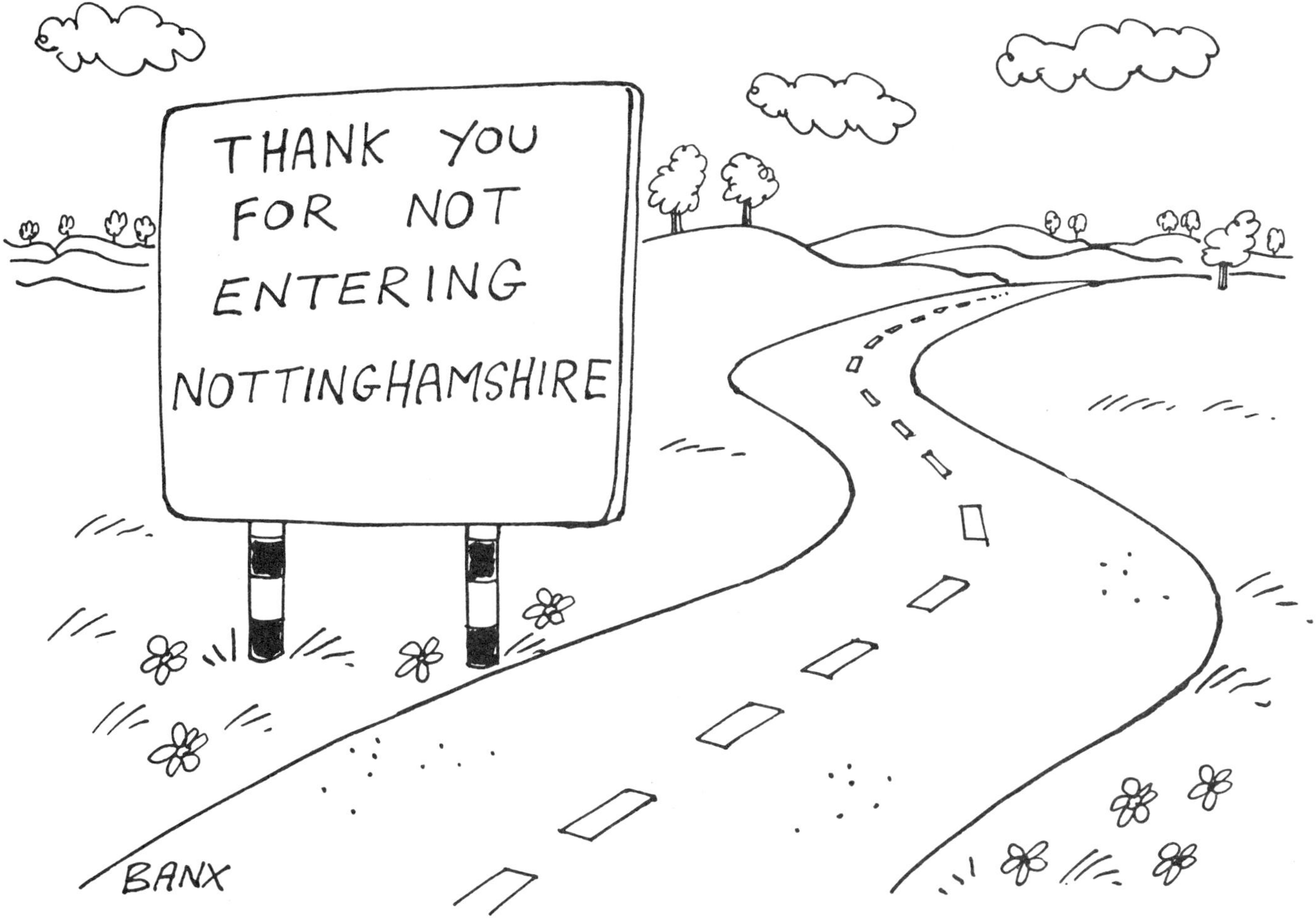
THANK YOU FOR NOT ENTERING NOTTINGHAMSHIRE
BANX

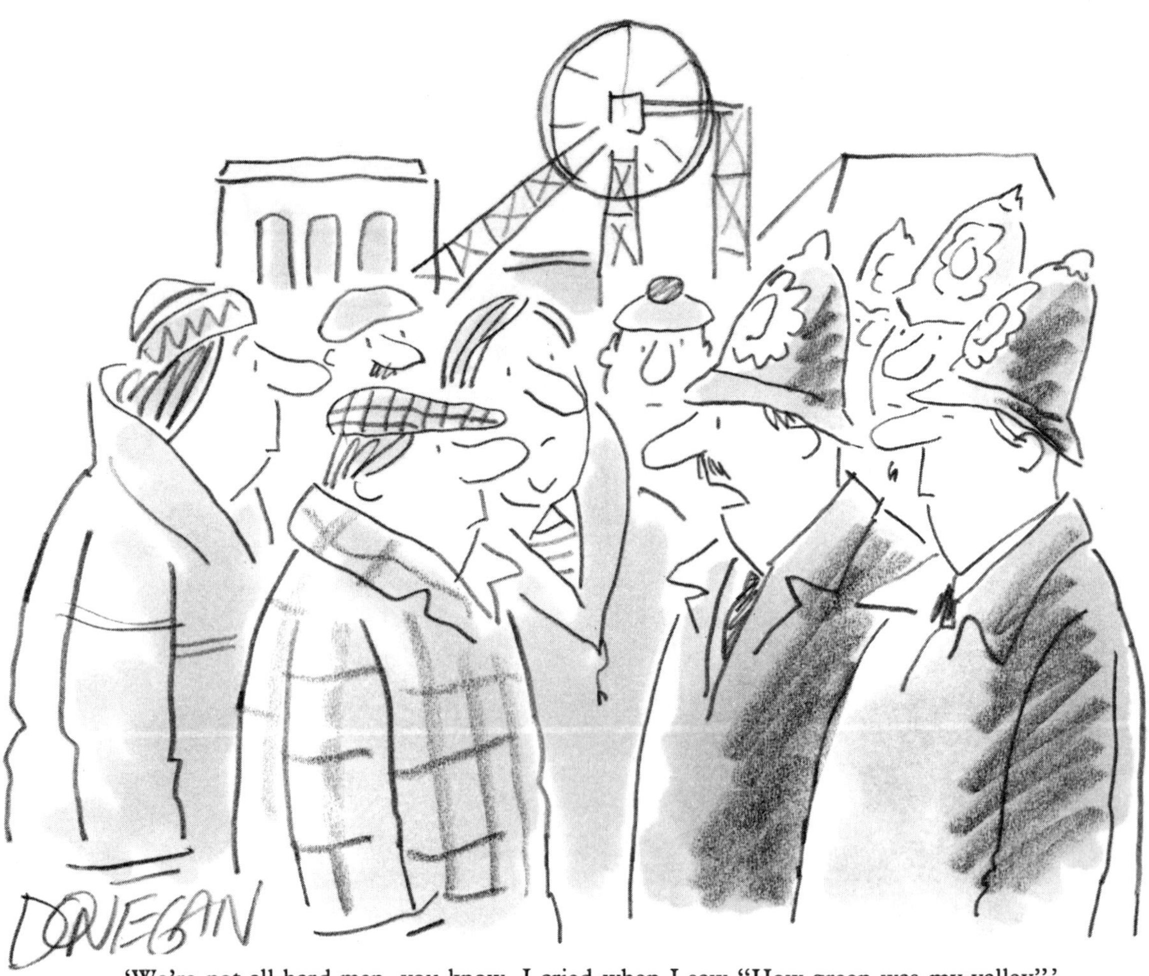
DONEGAN

'We're not all hard men, you know. I cried when I saw "How green was my valley"'

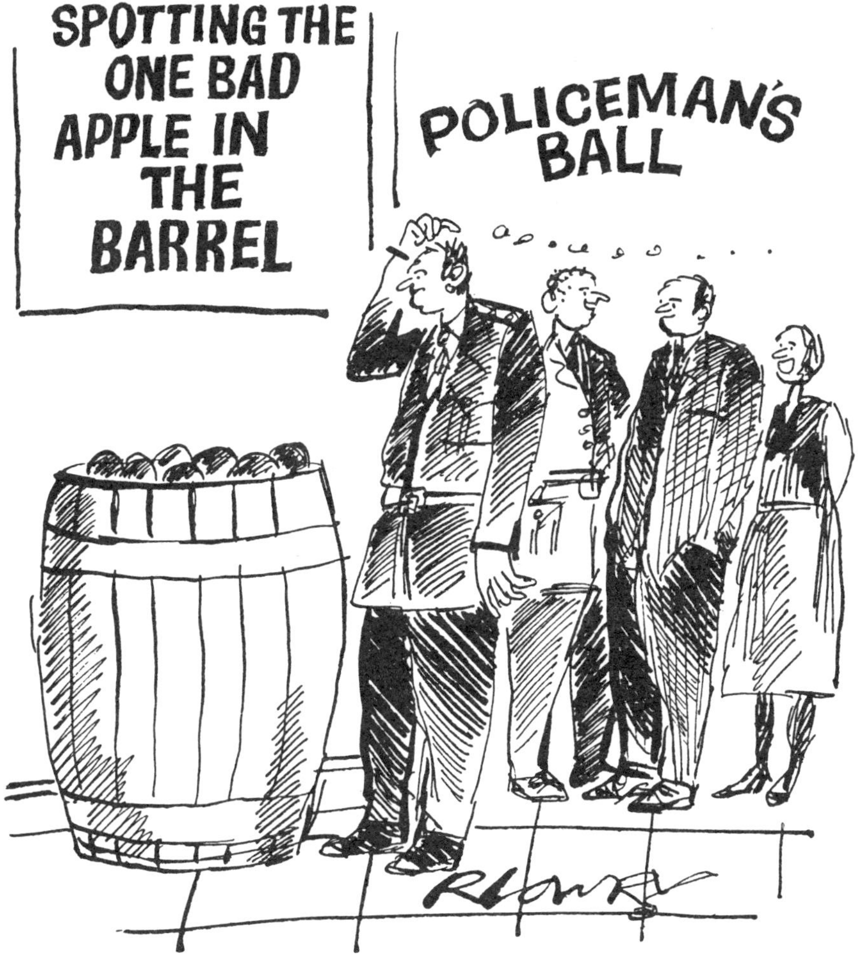
SPOTTING THE ONE BAD APPLE IN THE BARREL
POLICEMAN'S BALL

TUC
LABOUR PARTY
AT LEAST THEY'RE COMMITTED NOW
Ralph Edney

YOU SURE WE'RE ON THE RIGHT TRACK HERE SARGE — TRYING TO REGAIN THE CONFIDENCE OF THE COMMUNITY?
Ralph Edney

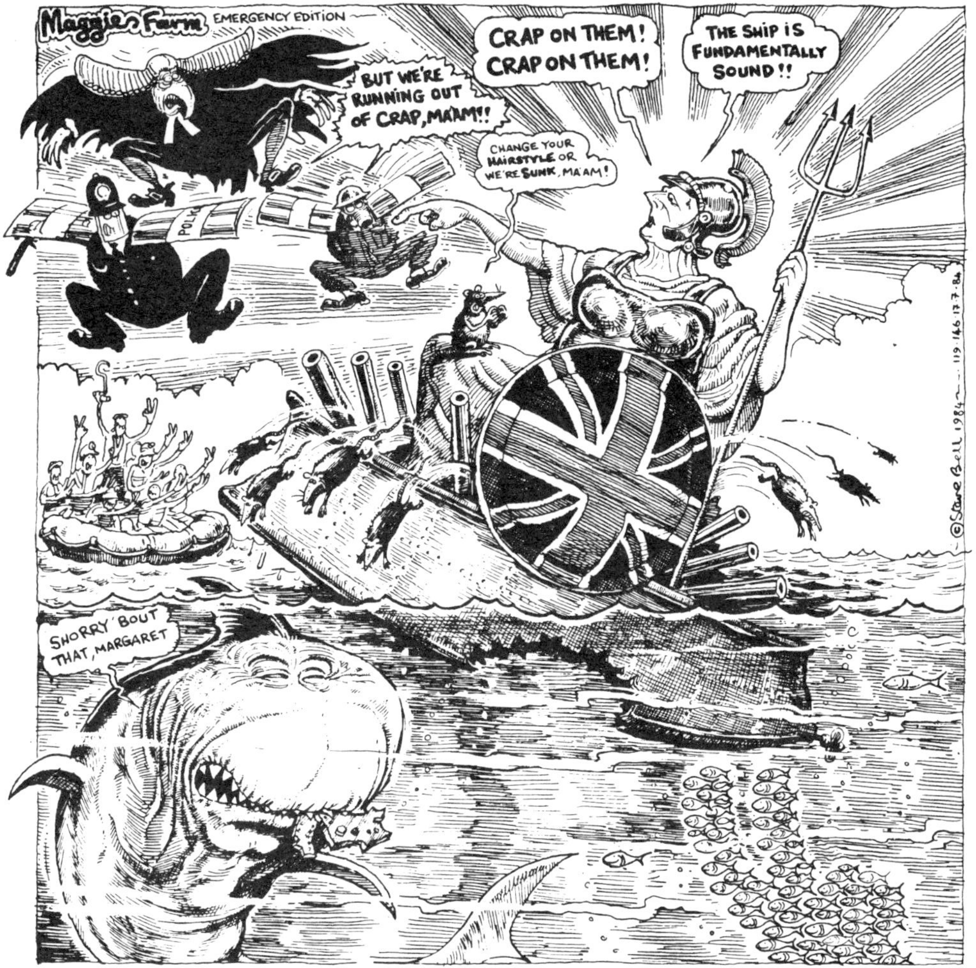
Maggie's Farm
EMERGENCY EDITION
BUT WE'RE RUNNING OUT OF CRAP, MA'AM!!
CRAP ON THEM! CRAP ON THEM!
THE SHIP IS FUNDAMENTALLY SOUND!!
CHANGE YOUR HAIRSTYLE OR WE'RE SUNK, MA'AM!
POLICE
SHORRY 'BOUT THAT, MARGARET
©Steve Bell 1984 119·146 17·7·84

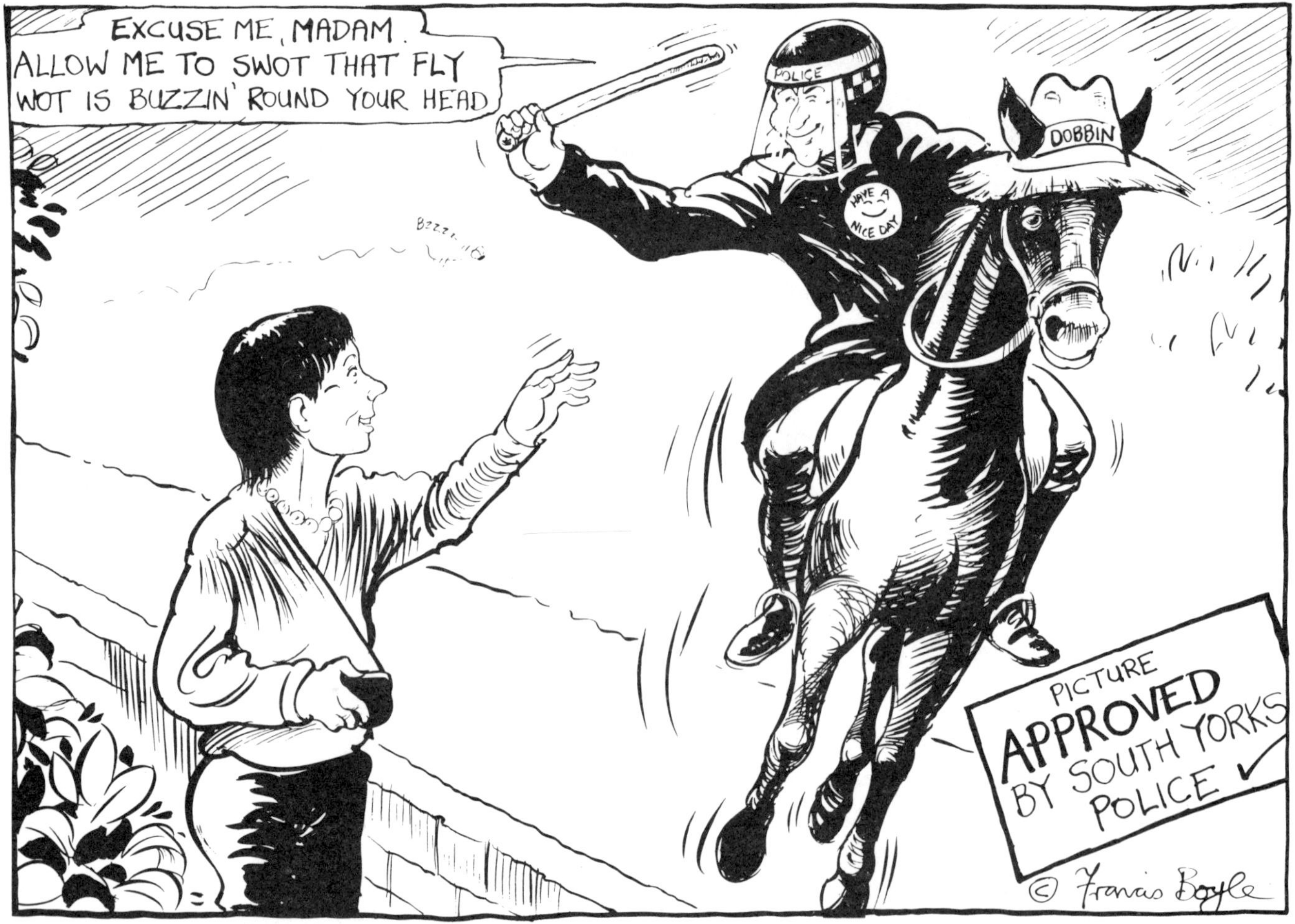
EXCUSE ME, MADAM. ALLOW ME TO SWOT THAT FLY WOT IS BUZZIN' ROUND YOUR HEAD
POLICE
HAVE A NICE DAY
DOBBIN
Bzzz..
PICTURE APPROVED BY SOUTH YORKS POLICE ✓
© Francis Boyle

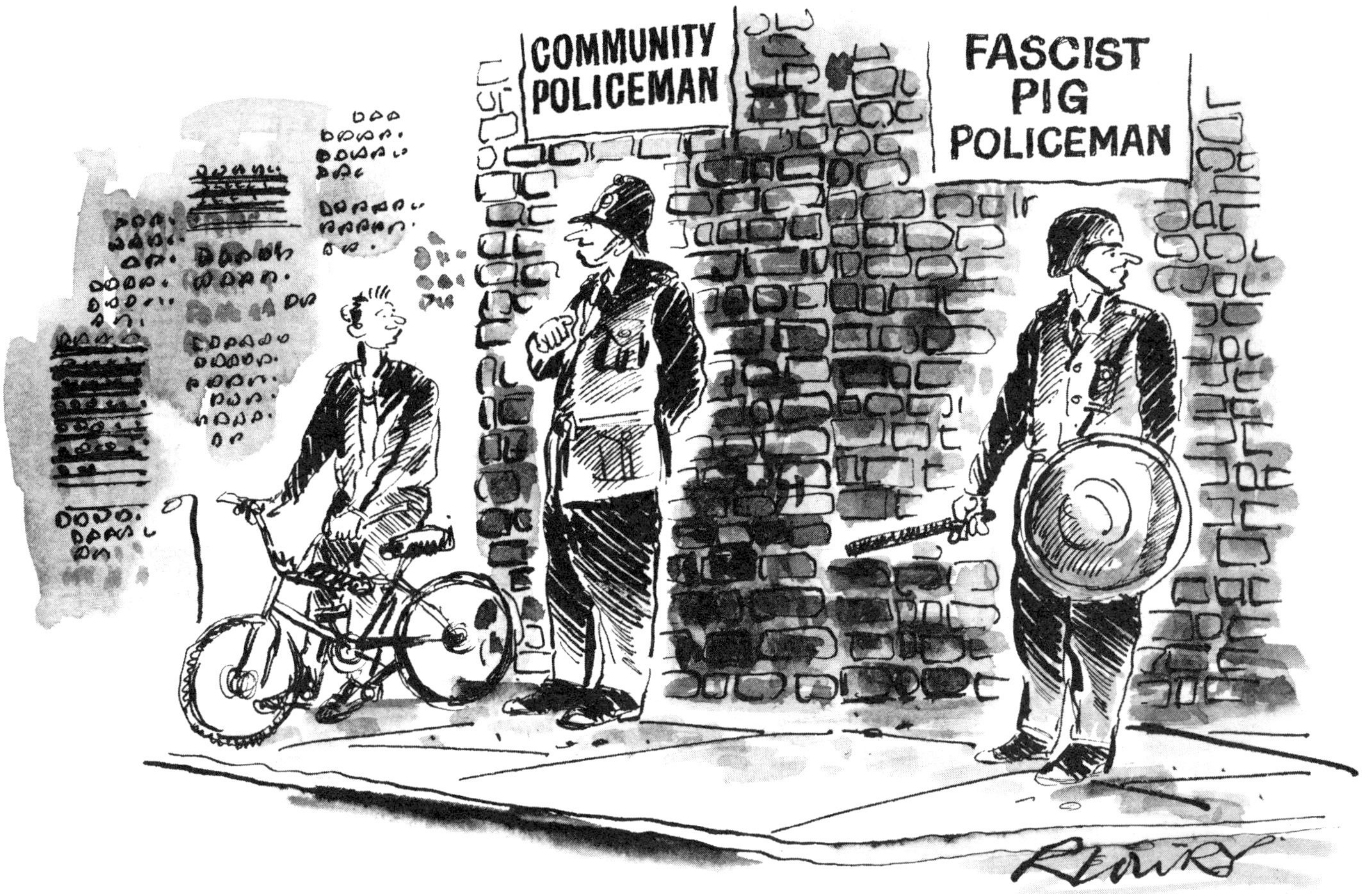
COMMUNITY POLICEMAN
FASCIST PIG POLICEMAN

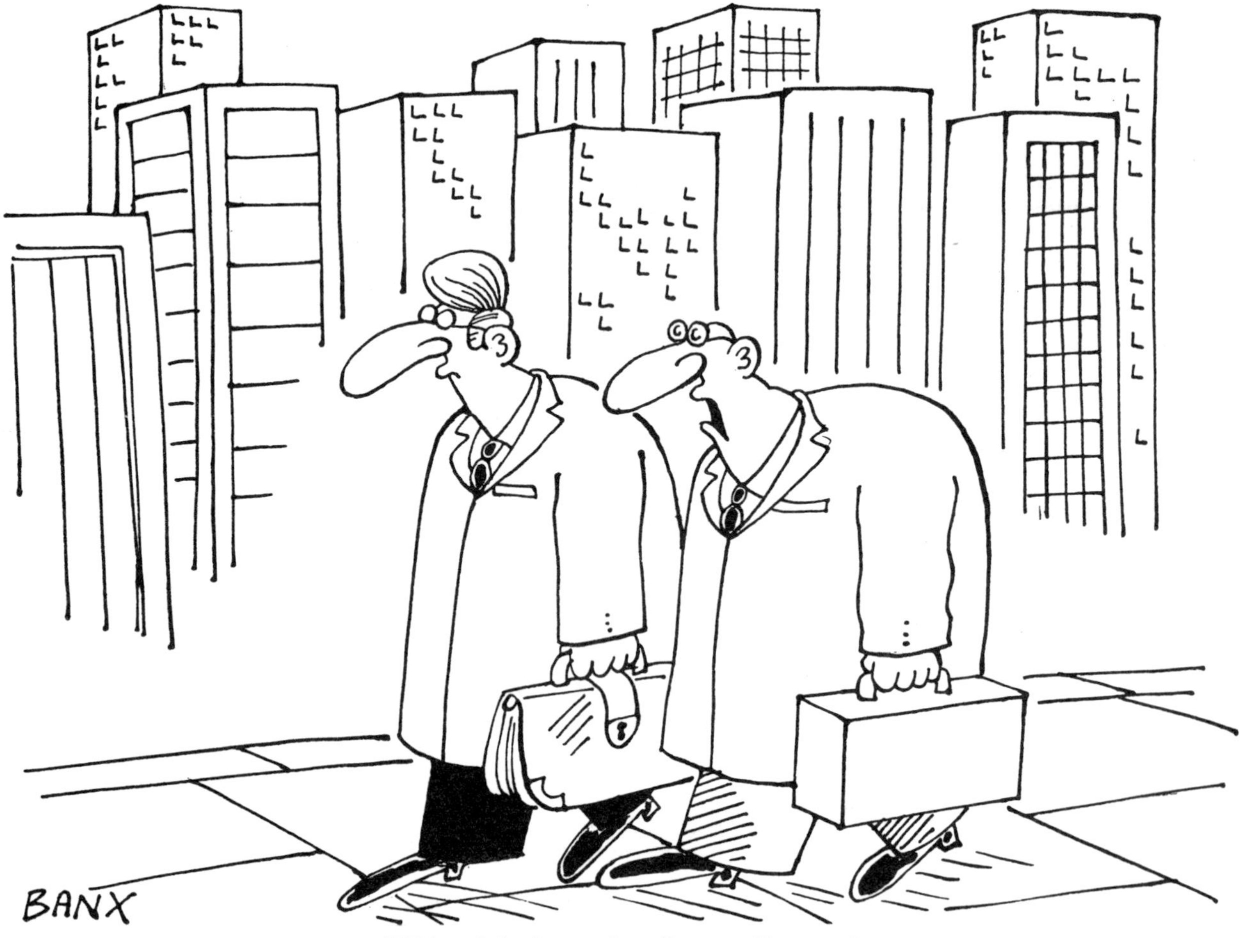
BANX

‘I’ll be glad when we’re all one police state’

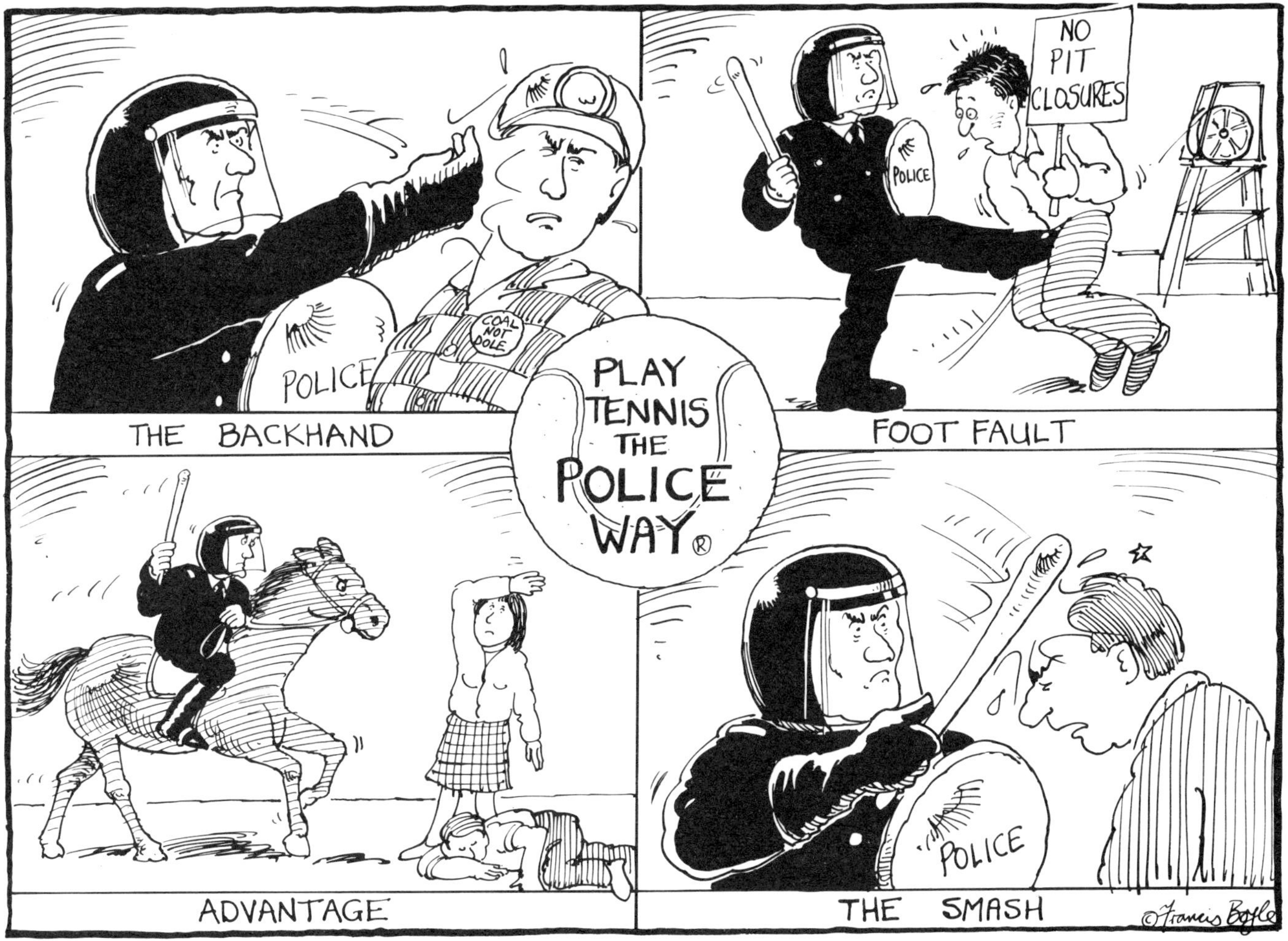
PLAY TENNIS THE POLICE WAY®
POLICE
COAL NOT DOLE
THE BACKHAND
NO PIT CLOSURES
POLICE
FOOT FAULT
ADVANTAGE
POLICE
THE SMASH
©Francis Boyle

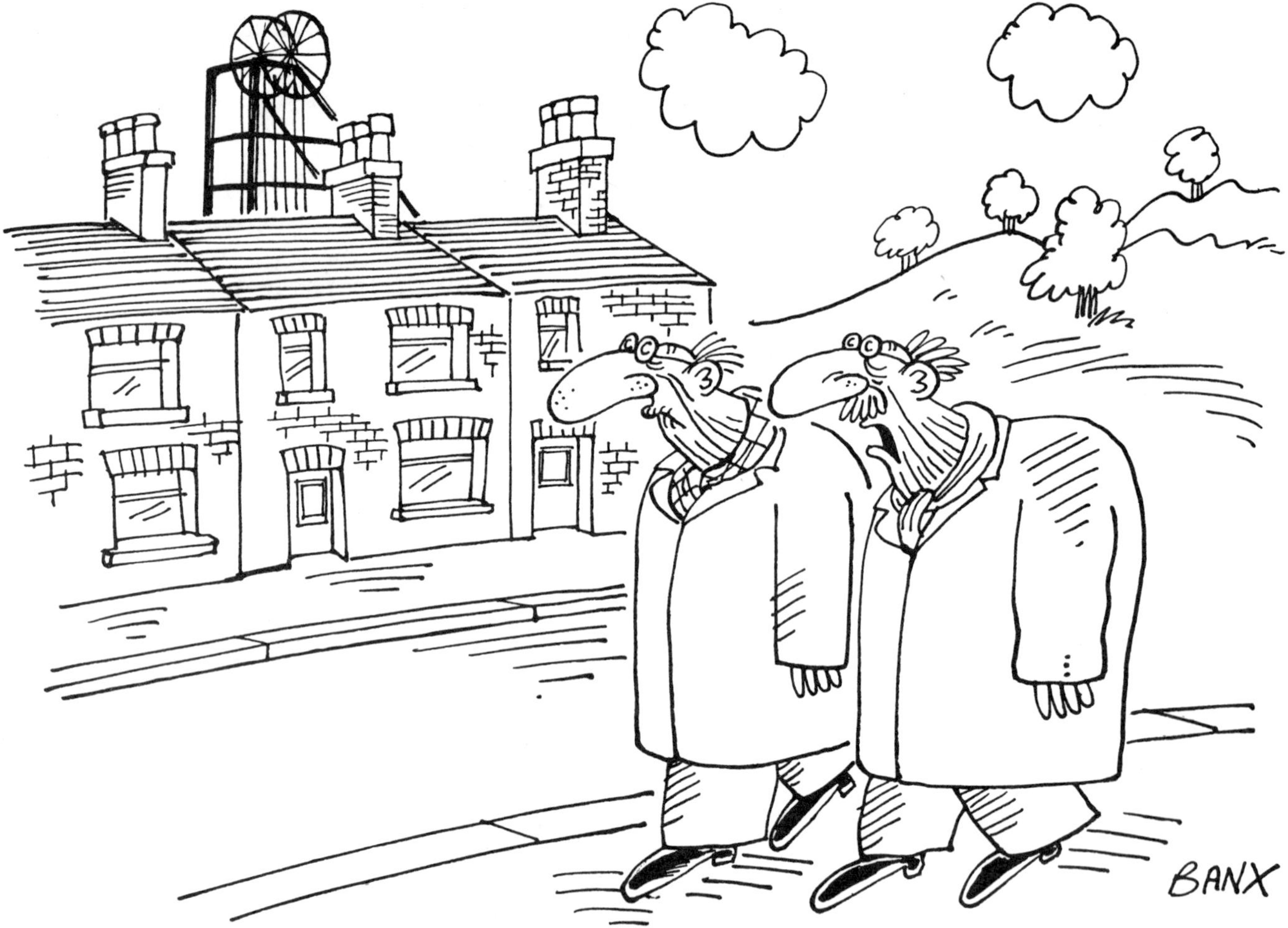
BANX

'Is it me or are the soldiers dressed as policemen getting younger?'

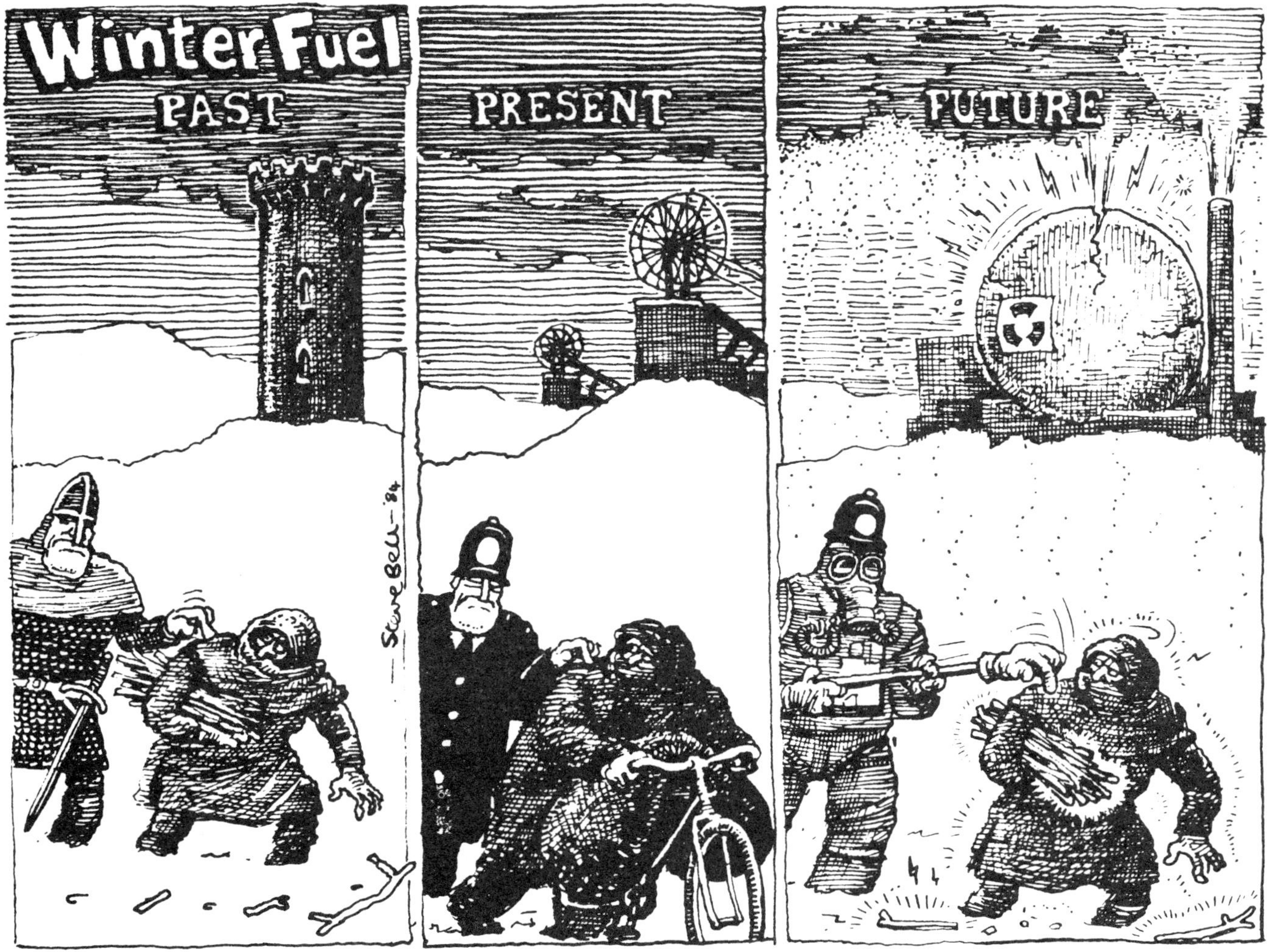

Winter Fuel
PAST
PRESENT
FUTURE
Steve Bell '84

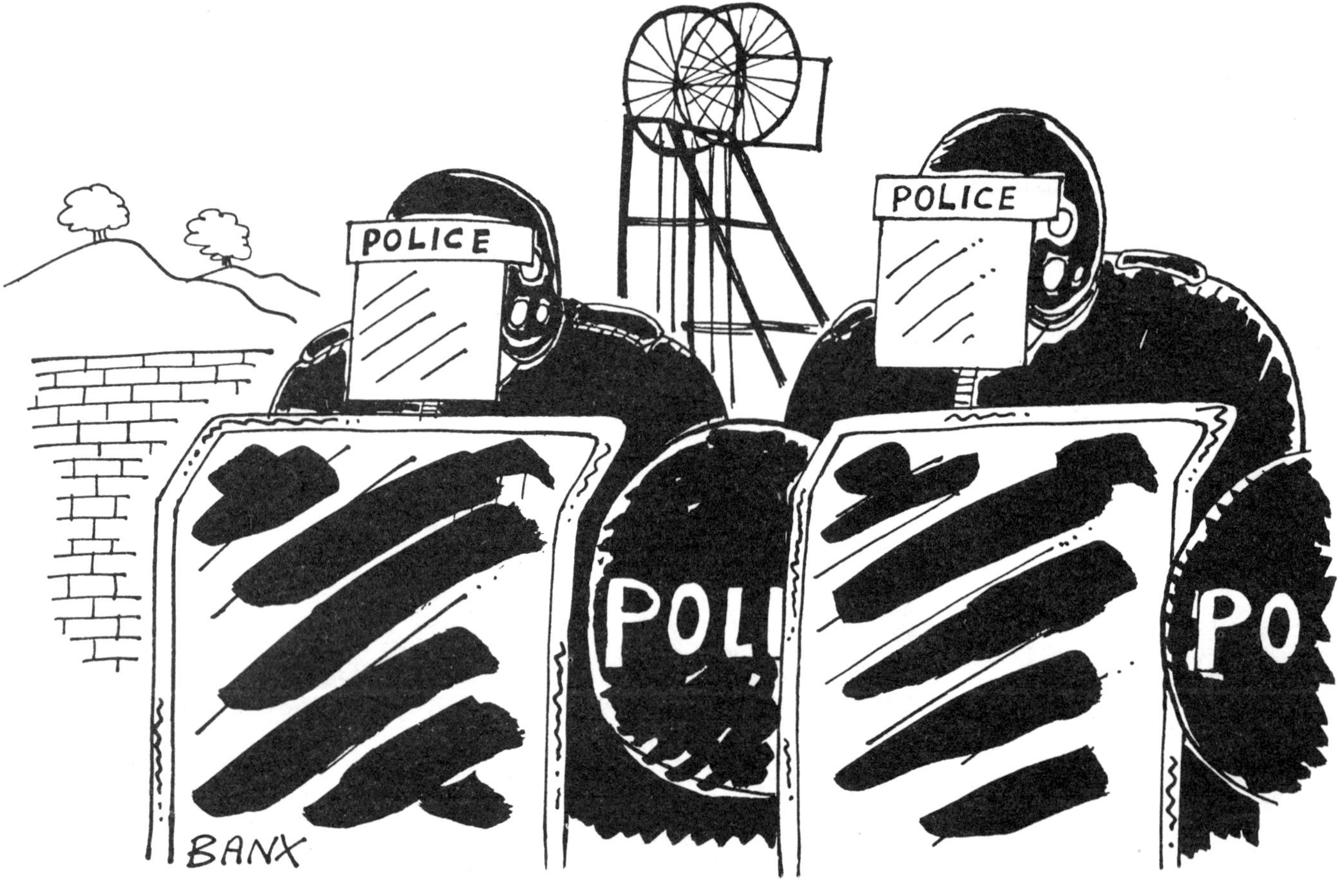
POLICE
POLICE
BANX

'I'd like to see someone ask me the bloody time now'

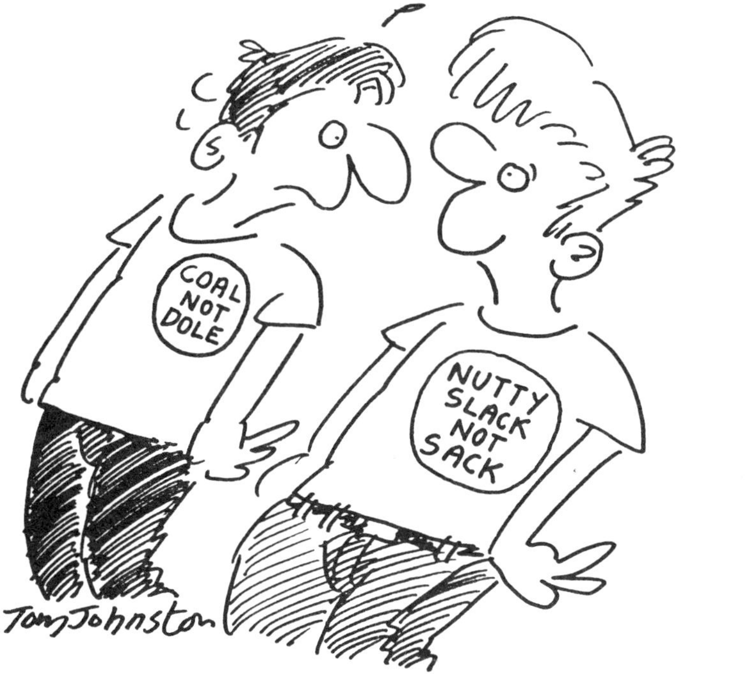
COAL NOT DOLE
NUTTY SLACK NOT SACK
Tom Johnston

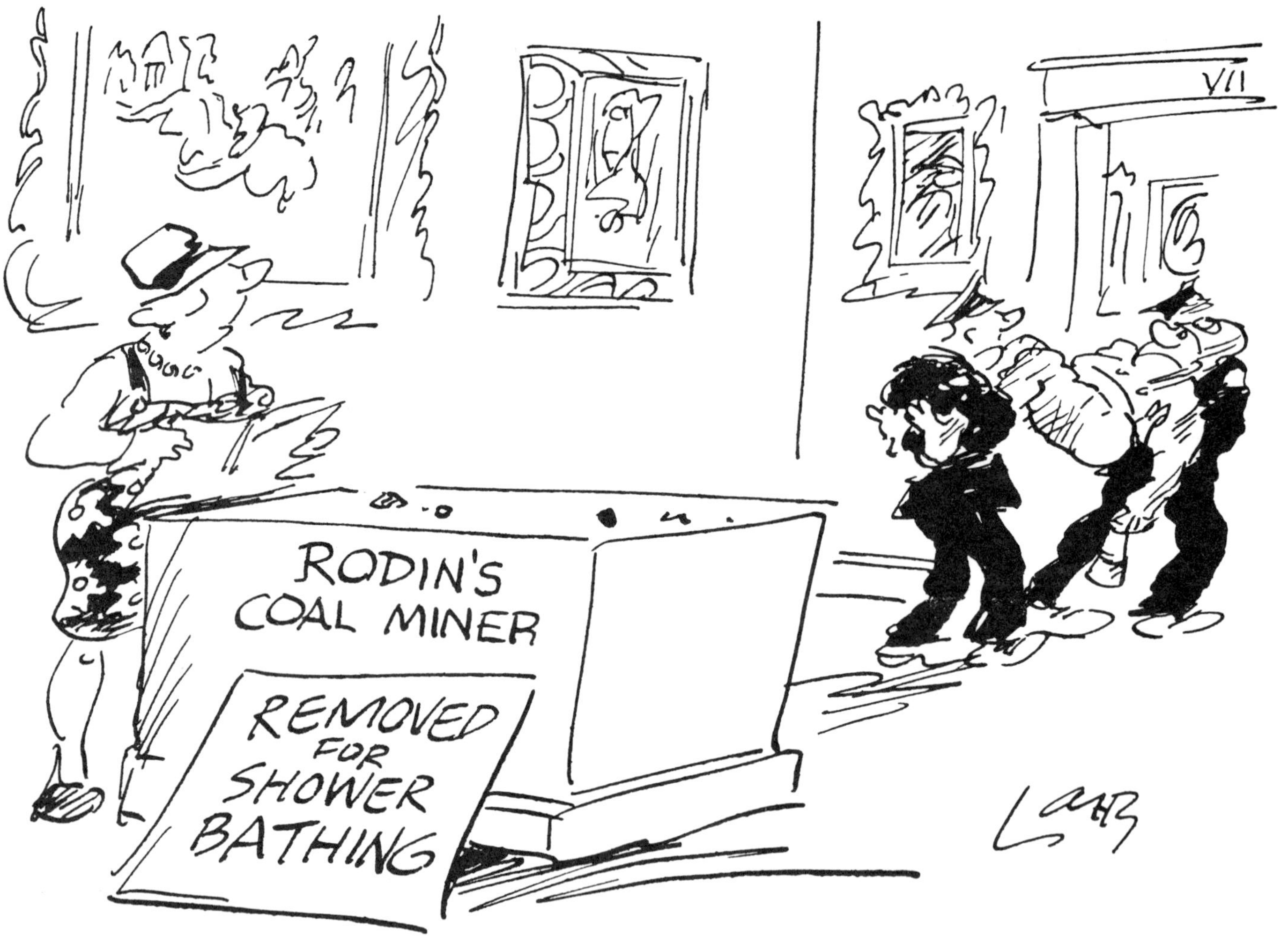
VII
RODIN'S
COAL MINER
REMOVED
FOR
SHOWER
BATHING
LAB

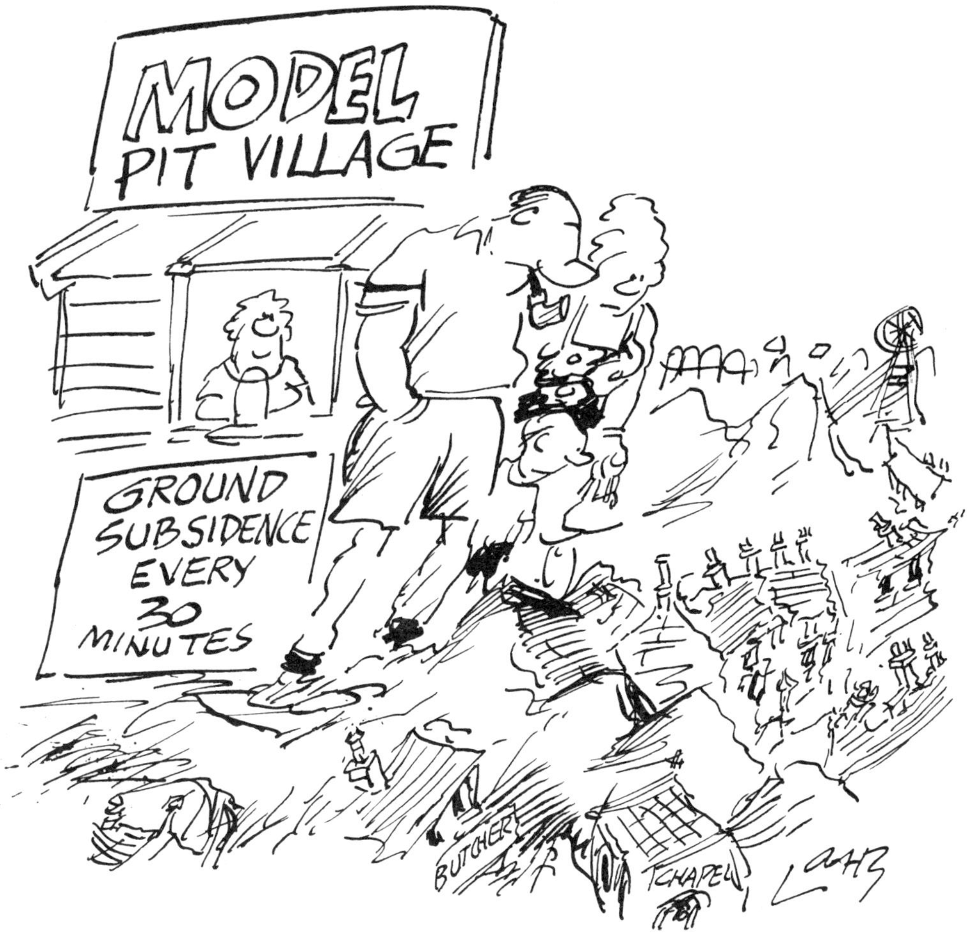
MODEL
PIT VILLAGE
GROUND SUBSIDENCE EVERY 30 MINUTES
BUTCHER
CHAPEL

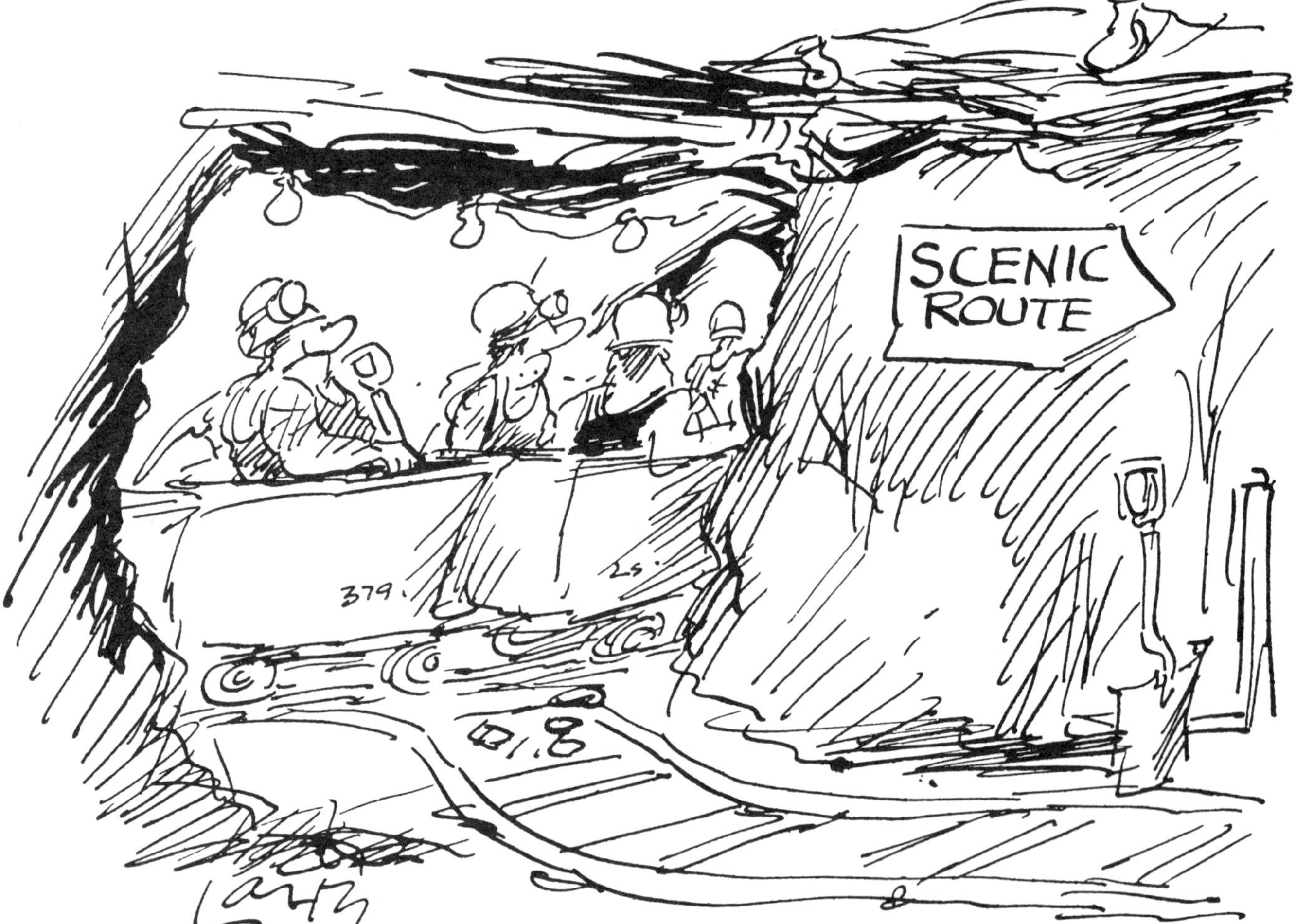
SCENIC ROUTE

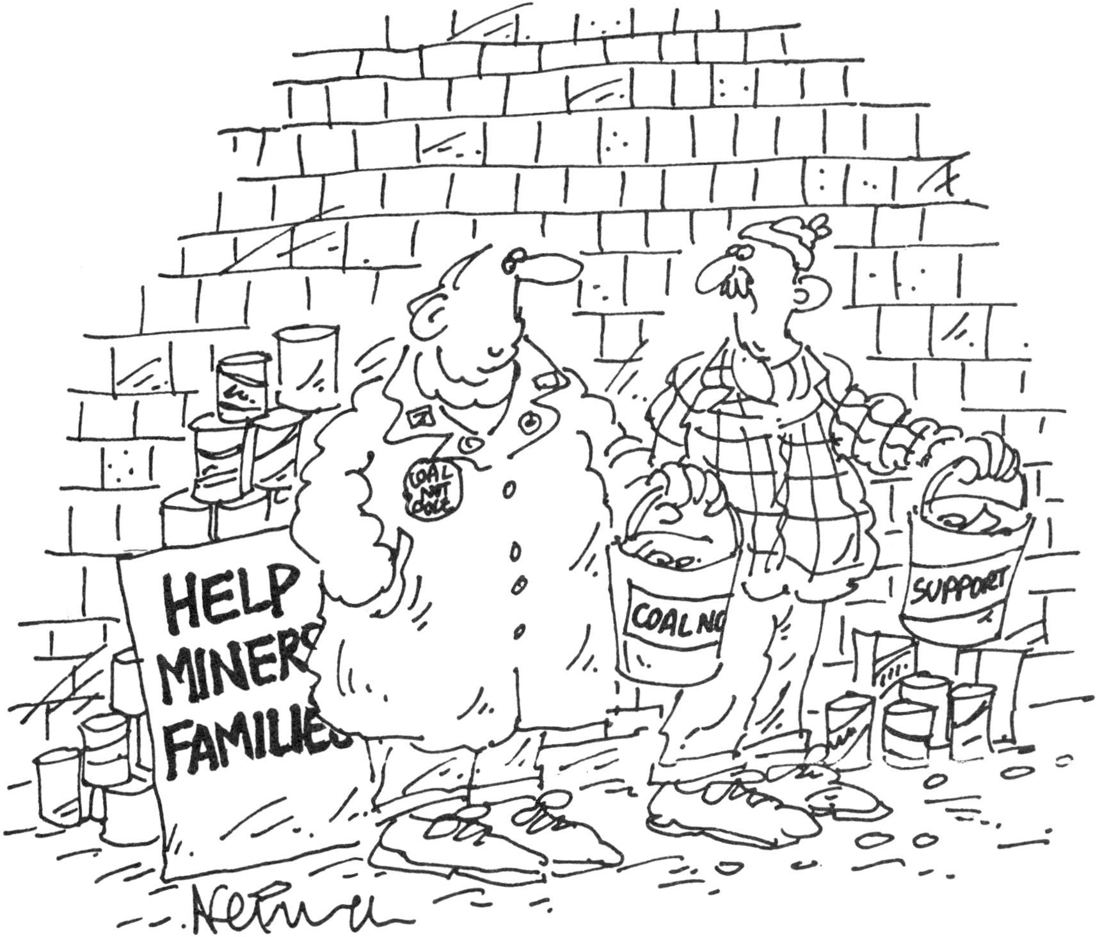
HELP MINERS FAMILIES
COAL NOT DOLE
COAL NO
SUPPORT

'Let's not make too much of our plight – we might get a visit from Bob Geldof'

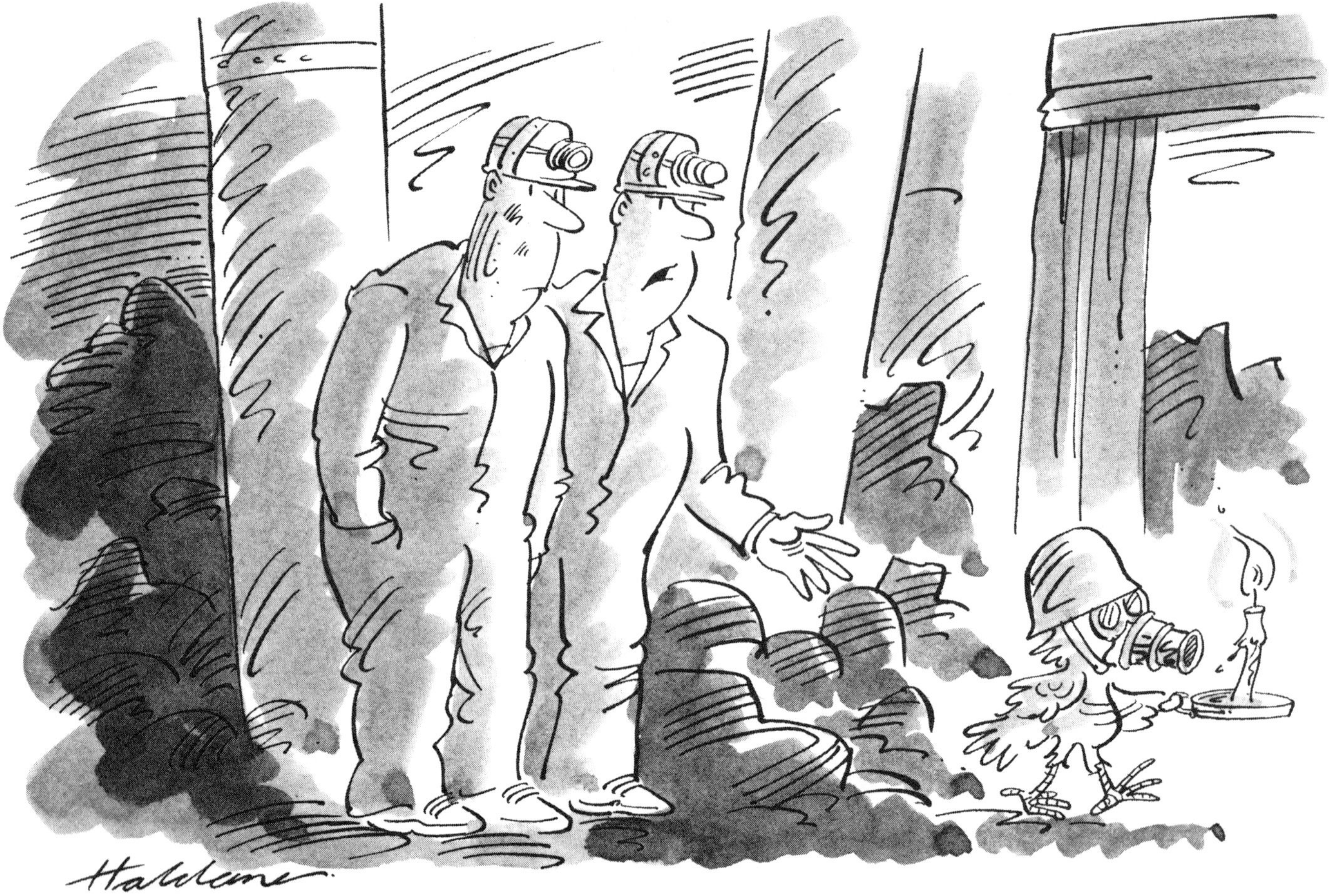
Haldane

'He's OK, but he'll never replace the canaries'

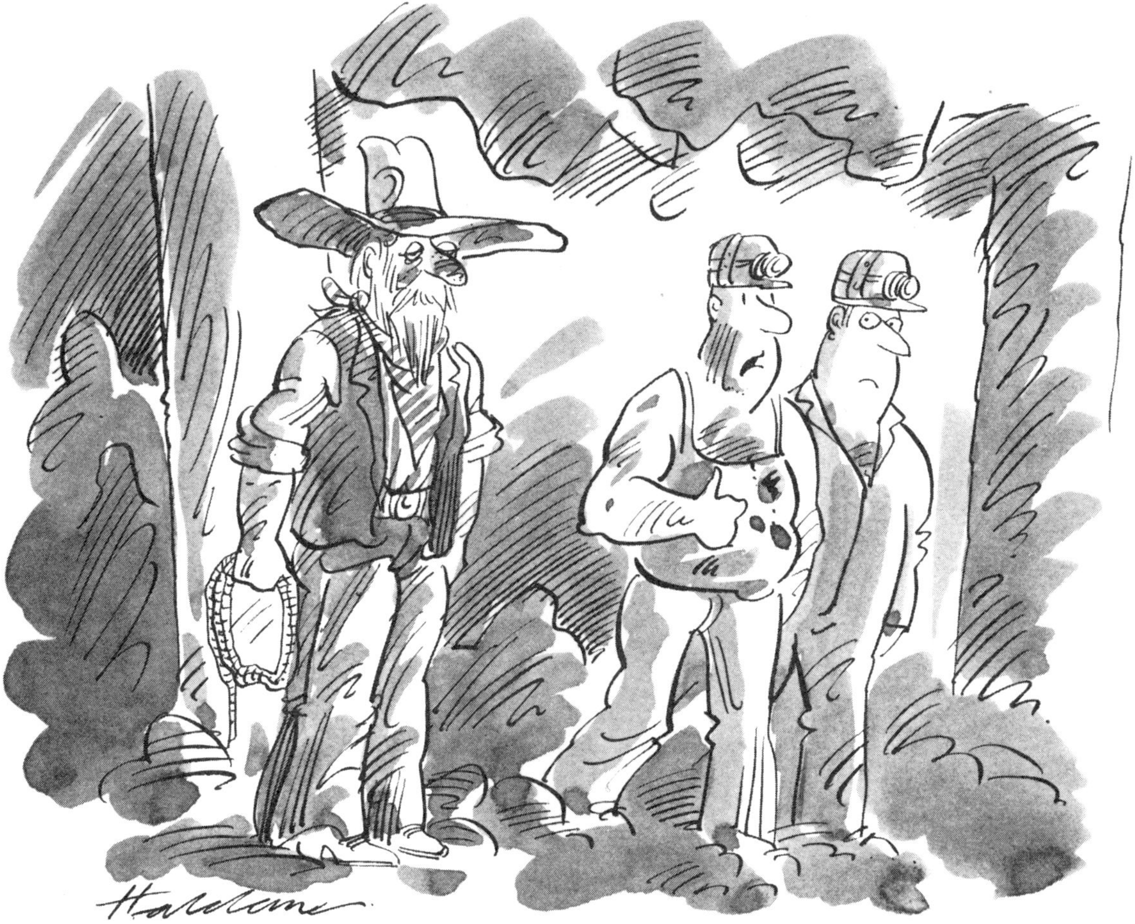
Haldane

'That's Charlie. He used to break the pit ponies'

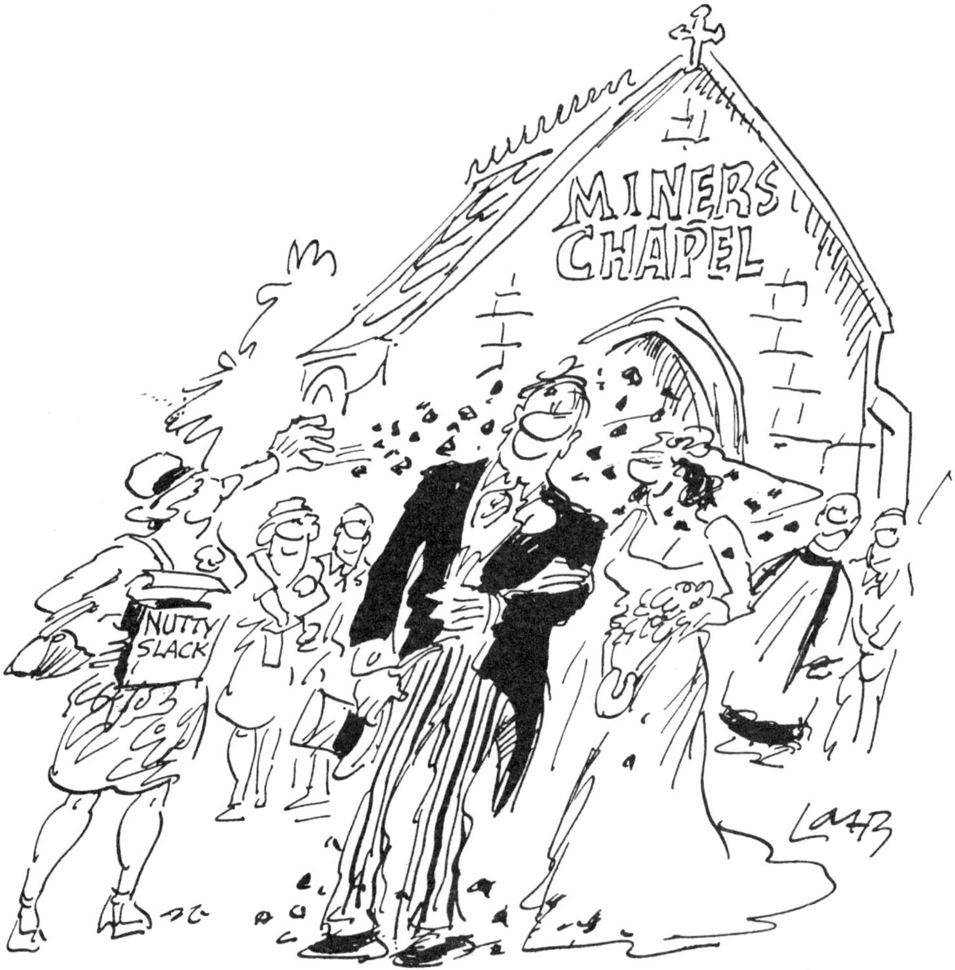

MINERS CHAPEL
NUTTY SLACK
LARB

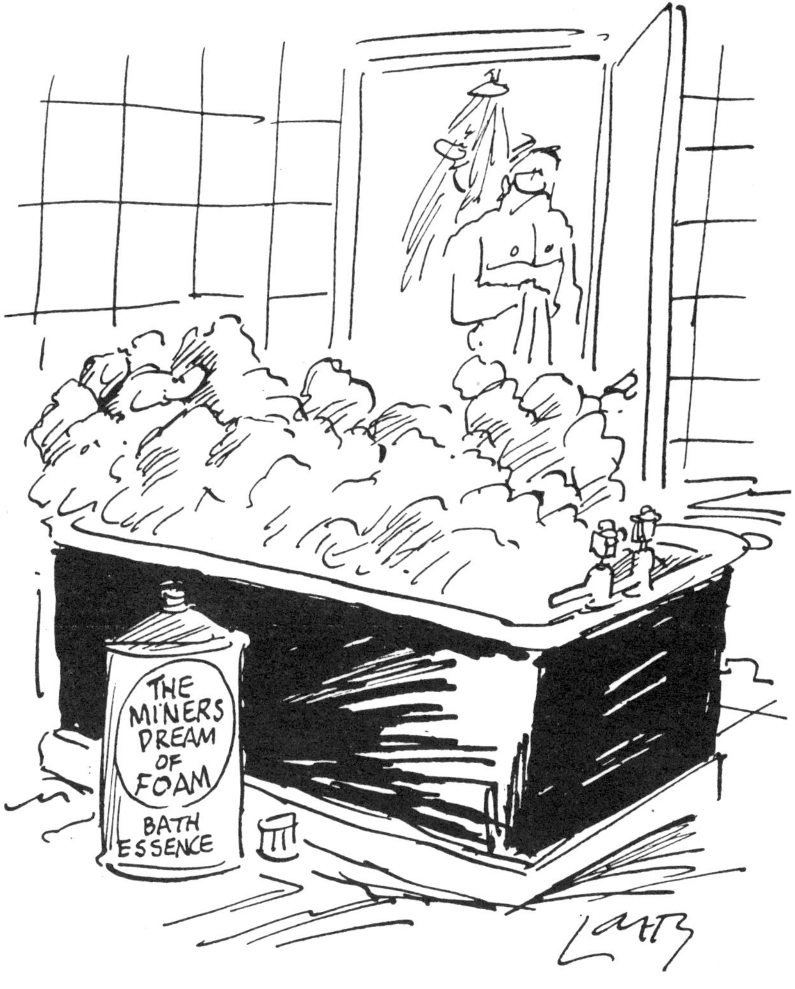
THE MINERS DREAM OF FOAM
BATH ESSENCE

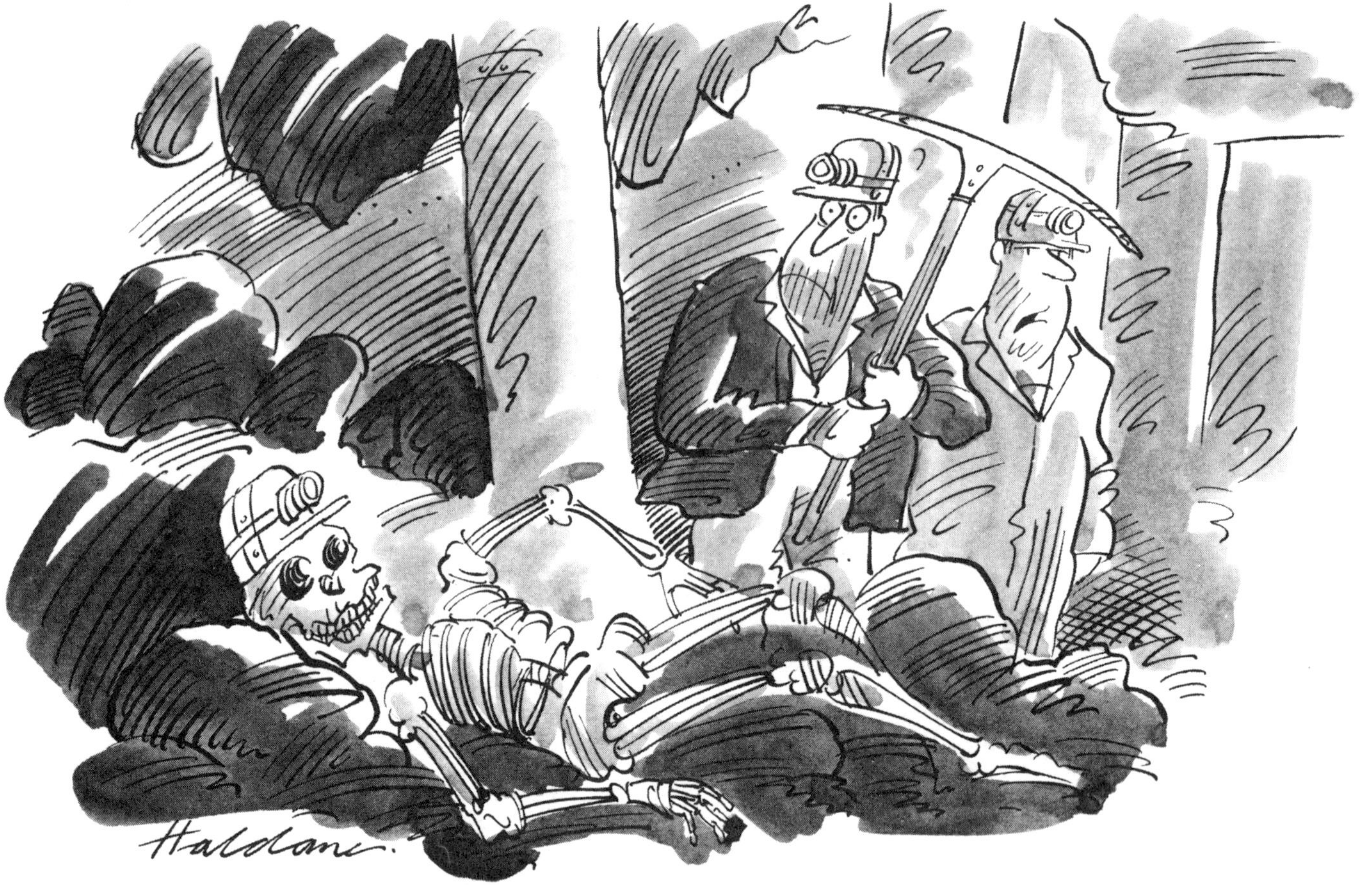
Haldane

'He's the last safety official we had down here'

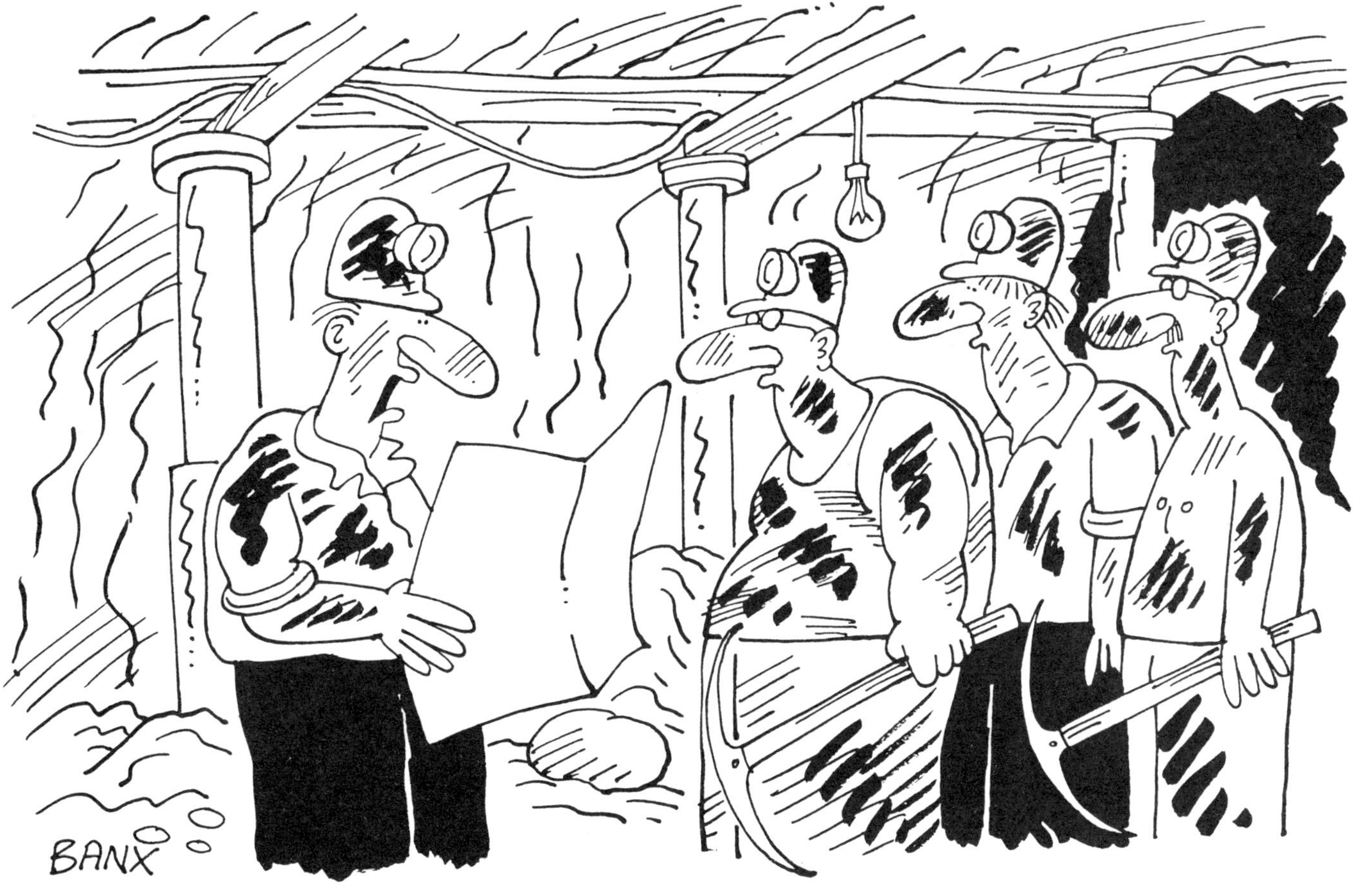
BANX

'According to this, we're supposed to be digging a shaft to the Polish coal fields'

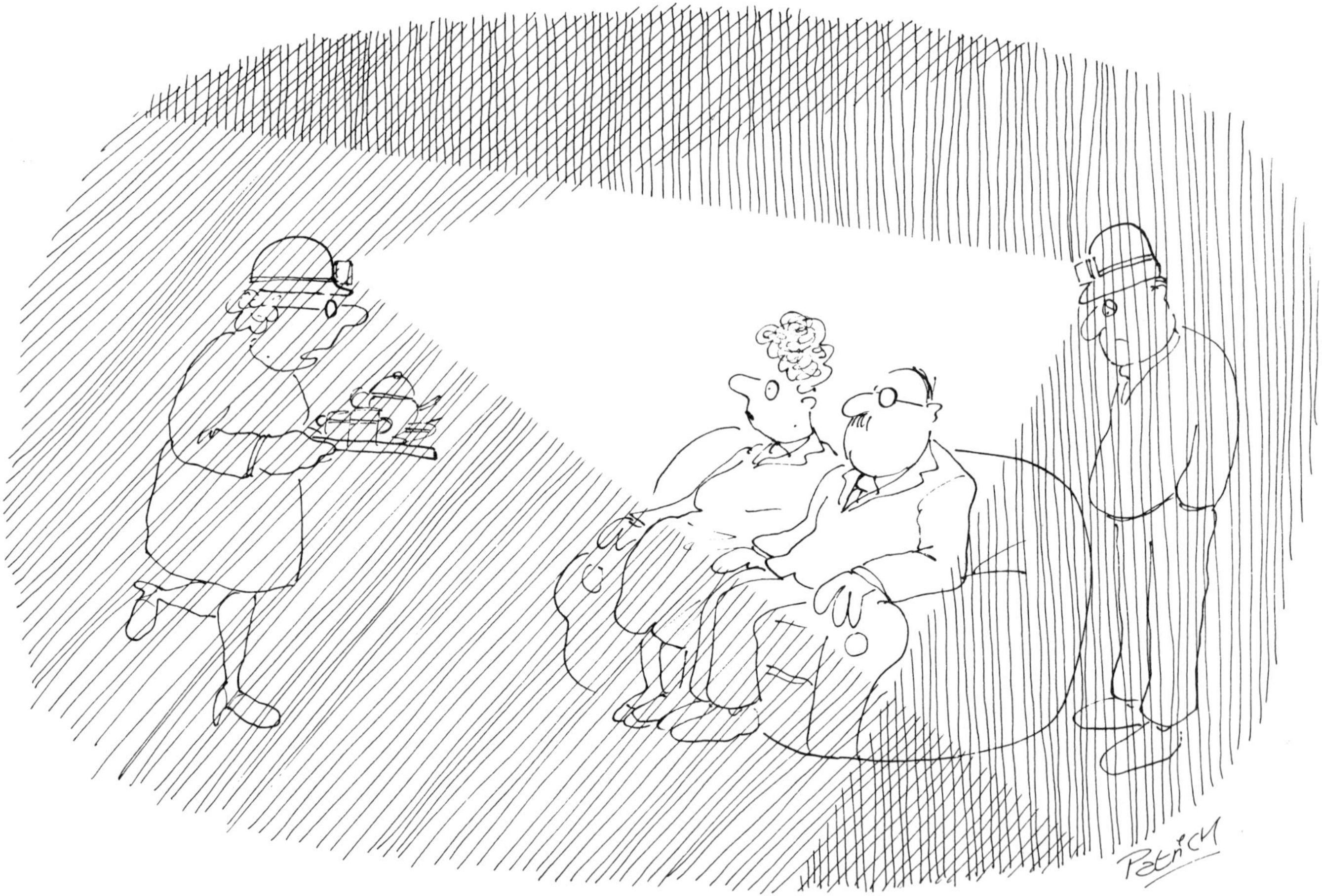
Patrick

'. . . and then it was only a matter of time before they came and cut us off'

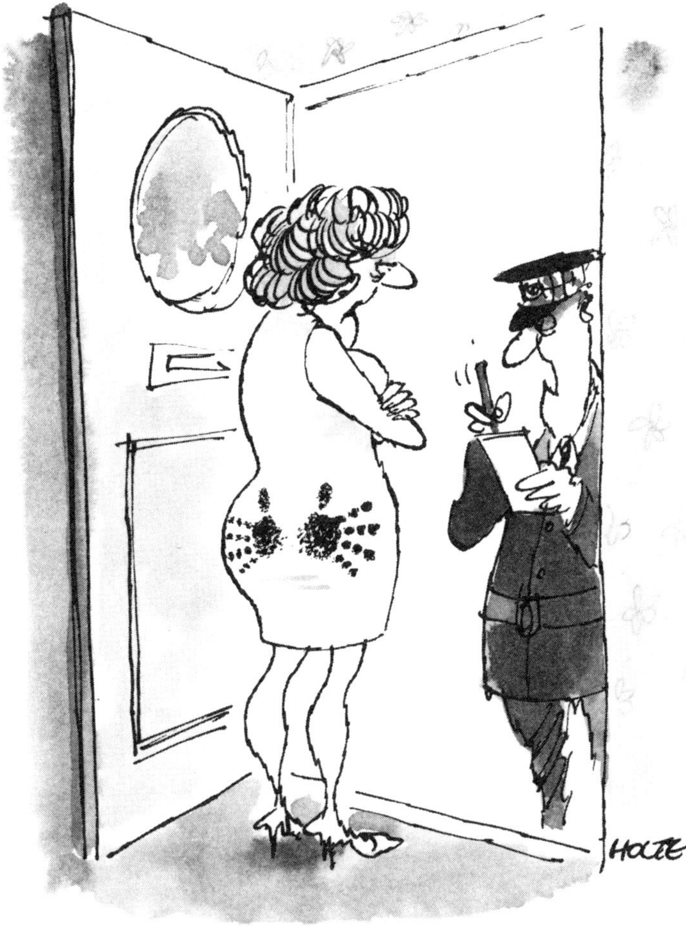
HOLTE

'If you didn't actually see him, how can you be sure it was a *working* miner?'

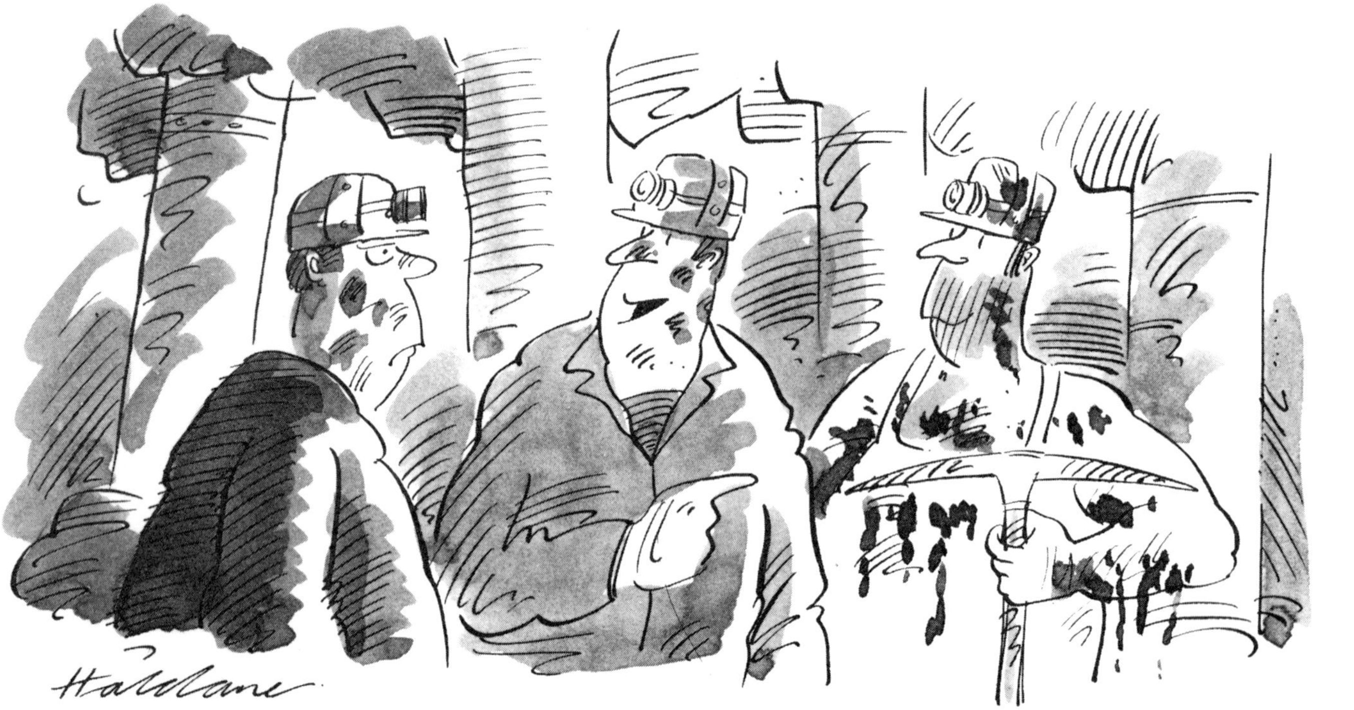
Haldane

'No more worry about the pit closing. Sid's just struck oil'

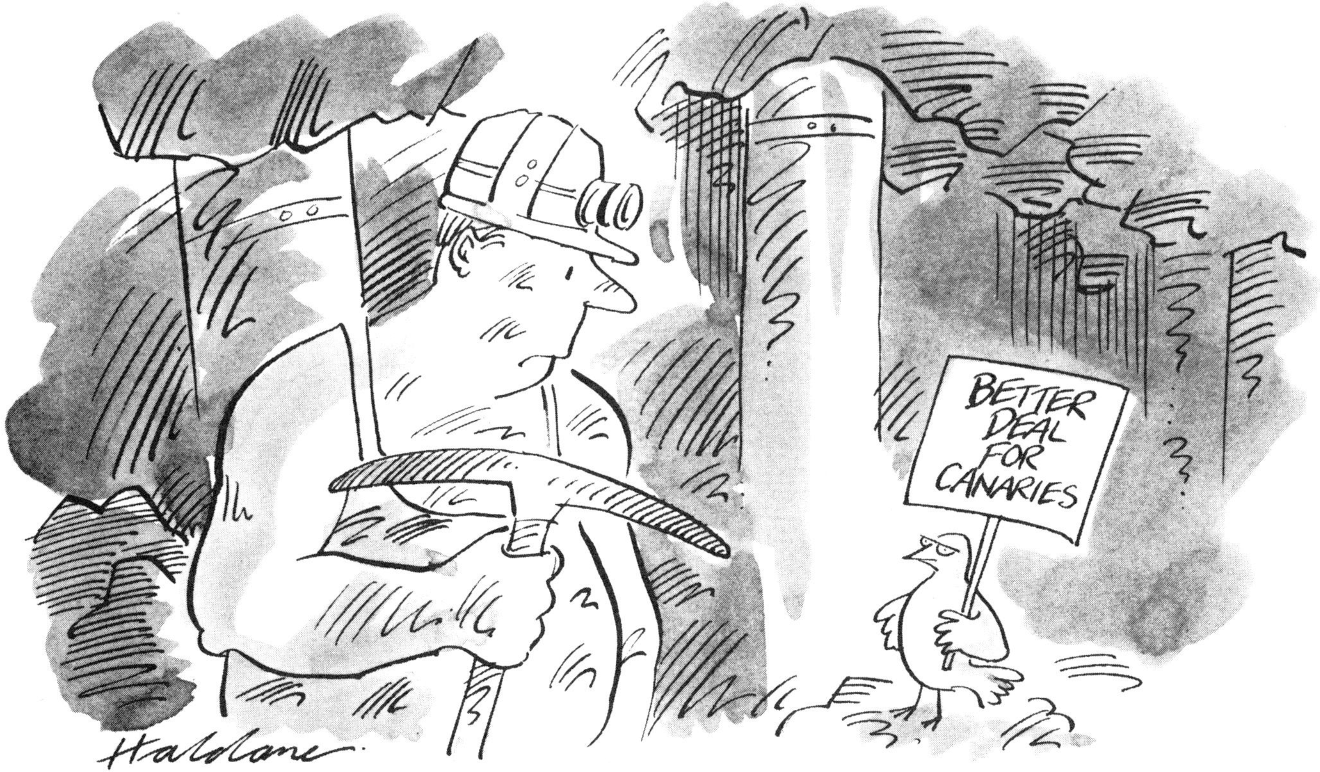
BETTER DEAL FOR CANARIES
Haldane

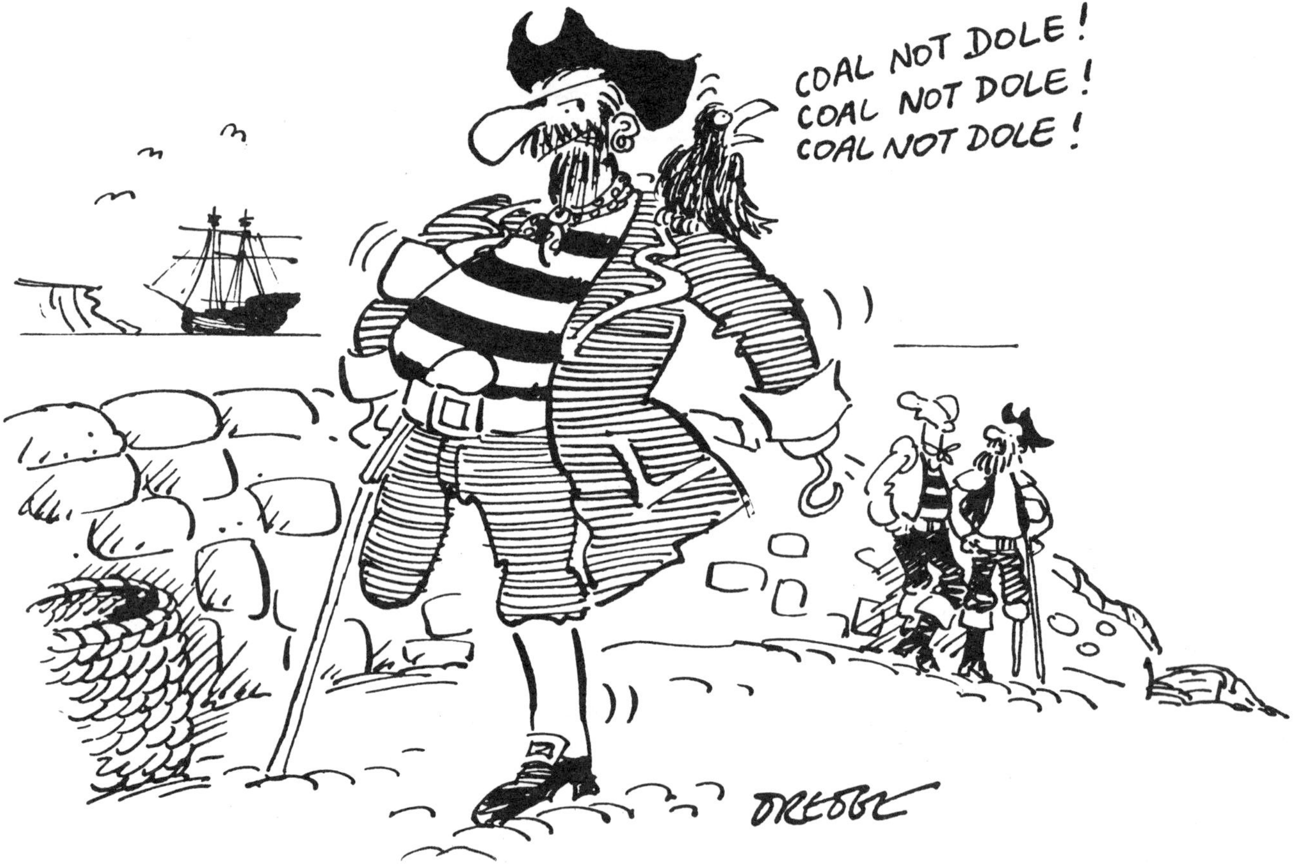
COAL NOT DOLE!
COAL NOT DOLE!
COAL NOT DOLE!
DREDGE

'Apparently he swopped his parrot for a mynah bird'

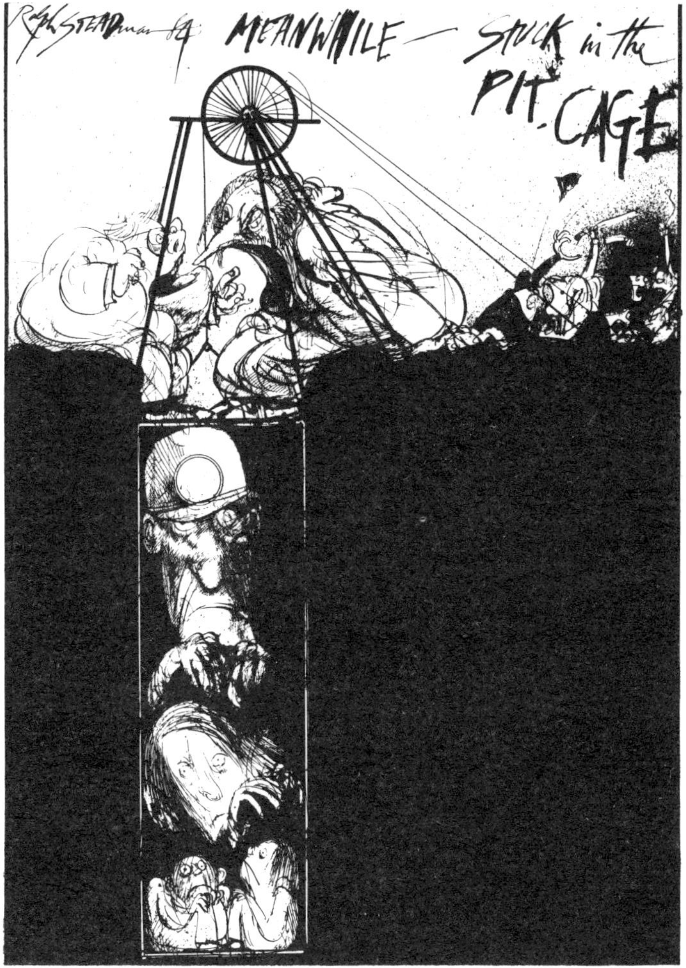
Ralph STEADman 84
MEANWHILE — STUCK in the PIT CAGE

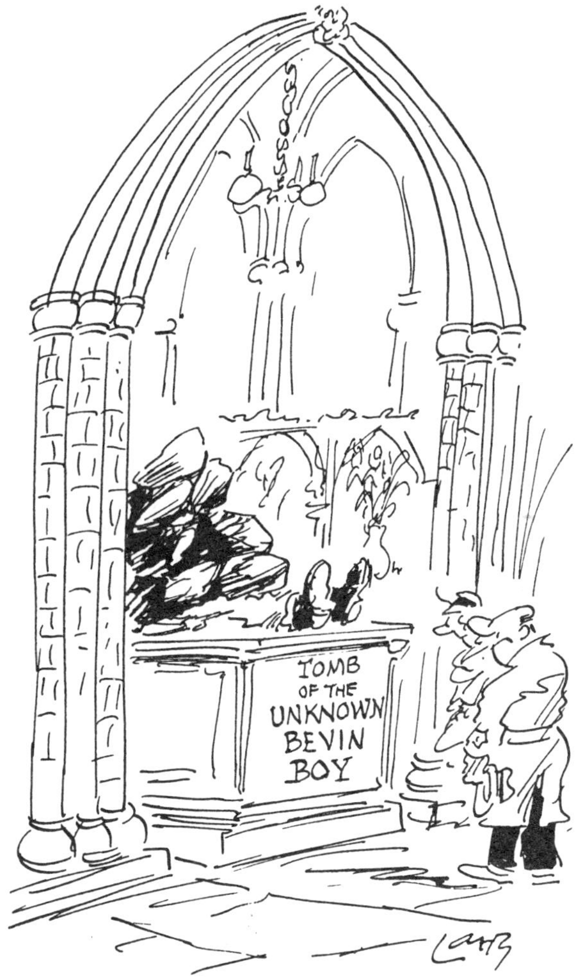
TOMB OF THE UNKNOWN BEVIN BOY
LAMB

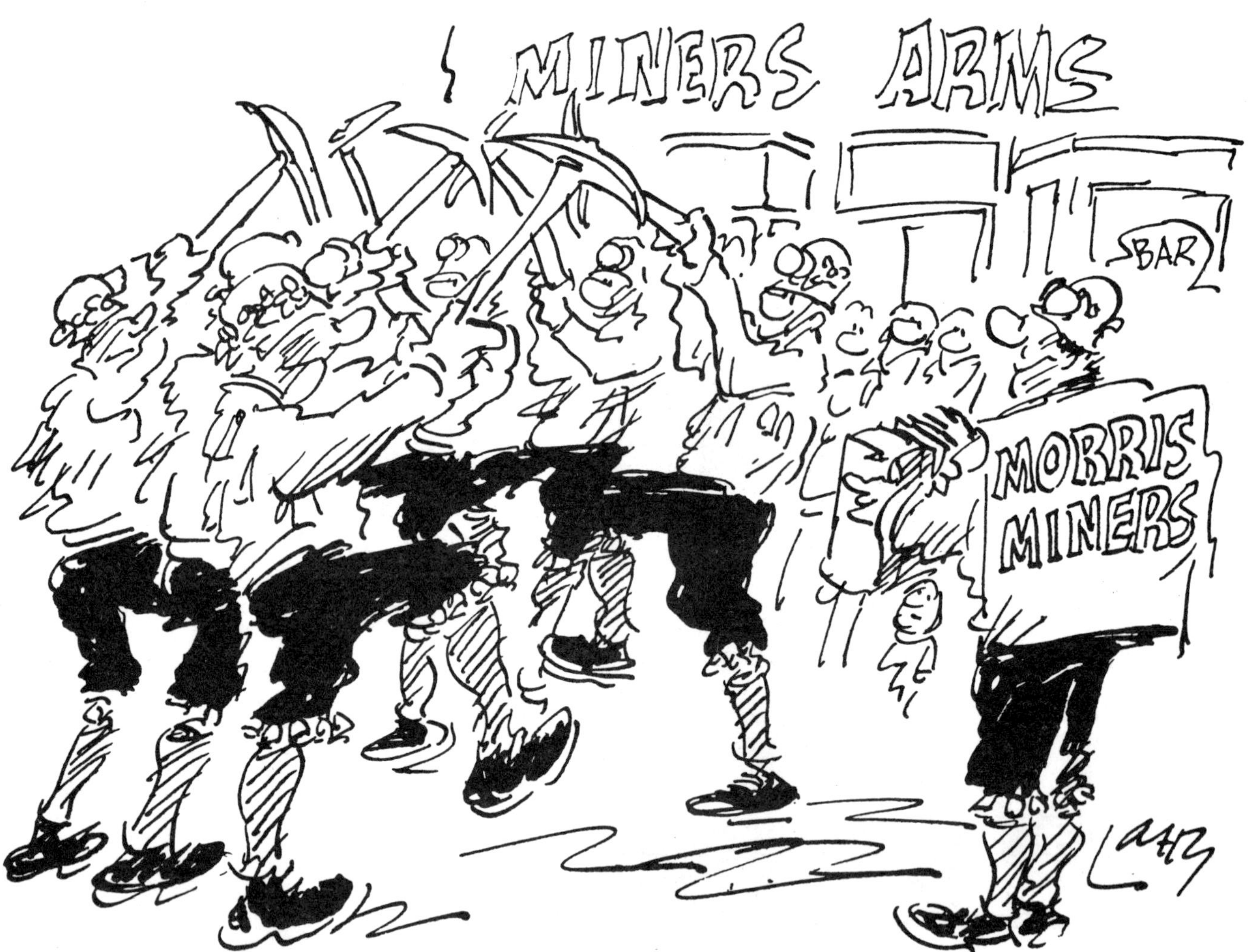
MINERS ARMS
BAR
MORRIS MINERS

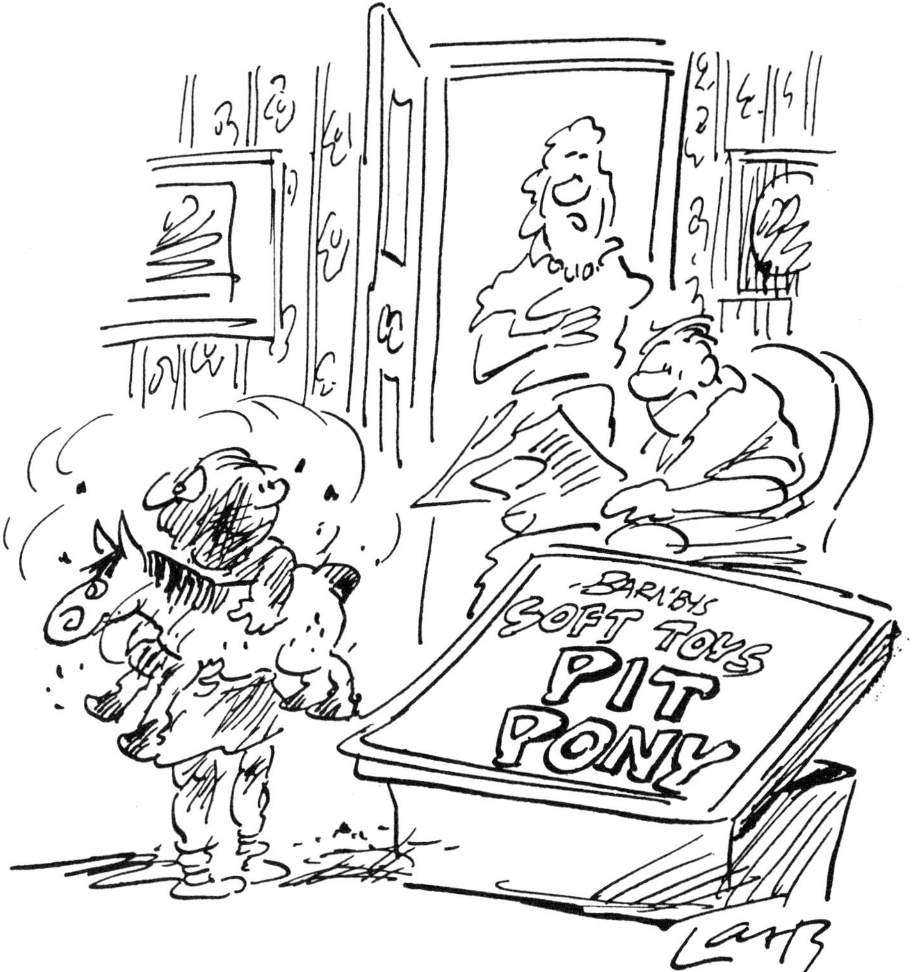
BARNBYS
SOFT TOYS
PIT
PONY
Larry

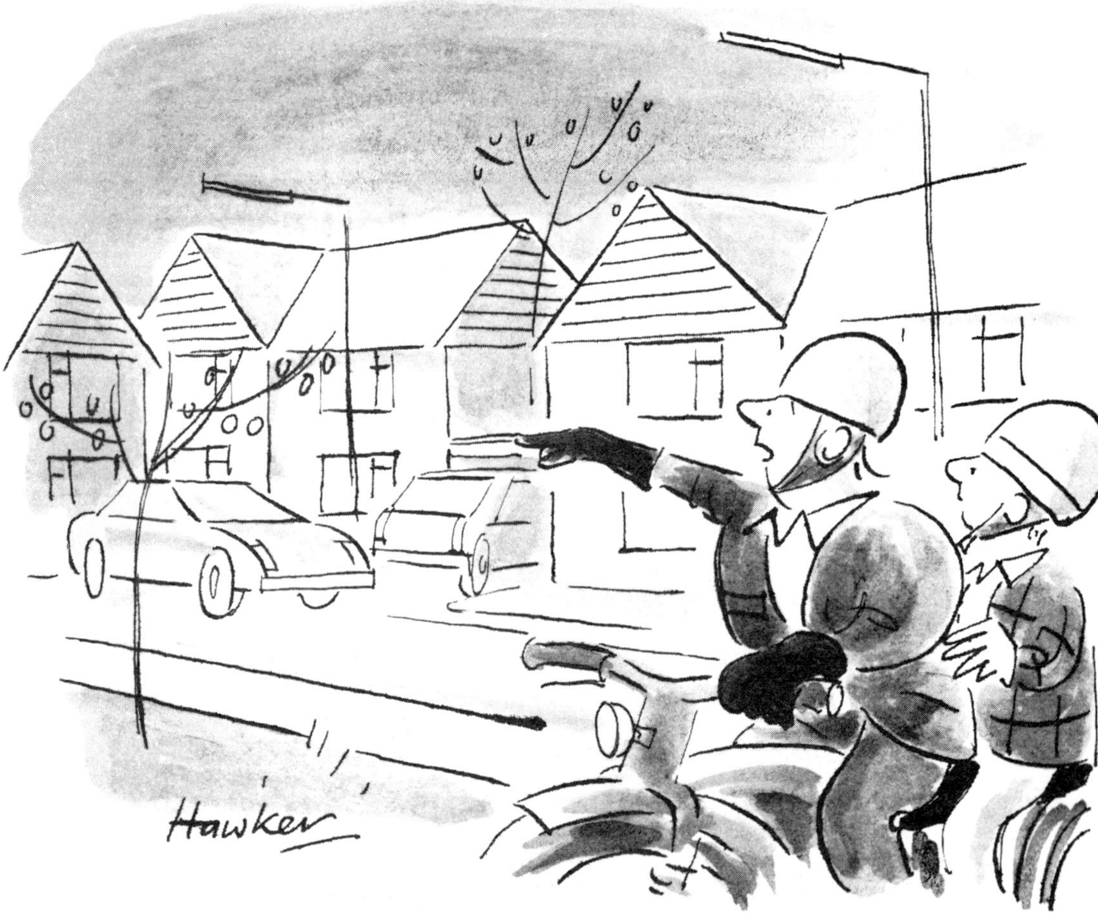
Hawker

'Son, this whole community is built on the paperwork involved in pit closures'

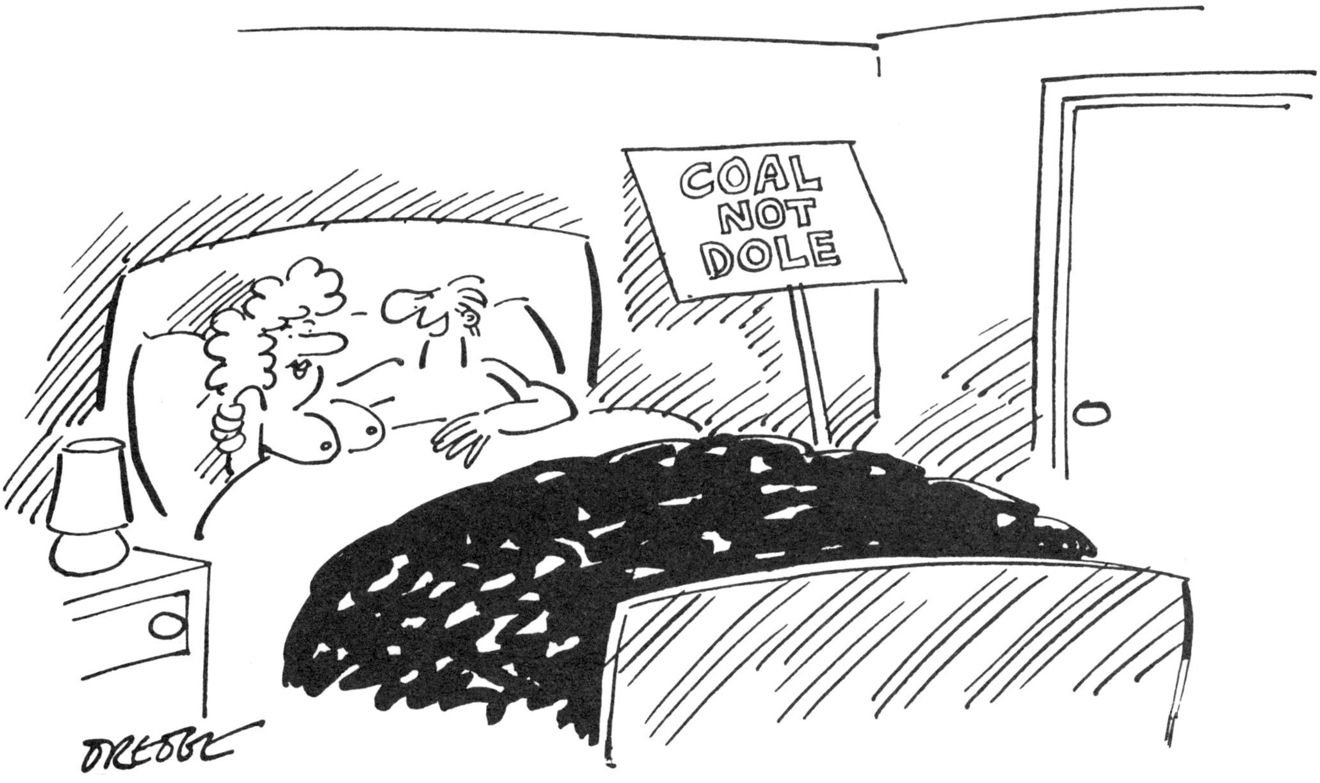
COAL NOT DOLE

'Stroke of luck your husband being a working miner, Gladys!'

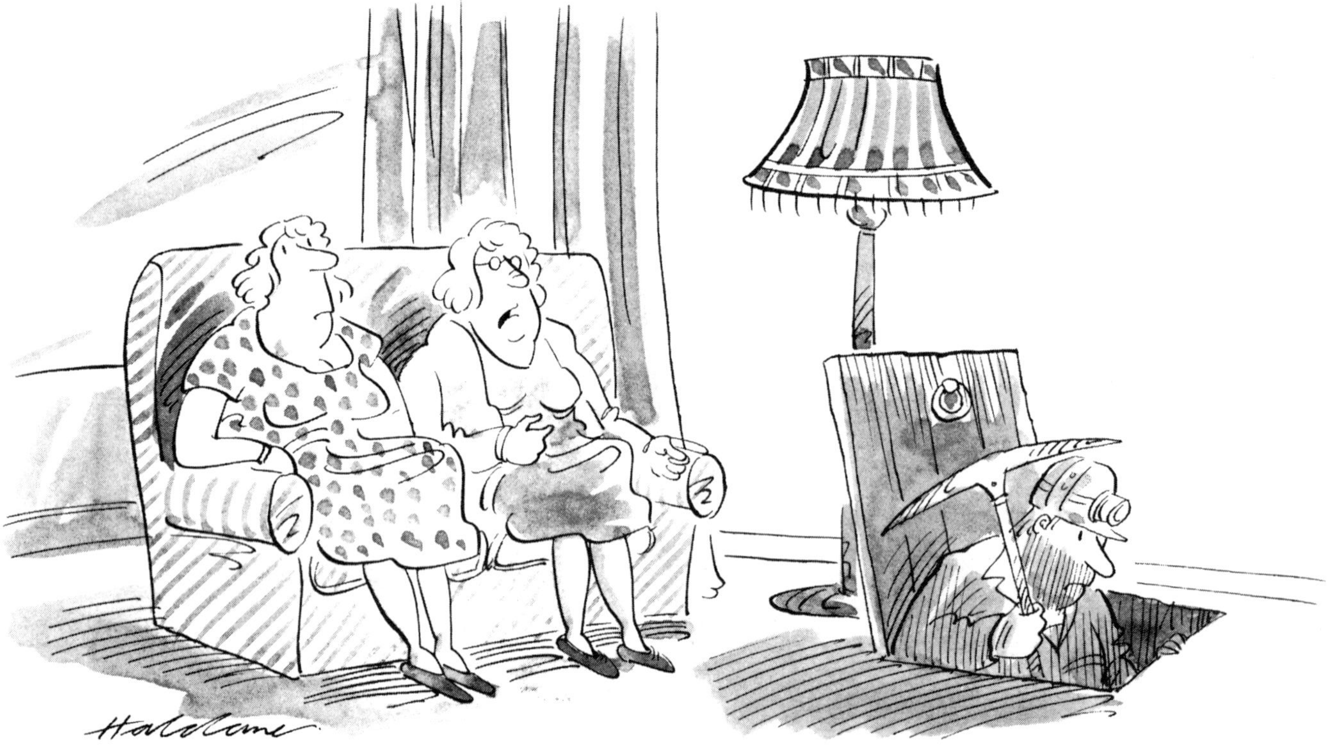

'After the dispute Billy decided to go freelance'

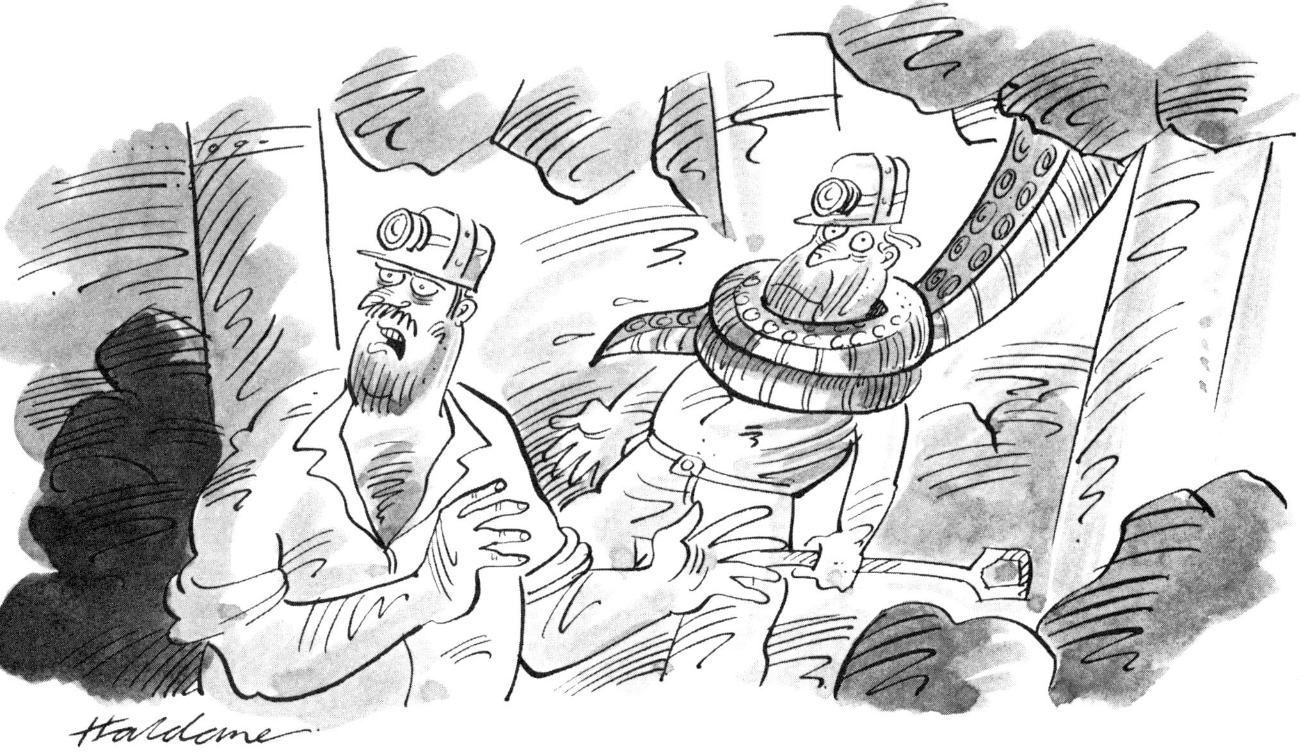
Haldane

'Er, Brian . . . How far out to sea is this seam?'

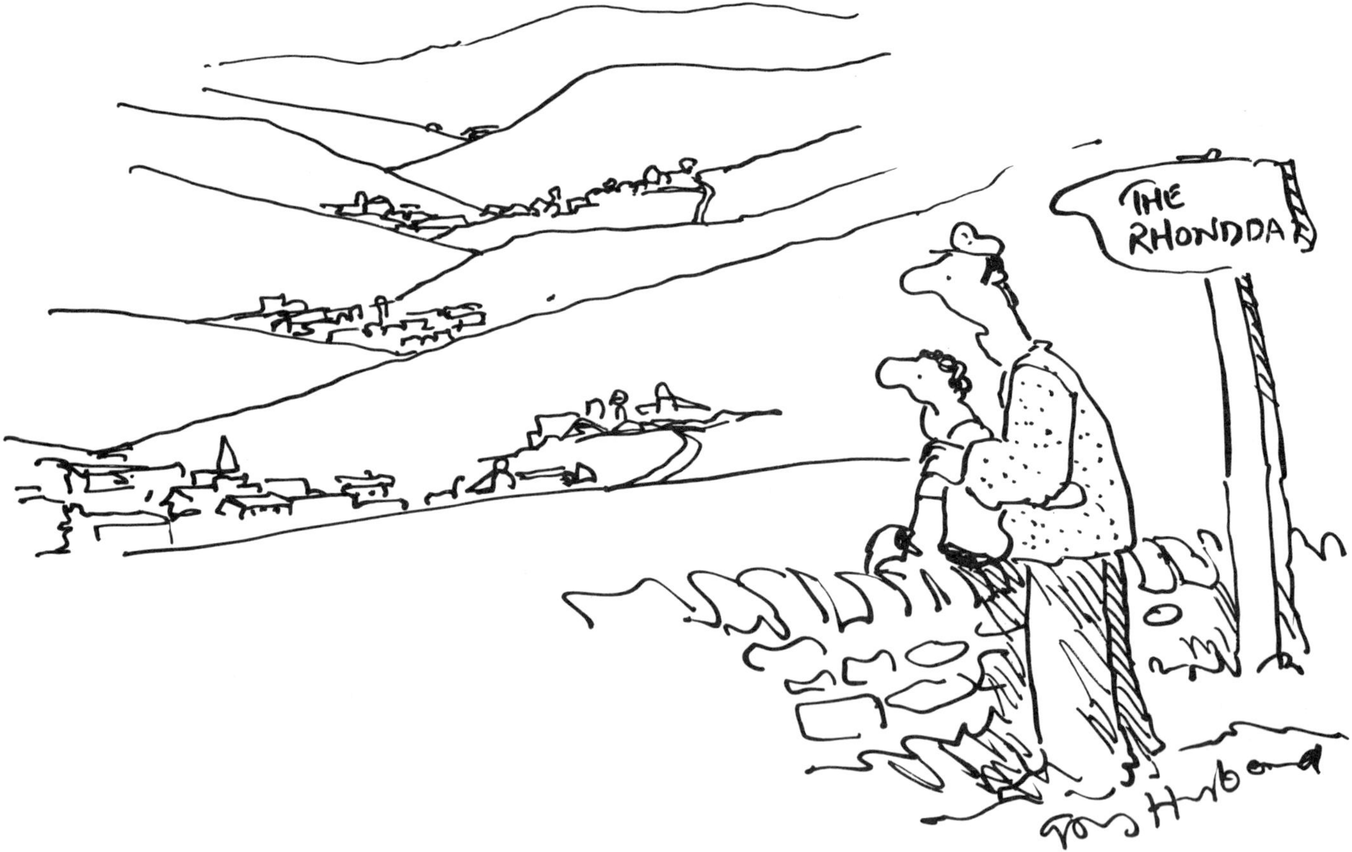
THE RHONDDA

'Some day, son, all this will be yours. Closed pits, no work, dying communities, no future'

THE ODEON
COMING SOON
IAN MACGREGOR
Vs
KING KONG
ACTION, STUNTS, SPECIAL EFFECTS
A BLOCKBUSTER ADULTS ONLY
Tony Husband

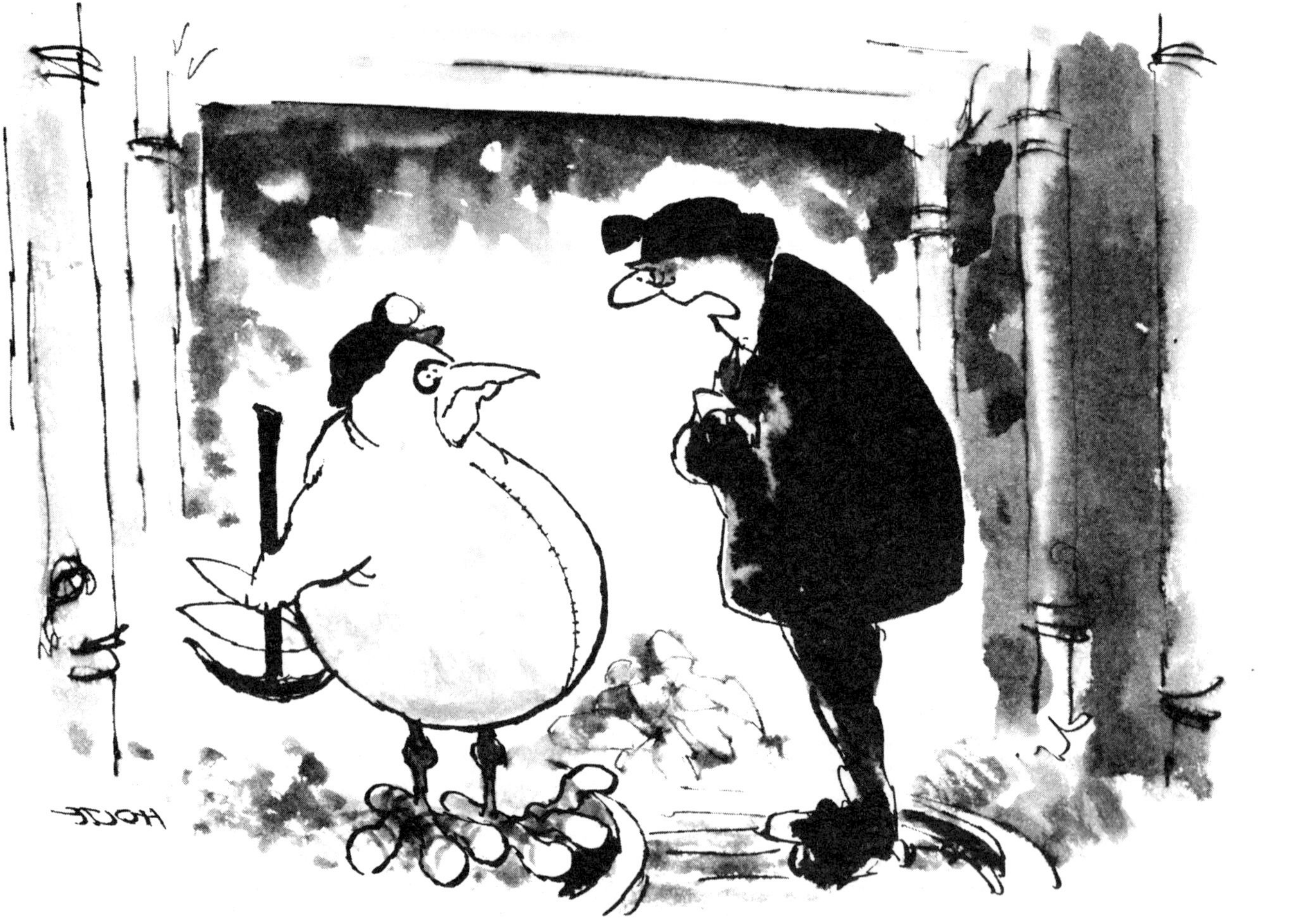

'Cut the "canary" bullshit, MacGregor . . . the game's up'

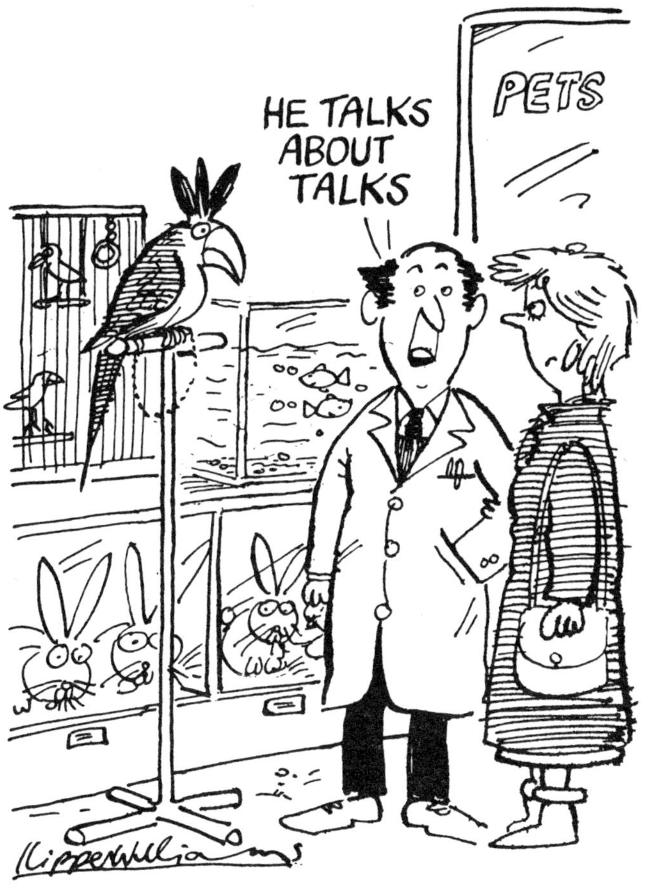
HE TALKS ABOUT TALKS
PETS

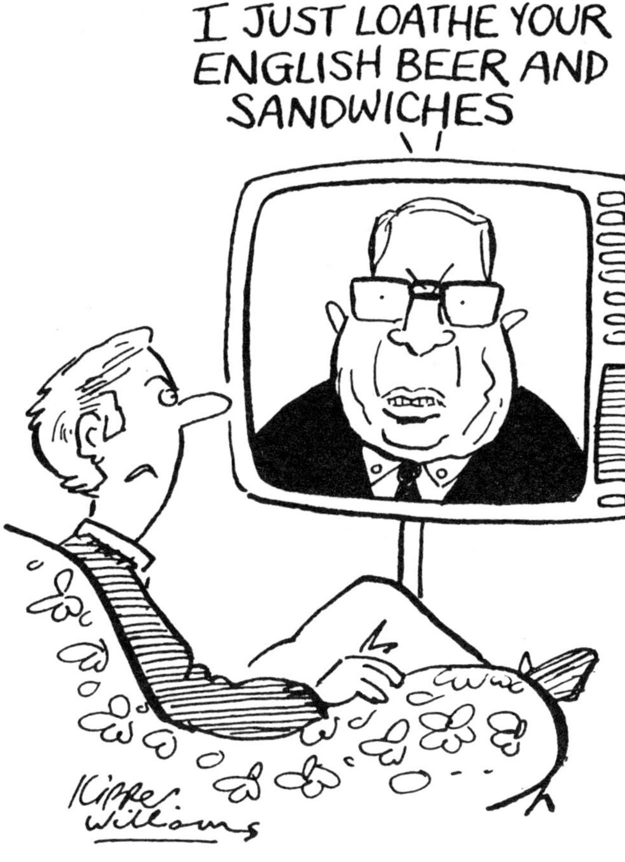
I JUST LOATHE YOUR ENGLISH BEER AND SANDWICHES

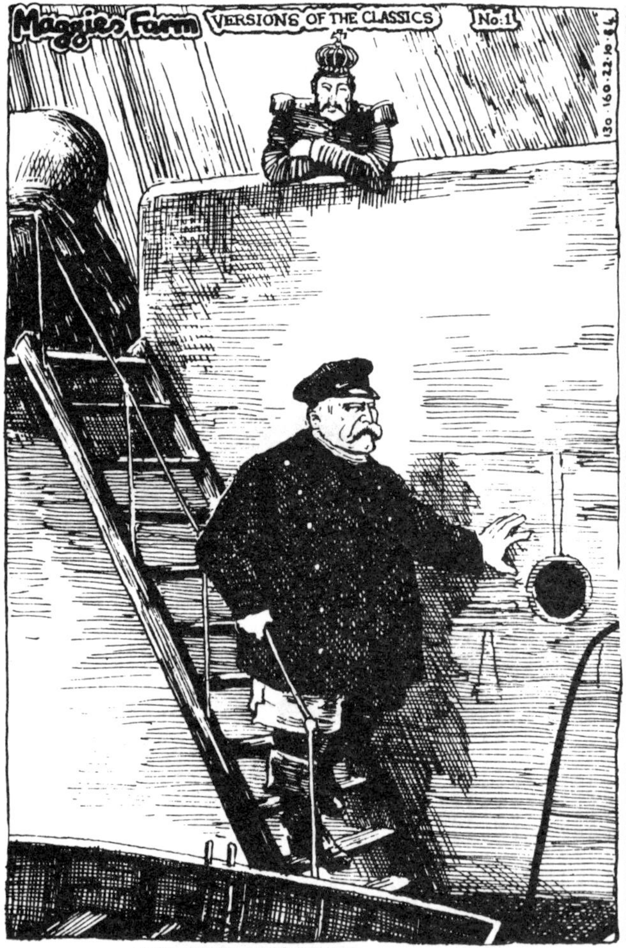
Maggies Farm
VERSIONS OF THE CLASSICS
No:1
130·160·22·10·84

DROPPING THE PILOT

AFTER SIR JOHN TENNIEL

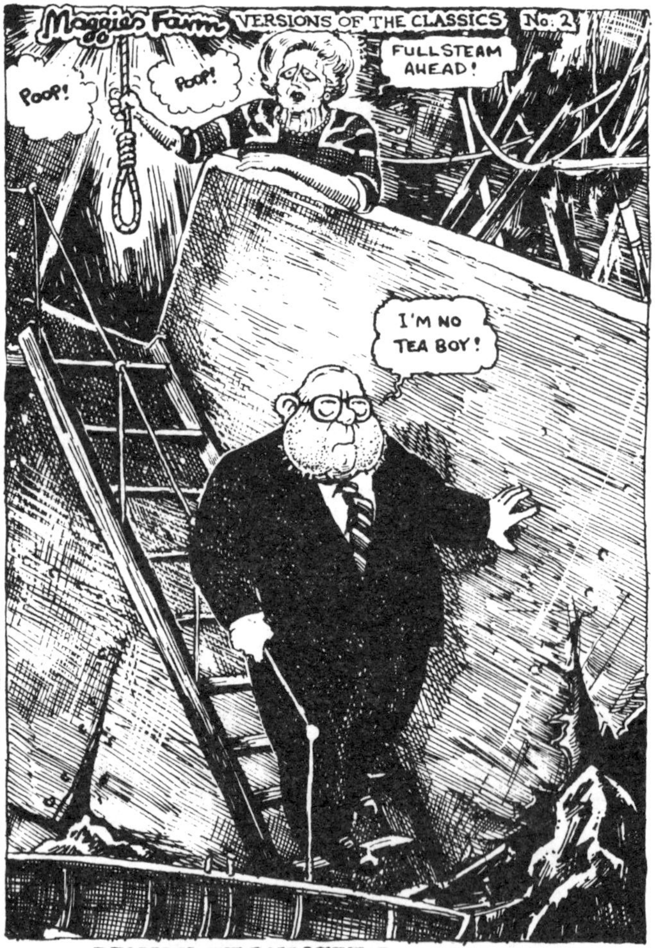
Maggies Farm
VERSIONS OF THE CLASSICS
No: 2
POOP!
POOP!
FULL STEAM AHEAD!
I'M NO TEA BOY!

DROPPING THE BOLLOCKHEAD

-©Steve Bell 1984-

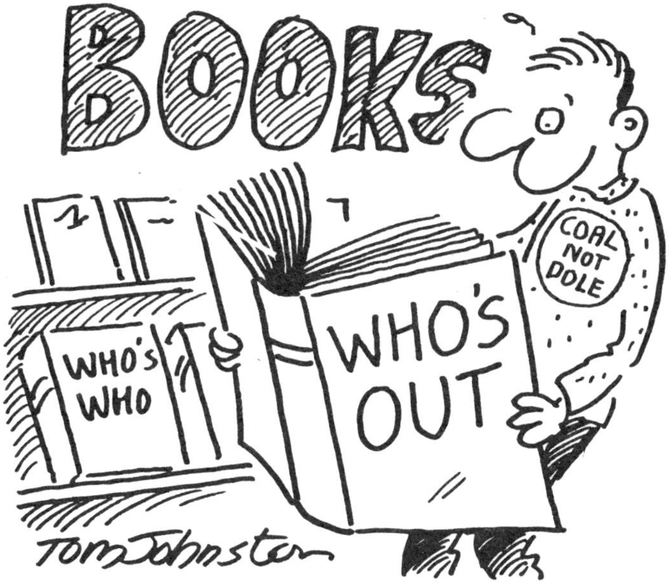
BOOKS
COAL NOT DOLE
WHO'S WHO
WHO'S OUT
Tom Johnston

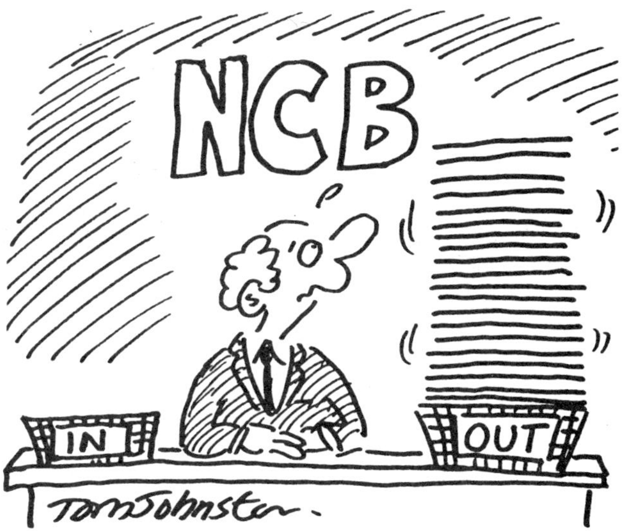
NCB
IN
OUT
Tom Johnston

MEANWHILE, BACK IN THE U.K.:
HEY– DUTCH ELM!! I WANNA WORD WITH YOU!!
JUST A MINUTE BOSS— I'M THINKING...
HMMM– -I NEED TO GO TO THE TOILET
DUTCH ELM
SNAP
ELDERLY Mac
...BUT I'D BETTER TAKE A BALLOT ON IT, JUST TO MAKE SURE...
"ALL THOSE IN FAVOUR OF GOING TO THE TOILET RAISE THEIR HANDS..!"
DUTCH ELM
C'MON– HURRY IT UP WILLYA!?
"ALL THOSE AGAINST?"
WELL, IT LOOKS LIKE IT'S UNANIMOUS– -I'M GOING TO THE TOILET.
DUTCH ELM
YOU'RE TAKIN' YOUR TIME FELLA!!
OOPS... TOO LATE!!
DUTCH ELM
JUST WHAT IN HELL DO YOU THINK YOU'RE DOIN' DUTCH ELM?
© Steve Bell 1984
882.

I'M GONNA CONFIDE SOMETHING IN YOU, DUTCH ELM–YOU CAN KEEP A SECRET CAN'T YOU?
YES BOSS
ELDERLY Mac
DUTCH ELM
883.
...I'M GONNA LEAVE THIS GODDAMN COUNTRY VERY SHORTLY, AND I STRONGLY ADVISE YOU TO DO THE SAME....
YES BOSS?
DUTCH ELM
...THE WHOLE GODDAMN PLACE IS SHOT THROUGH WITH GOD-DAMN COMMIES – THE GODDAMN COAL BOARD IS FULLA' COMMIES! I'M GOIN' BACK TO WHERE A MAN CAN WIELD A HATCHET IN AN ATMOSPHERE OF TRUE FREEDOM!
© Steve Bell 1984
YOU'RE GOIN' BACK TO AMERICA THEN, BOSS?
NO, I'M GOIN' RIGHT BACK HOME TO URANUS!
ELDERLY Mac

AT A MEETING OF THE WORKING MINERS COMMITTEE:
JUST A MOMENT, MY FELLOW SUPERHEROES – – I'M GETTING SOME IMPORTANT LEGAL ADVICE FROM OUR FRIEND FROM THE FREEDOM ASSOCIATION.
BZZZBZZ BZZBZZ
NNNN
NNN
NNNN
RRRRR
NNNNN
DUTCH ELM
SNAPPED-OFF TWIG
BURNING BUSH
TWO SHORT PLANKS
BUNDLE OF STICKS
ROTTING STUMP
© Steve Bell 1984
884
HE'S INFORMED ME THAT IF WE SET FIRE TO OURSELVES HERE AND NOW, WE'D HAVE A PRIMA FACIE CASE OF ARSON AGAINST ARTHUR SCARGILL. WE COULD HAVE HIM ARRESTED WITHIN THE HOUR. WHAT'S THE FEELING, SUPERHEROES?
MY HEAD FEELS NUMB
I FEEL ALL LUMPY
TAKE THE MONEY
OPEN THE BOX
TAKE THE MONEY
OPEN THE BOX
TAKE THE BOX
OPEN THE MONEY
ROTTING STUMP
DISEASED LARCH
LONESOME PINE
MANKY MULBERRY
DUTCH ELM

WALK TALL – THE DUTCH ELM WAY
STRAWFOOT BOBBLEFOOT STRAWFOOT BOBBLEFOOT
STRAWFOOT BOBBLEFOOT STRAWFOOT BOBBLEFOOT
DUTCH ELM
885
STAND PROUD – THE DUTCH ELM WAY
TIMBERRRR!
© Steve Bell 1984
SUPPORT YOUR UNION – THE DUTCH ELM WAY
I'M ALRIGHT JACK!
SUPPORT YOUR FRIENDS – THE DUTCH ELM WAY
YOU ARE THE MOTHER OF THE NATION MA'AM!
HOW TRUE!

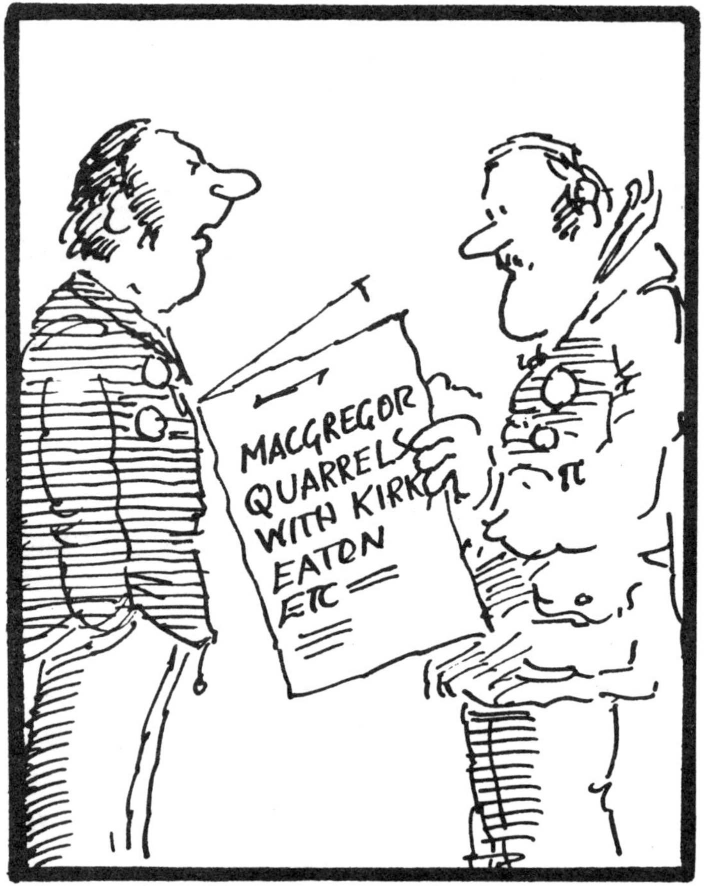
MACGREGOR
QUARRELS
WITH KIRK
EATON
ETC

‘It’s a race between the drift back in the NUM and the drift apart in the NCB’

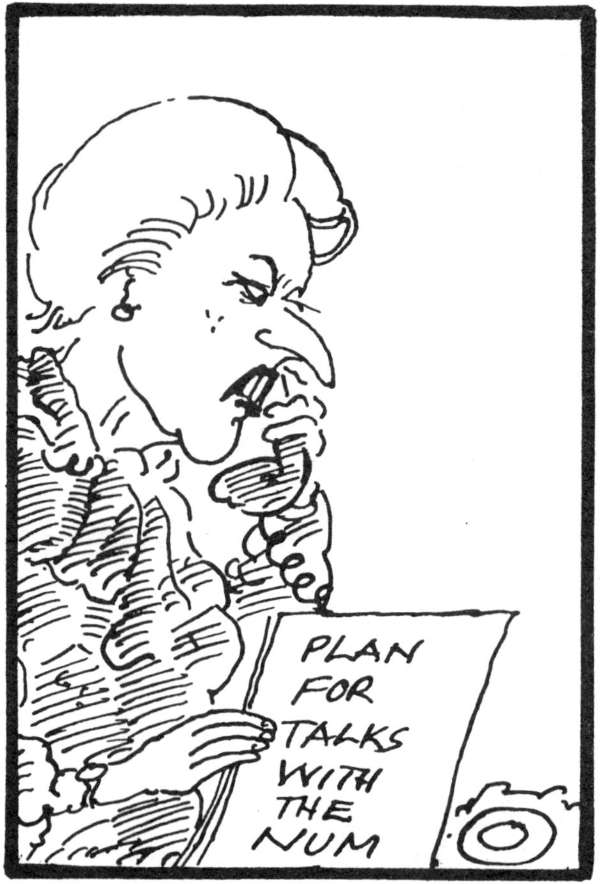
PLAN
FOR
TALKS
WITH
THE
NUM

‘I told you MacGregor, I want law, law, not jaw, jaw’

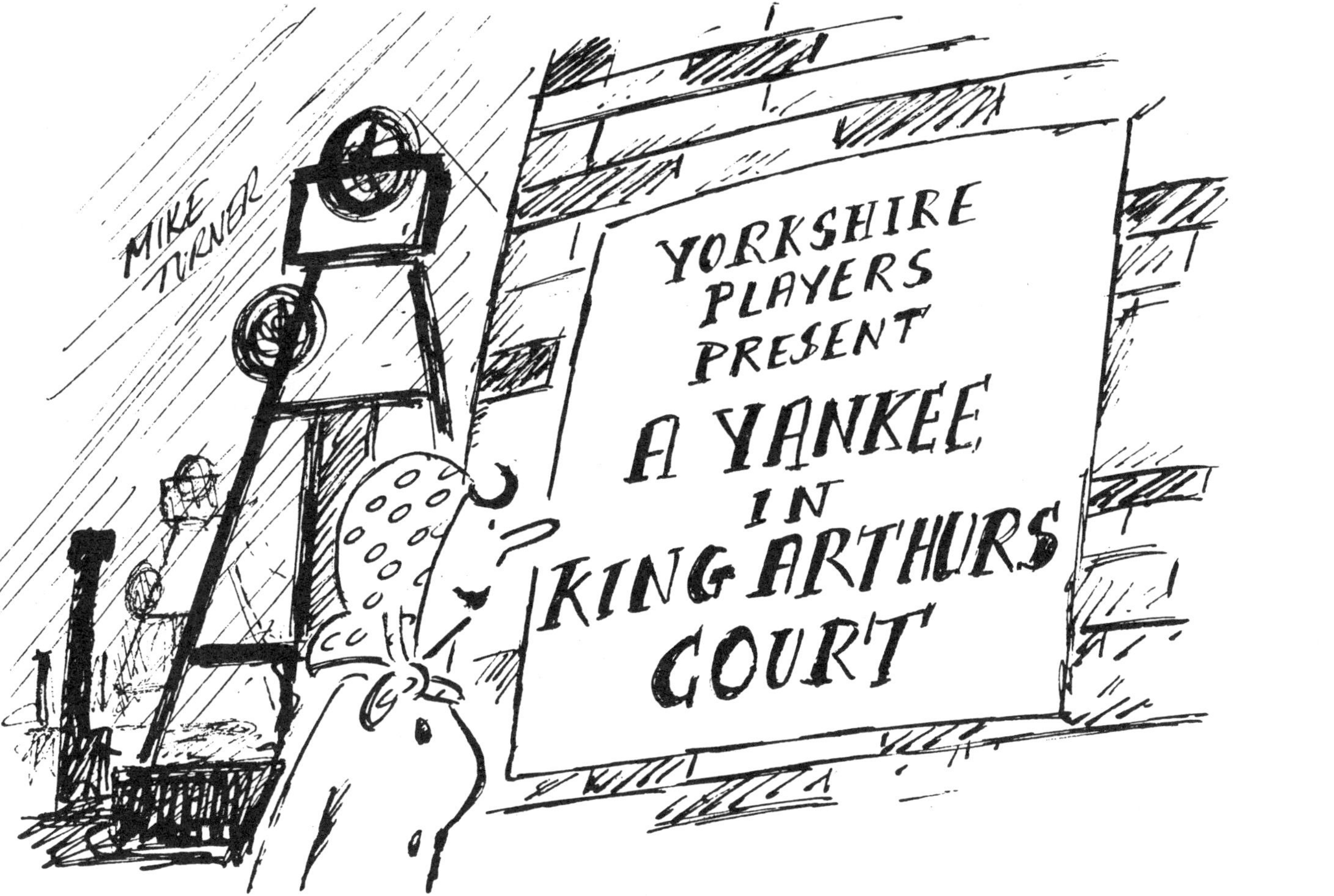
MIKE TURNER
YORKSHIRE PLAYERS PRESENT
A YANKEE IN KING ARTHURS COURT

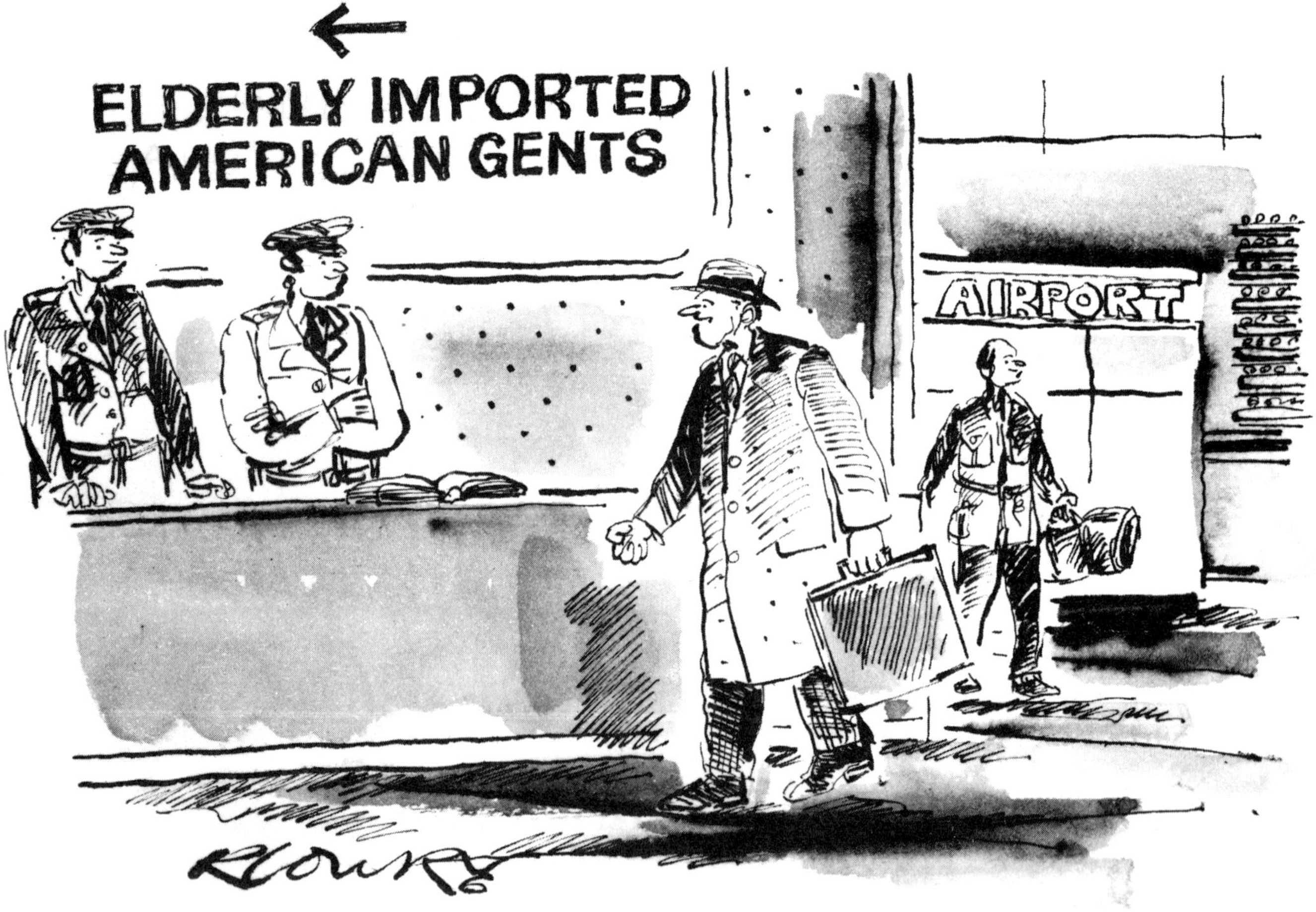
ELDERLY IMPORTED
AMERICAN GENTS
AIRPORT

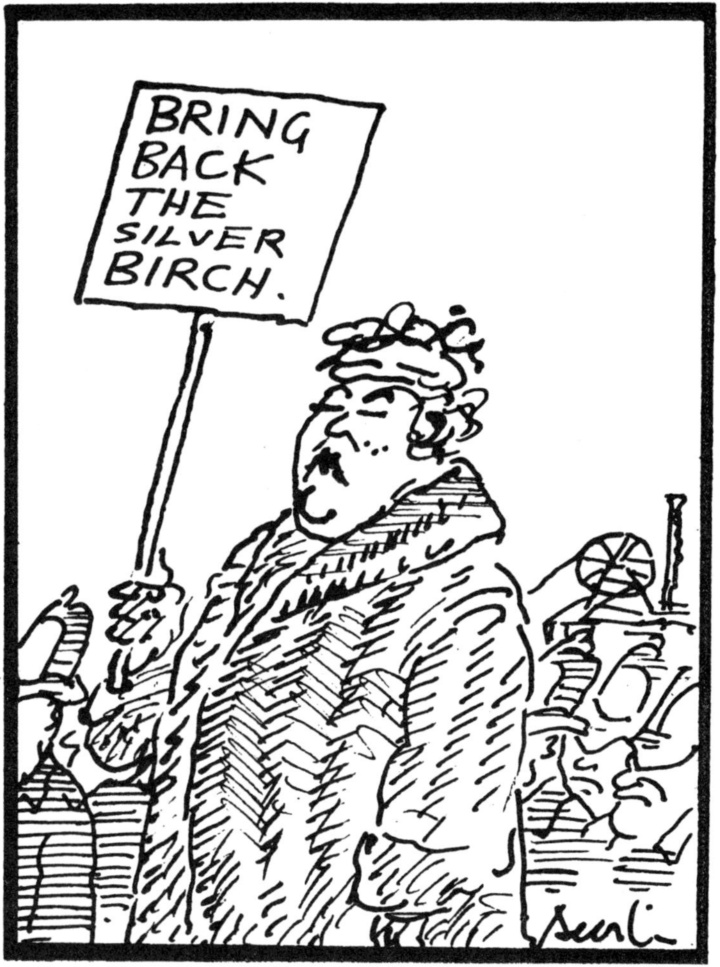
BRING BACK THE SILVER BIRCH.

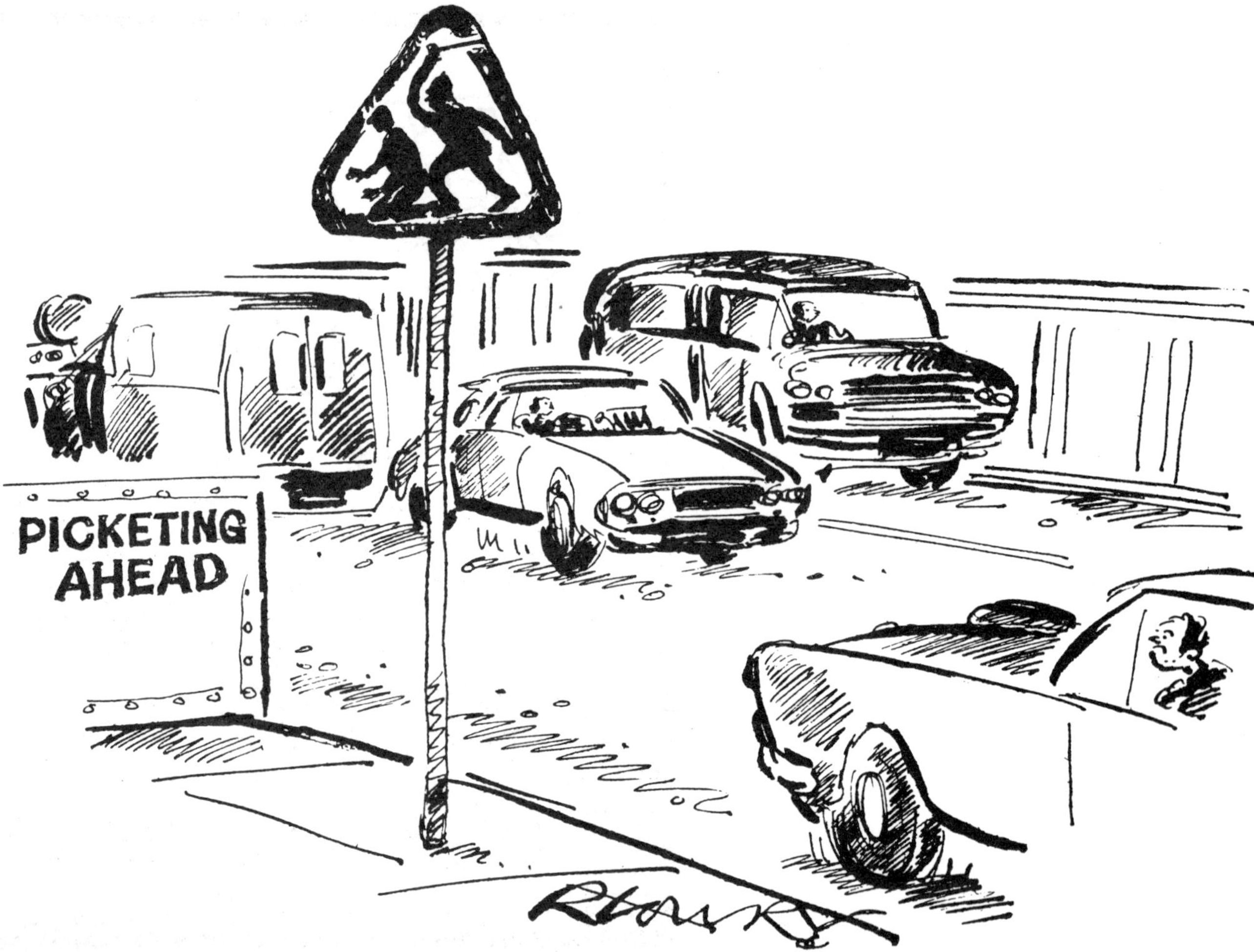
PICKETING
AHEAD

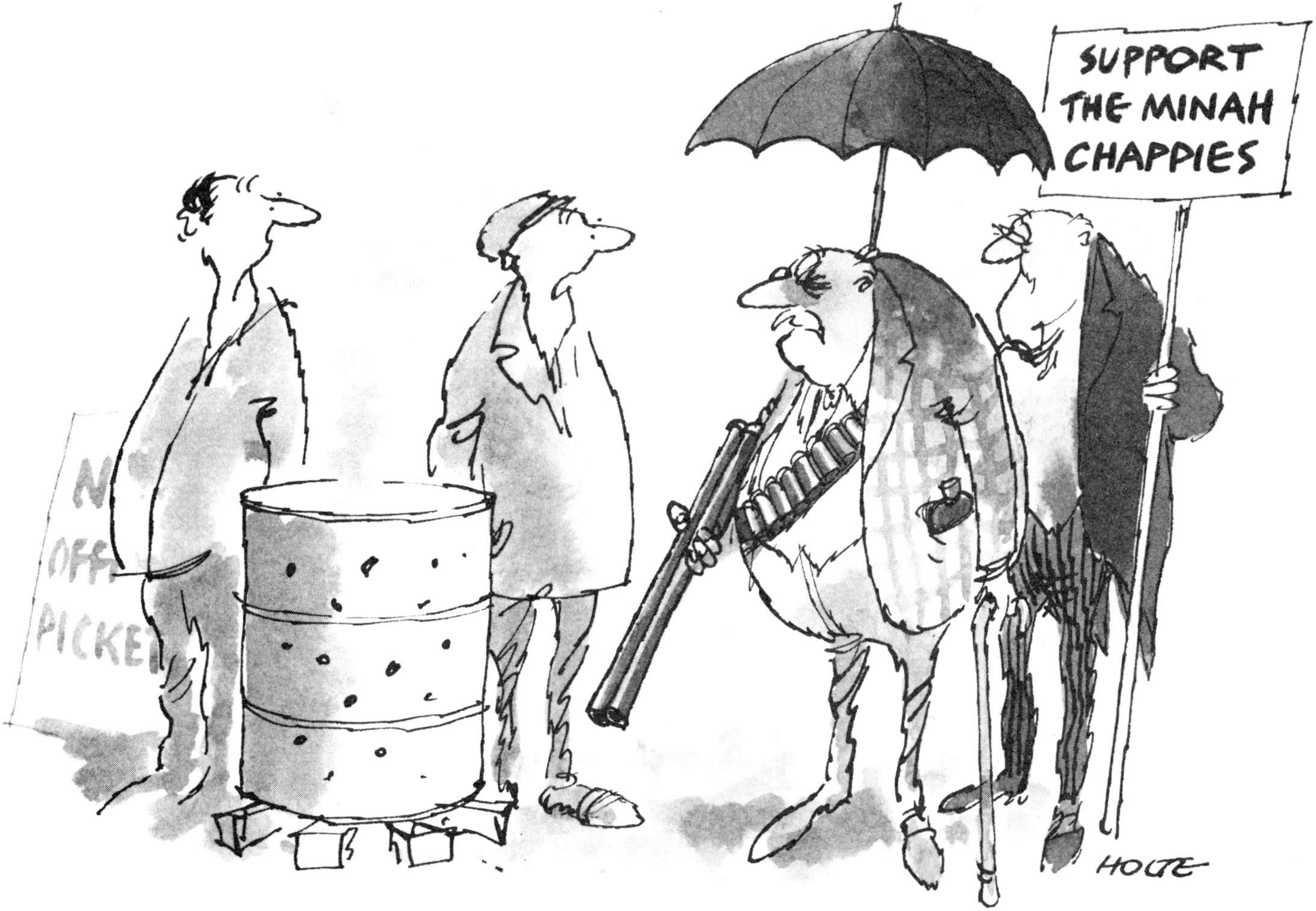
SUPPORT
THE MINAH
CHAPPIES
HOLTE

'Sorry to disappoint you Brigadier, but we aren't actually expecting any trouble'

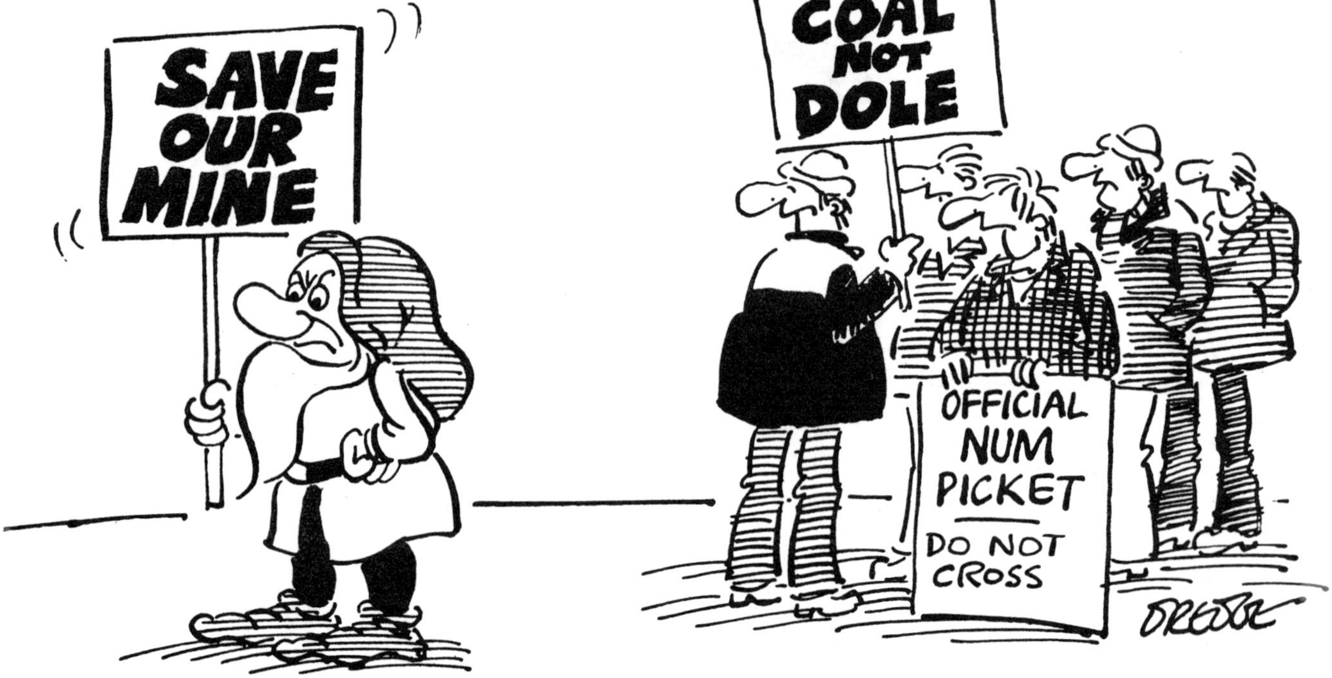
SAVE OUR MINE
COAL NOT DOLE
OFFICIAL NUM PICKET
DO NOT CROSS

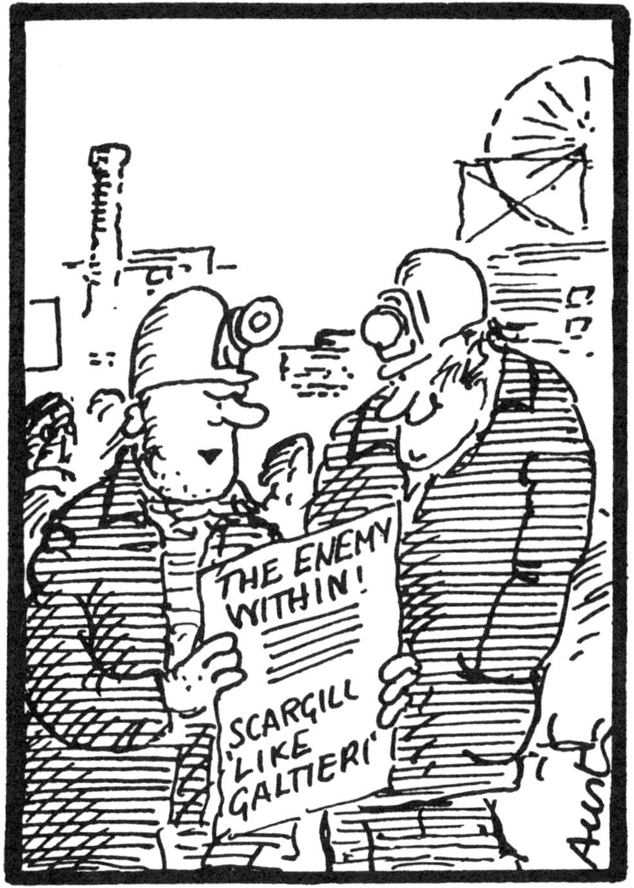
THE ENEMY WITHIN!
SCARGILL 'LIKE GALTIERI'

'I suppose they'll start to call us Scargies'

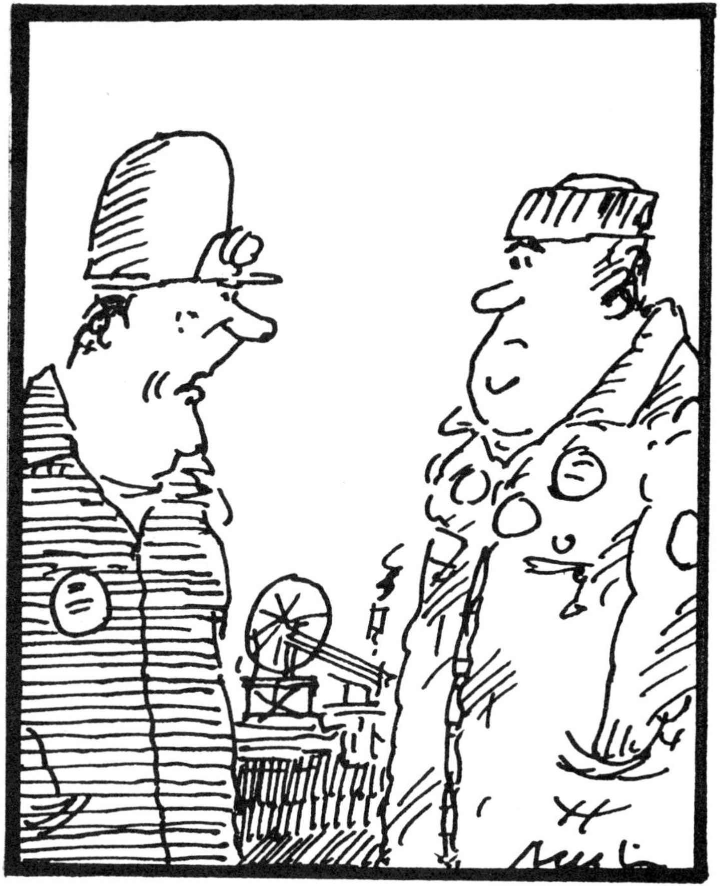

'If we'd bought Telecom shares we could have stayed out for a couple more years'

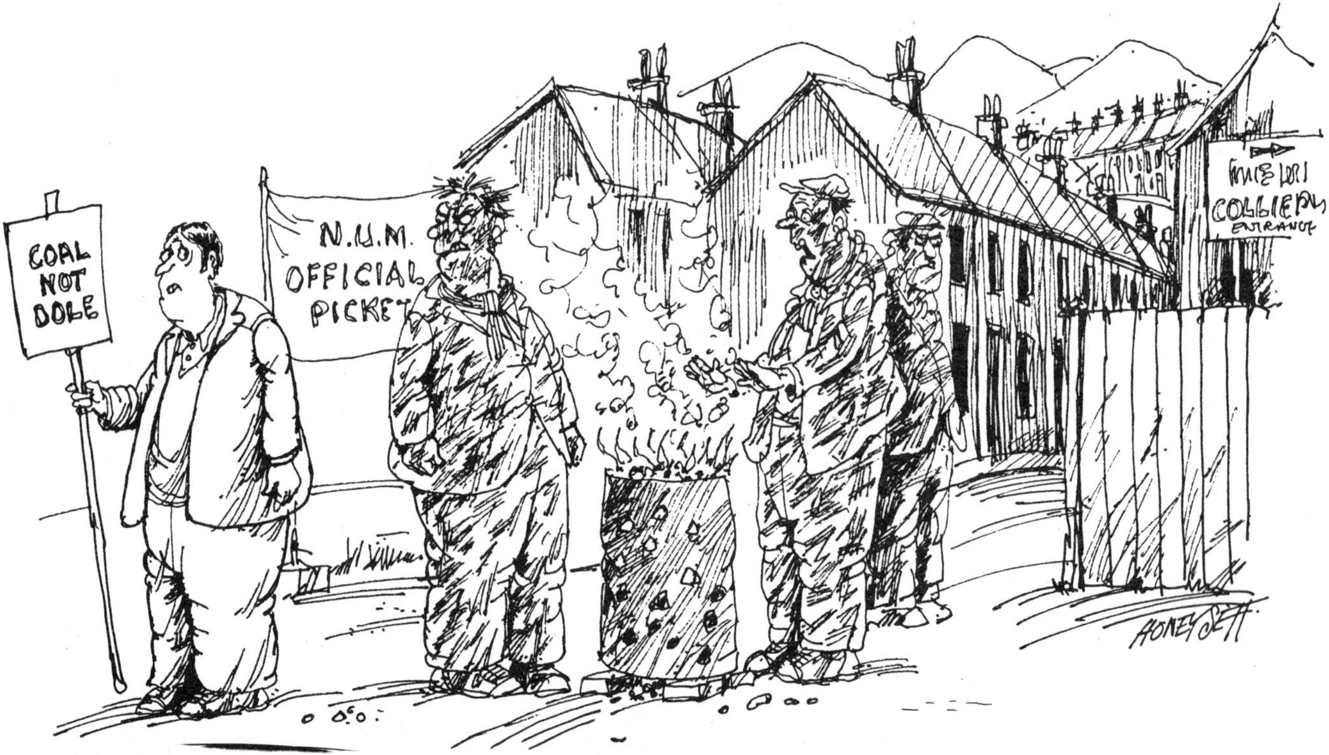
COAL NOT DOLE
N.U.M. OFFICIAL PICKET
COLLIERY ENTRANCE
HONEYSETT

'Be fair, Jim, he only went back to work for one day, so he could have a bath'

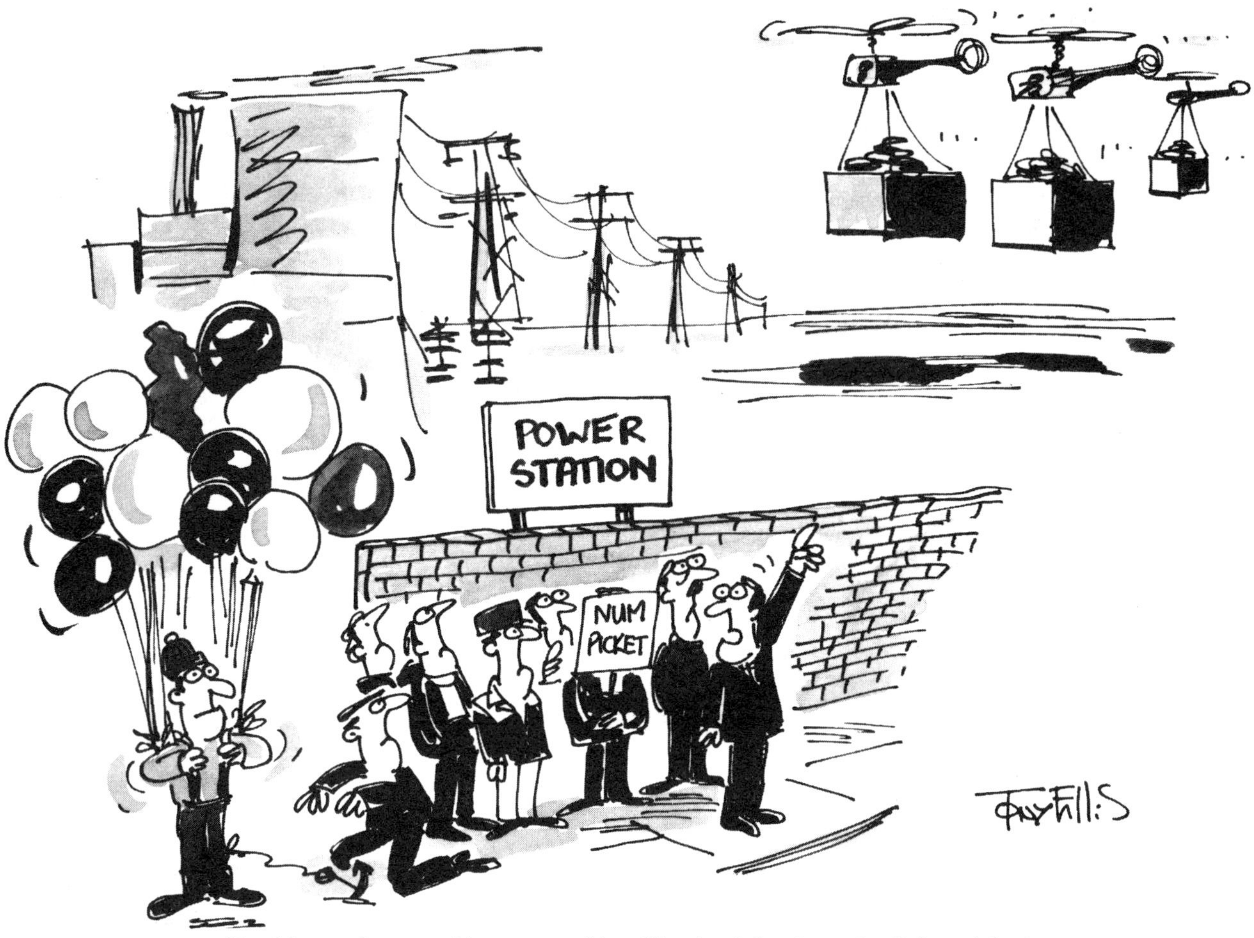
POWER STATION
NUM PICKET

'I told you they would try something like that! Send up the flying picket'

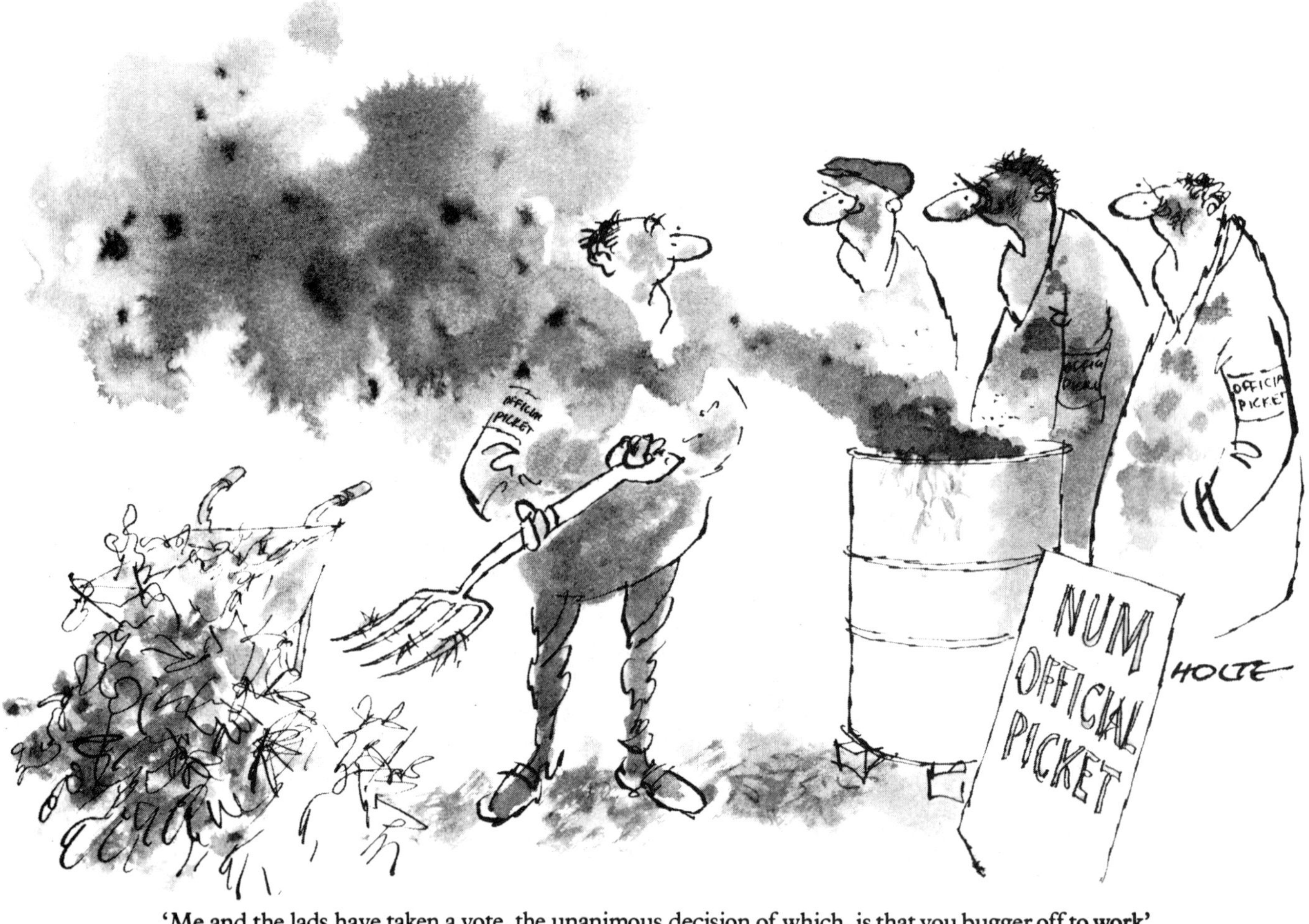
OFFICIAL PICKET
OFFICIAL PICKET
NUM OFFICIAL PICKET
HOLTE

'Me and the lads have taken a vote, the unanimous decision of which, is that you bugger off to work'

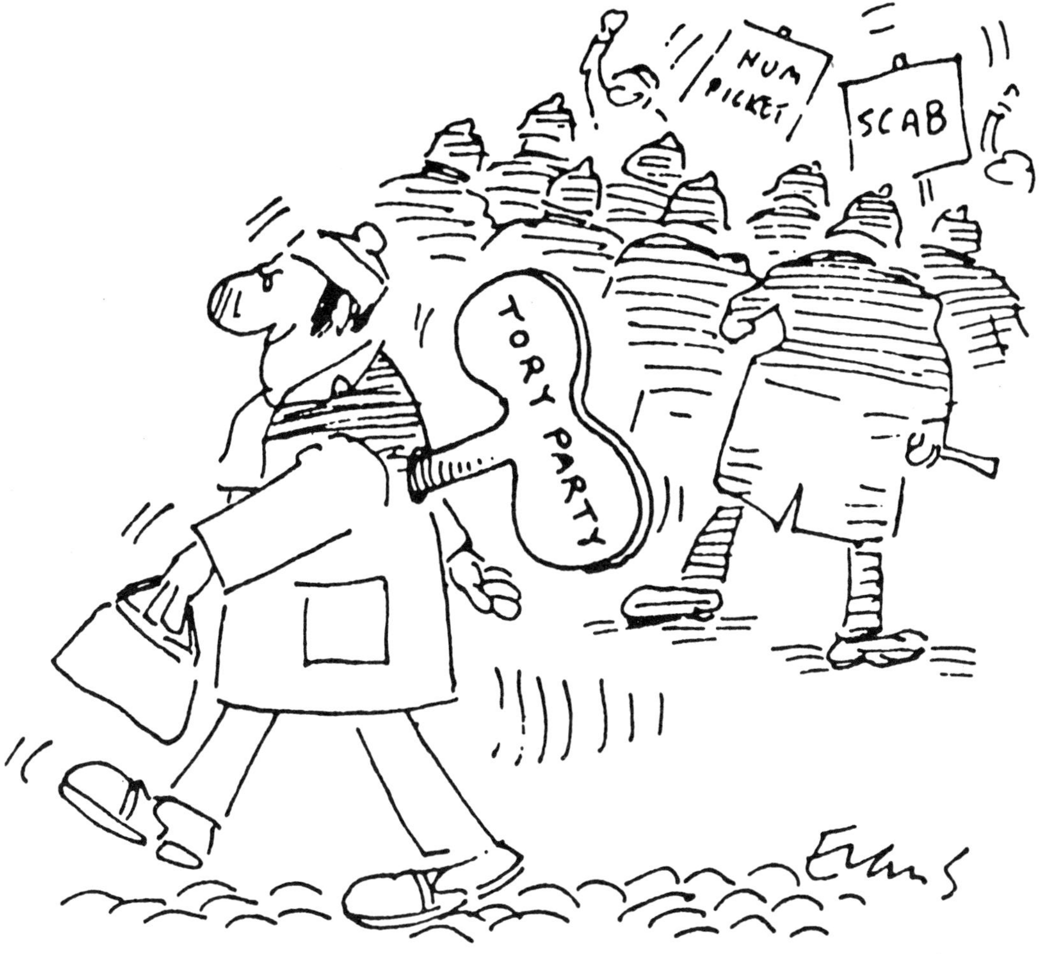
NUM PICKET
SCAB
TORY PARTY
Evans

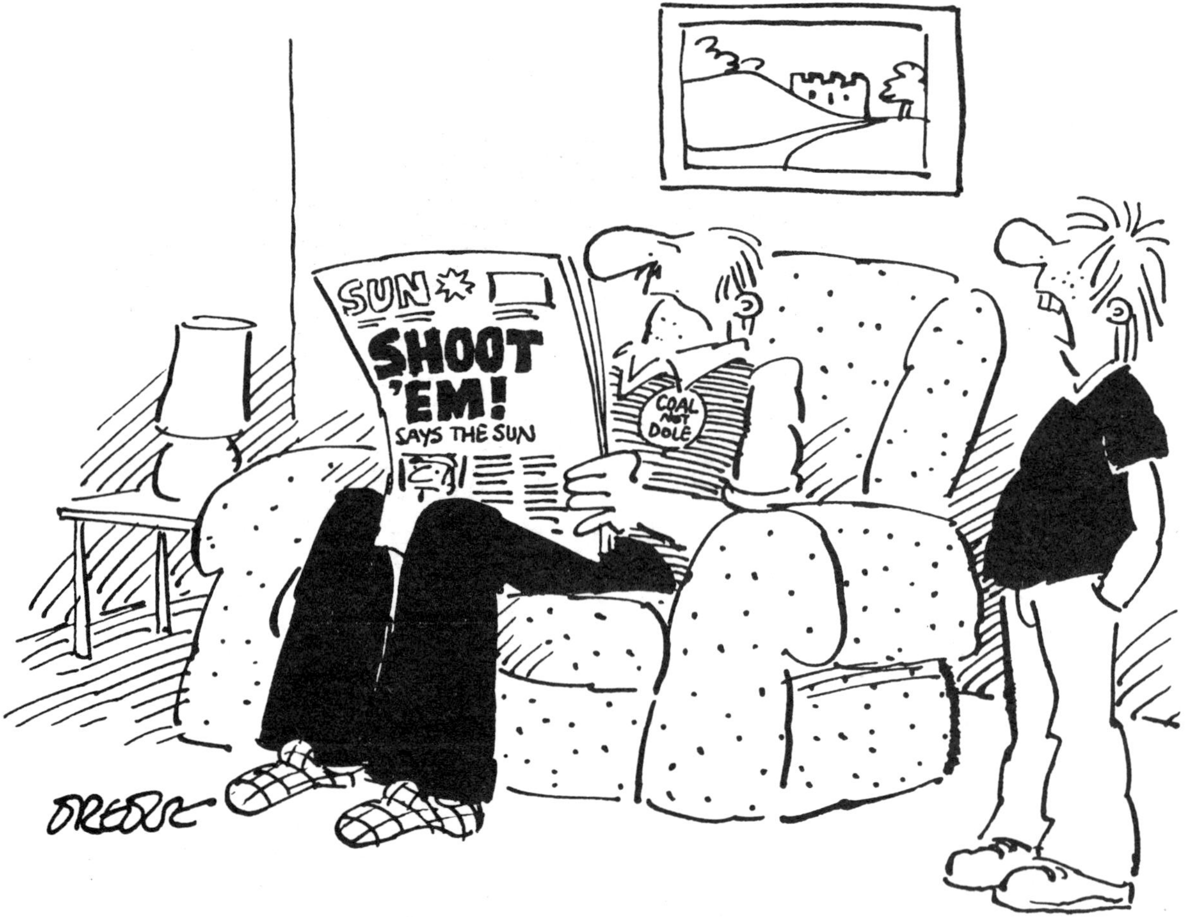
SUN
SHOOT 'EM!
SAYS THE SUN
COAL NOT DOLE

'What came first Dad – the picket or the scab?'

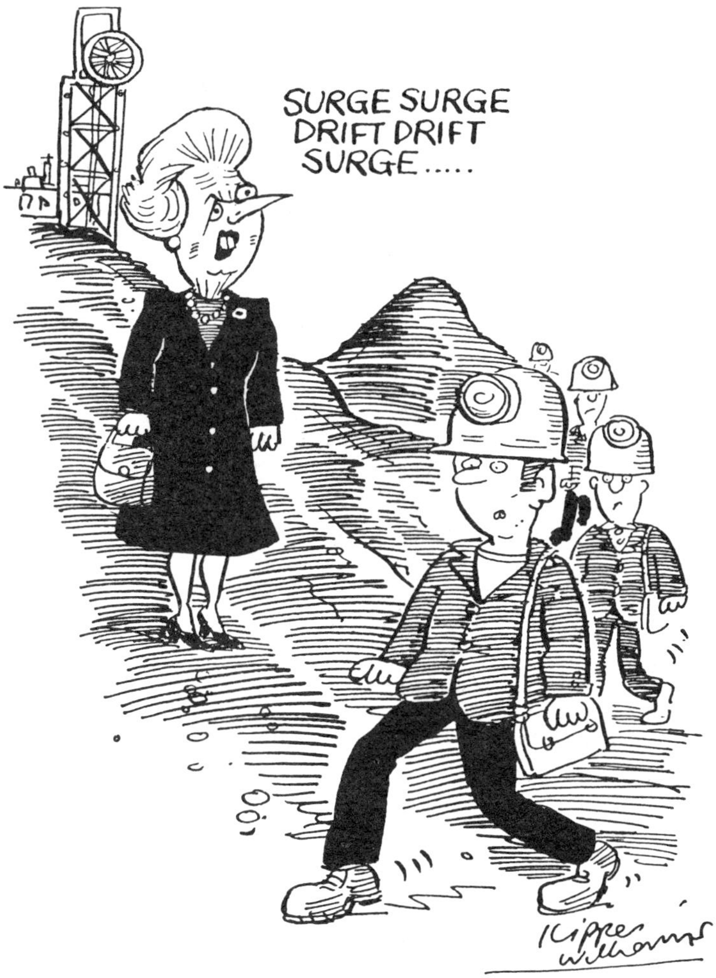
SURGE SURGE
DRIFT DRIFT
SURGE.....

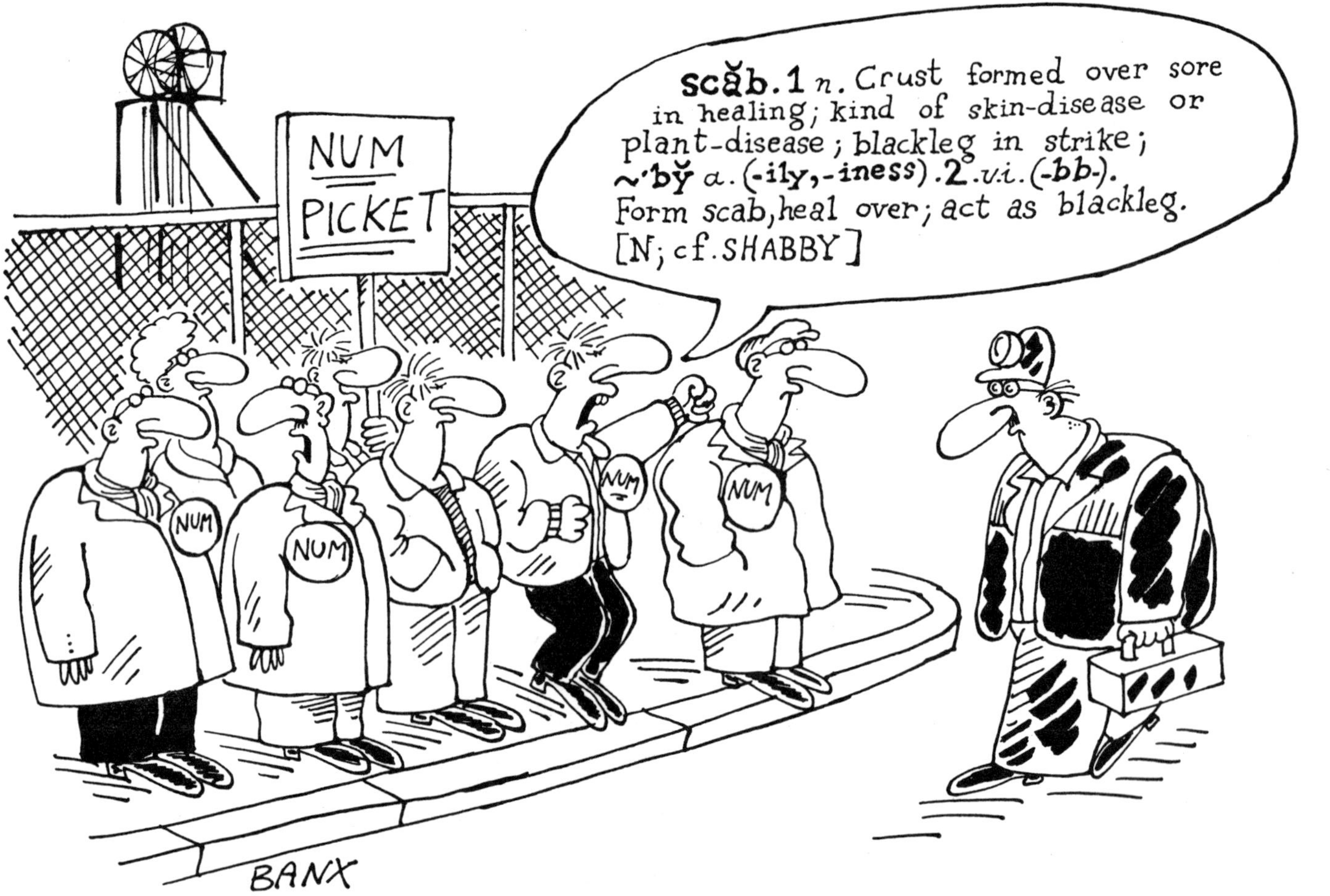
scăb.1 n. Crust formed over sore in healing; kind of skin-disease or plant-disease; blackleg in strike; ~'bў a. (-ily, -iness). 2. v.i. (-bb-). Form scab, heal over; act as blackleg. [N; cf. SHABBY]
NUM PICKET
NUM
NUM
NUM
NUM
BANX

'You get a better class of picket in the southern coal fields'

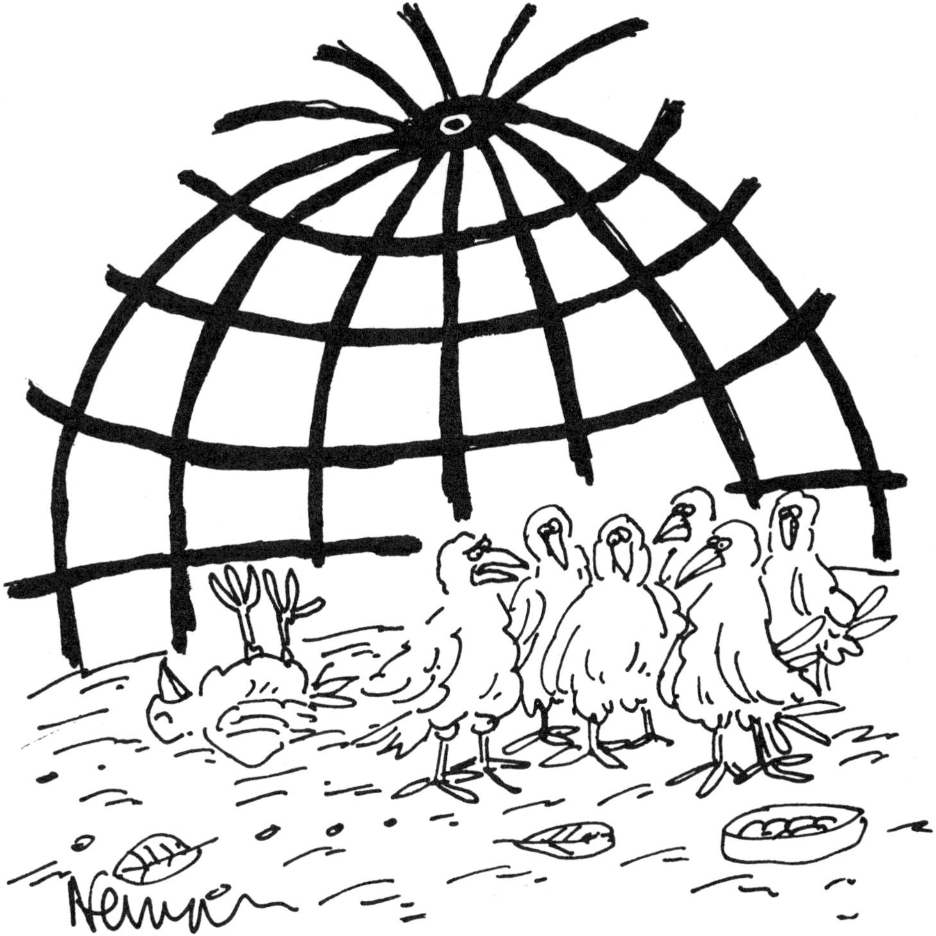
Newman

'I refuse to have anything to do with a working canary'

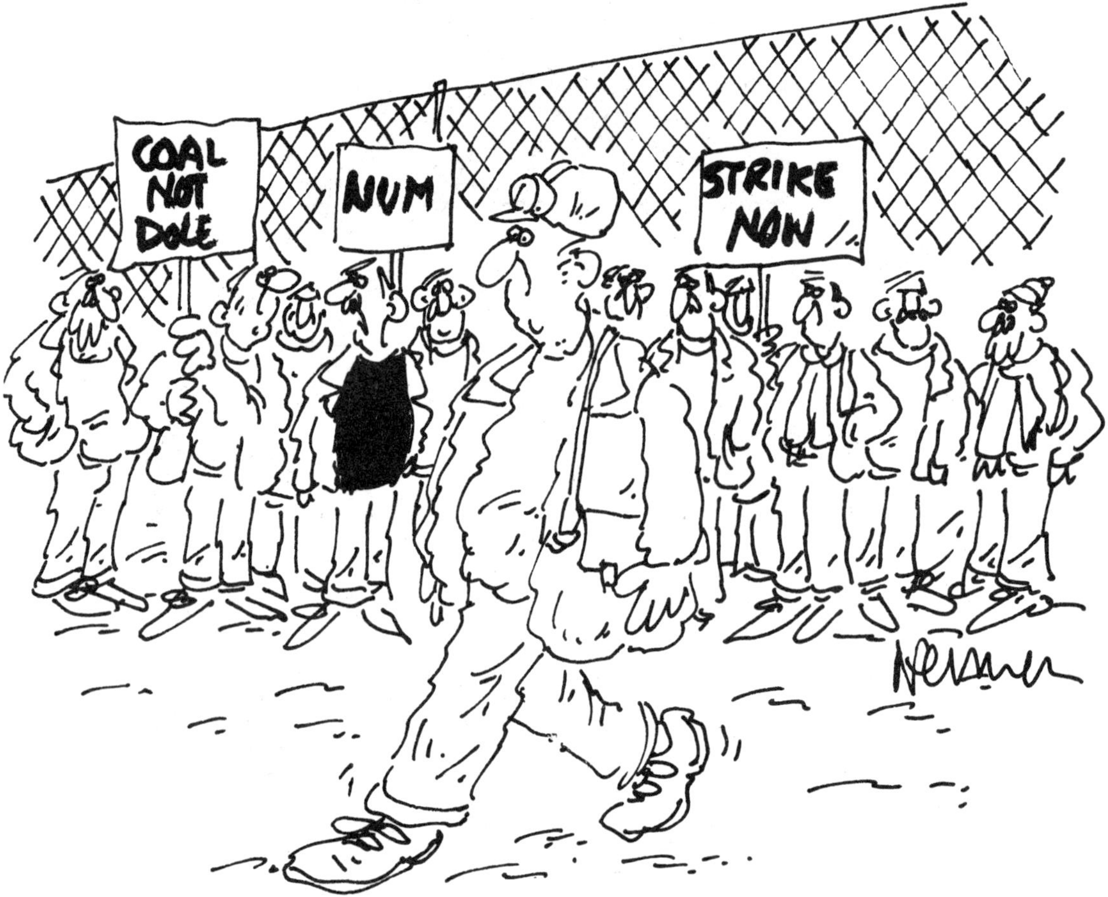
COAL NOT DOLE
NUM
STRIKE NOW

'We don't call him a scab – we haven't spoken to his family since the 1926 strike'

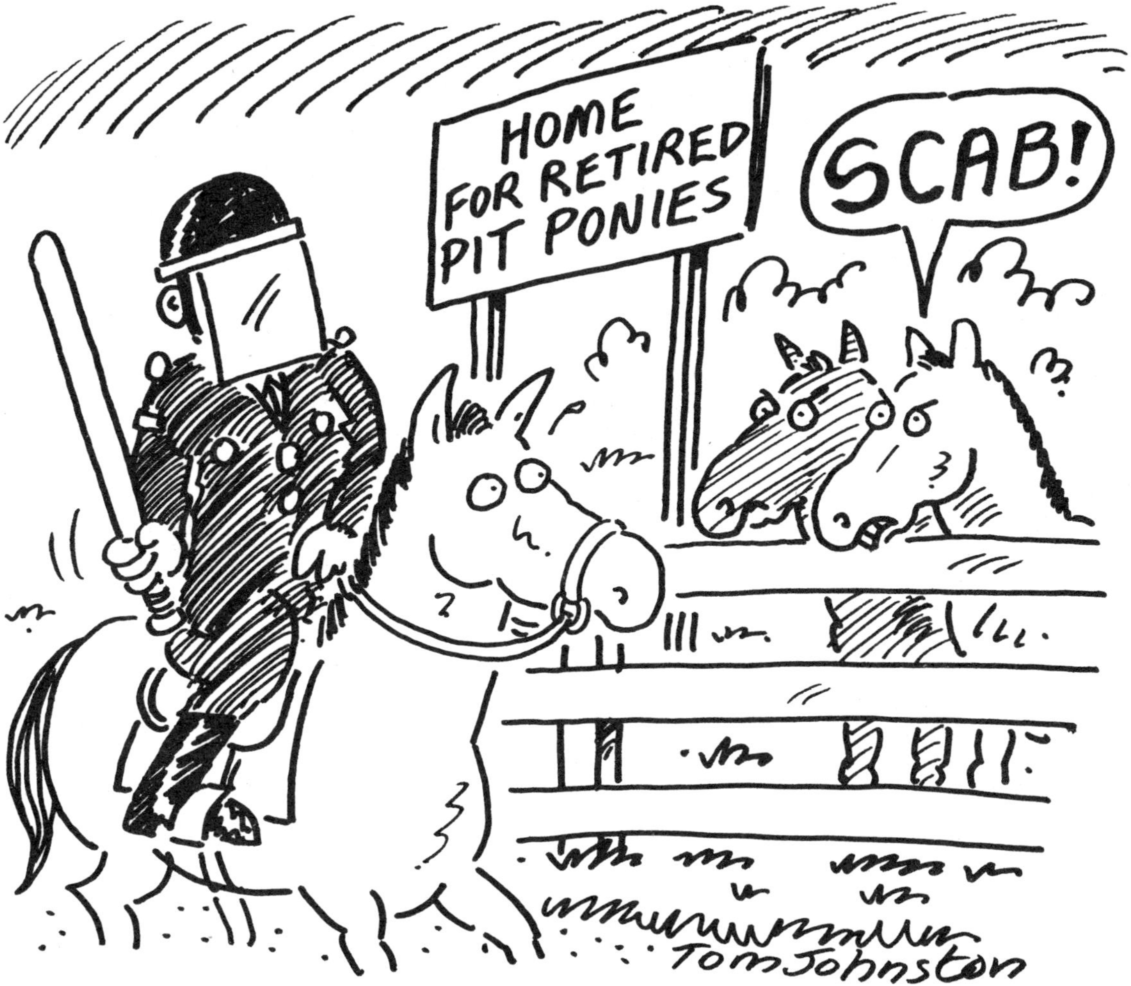
HOME FOR RETIRED PIT PONIES
SCAB!
Tom Johnston

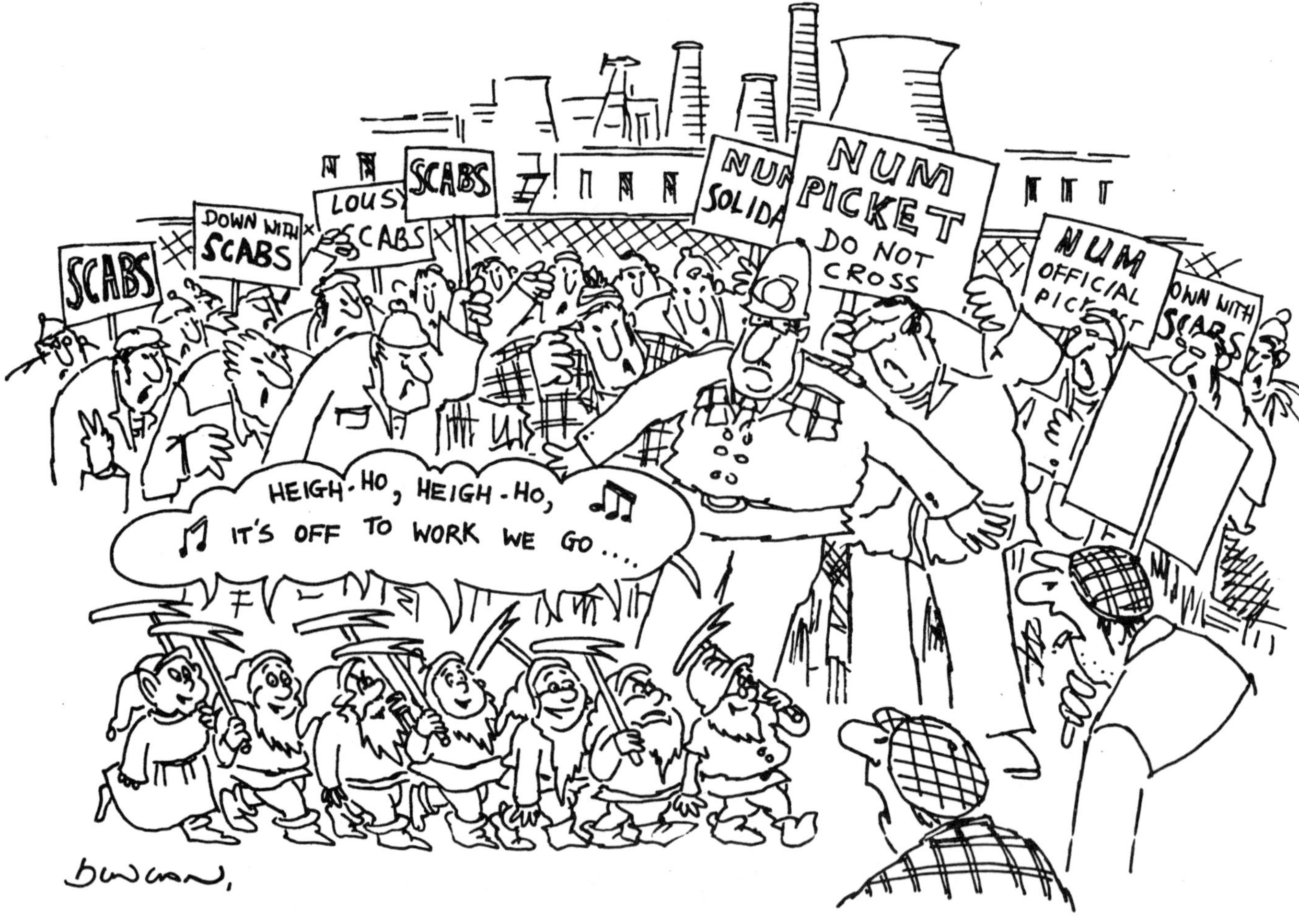
SCABS
DOWN WITH SCABS
LOUSY SCABS
SCABS
NUM SOLIDA
NUM PICKET DO NOT CROSS
NUM OFFICIAL PICK
OWN WITH SCABS
HEIGH-HO, HEIGH-HO, IT'S OFF TO WORK WE GO....
DUNCAN.

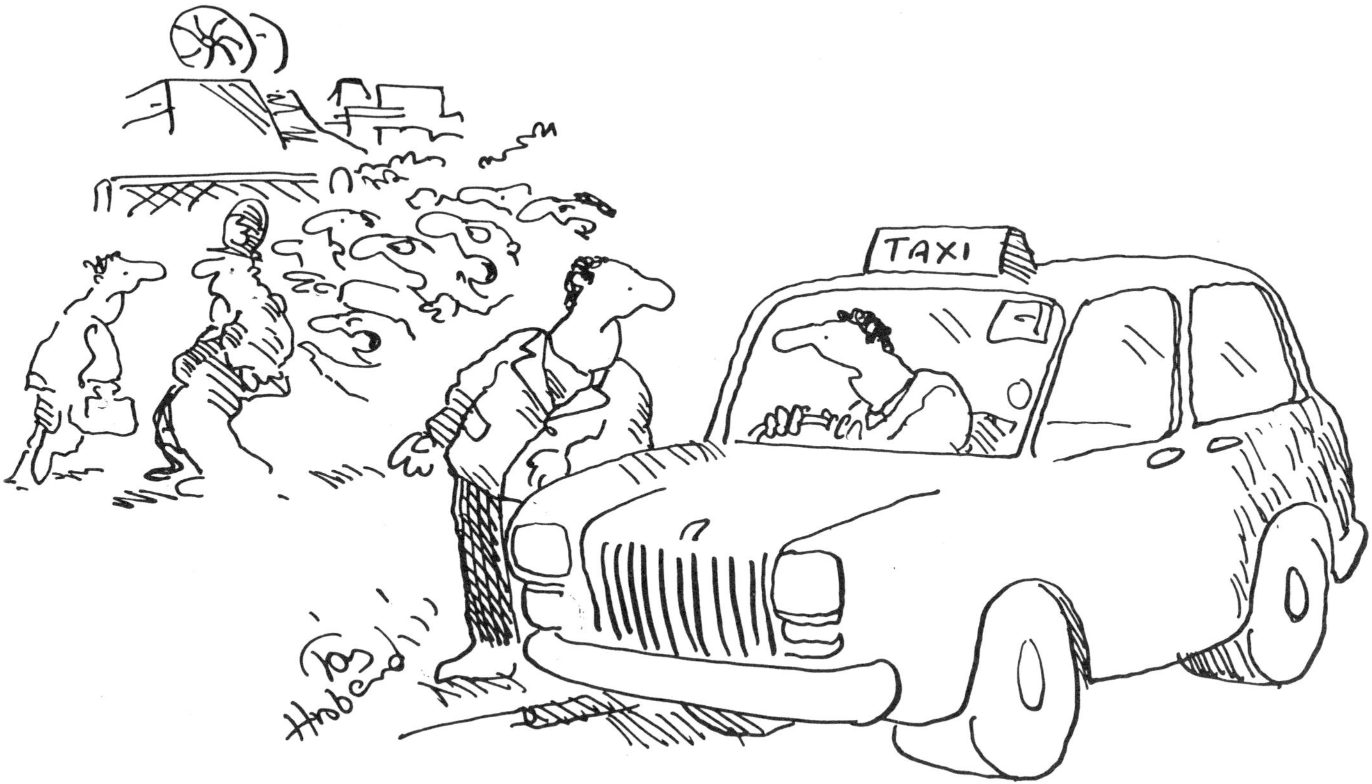
TAXI

'Oh, scab. Sorry, I thought you shouted cab'

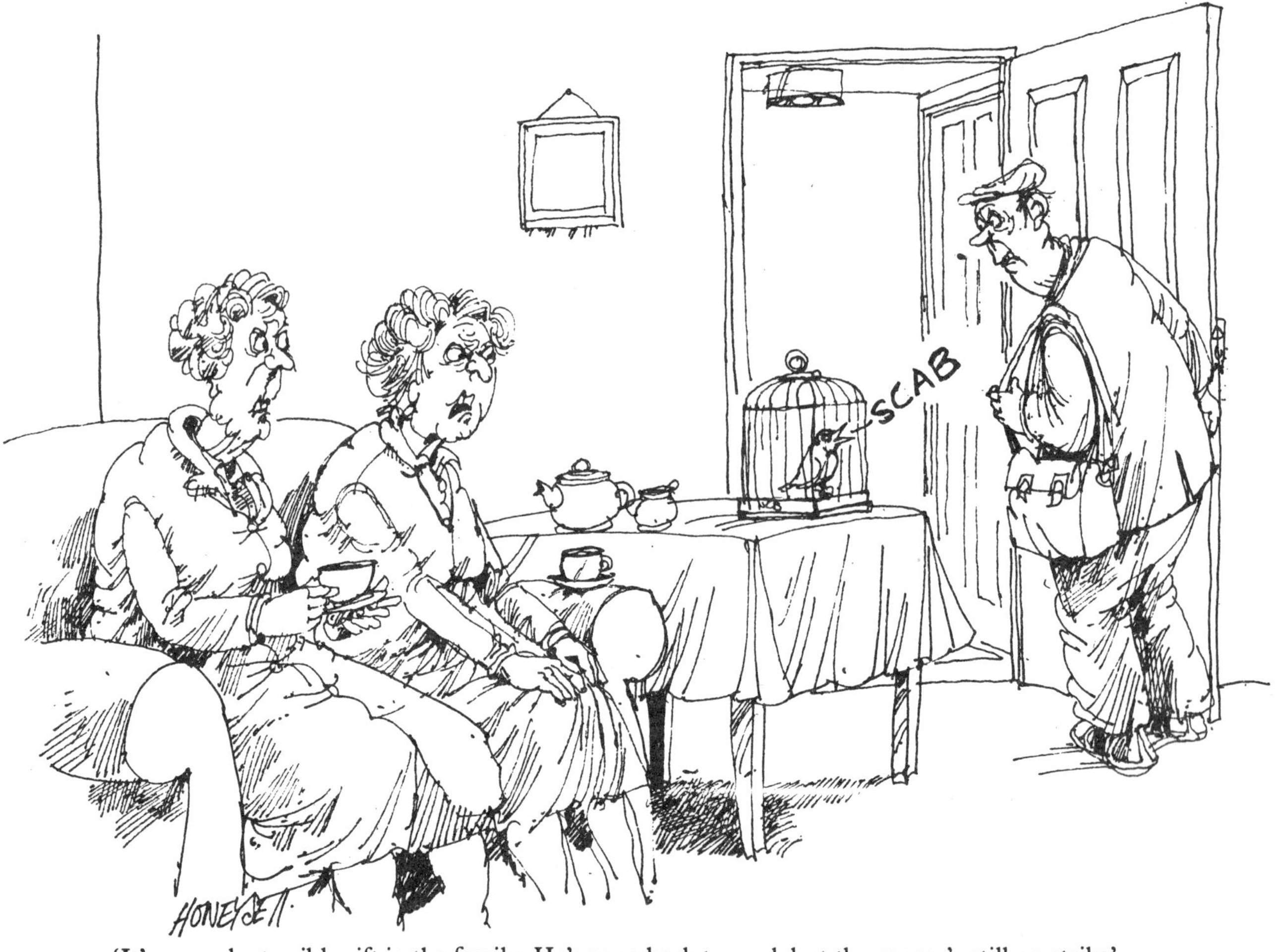
SCAB
HONEYSETT

'It's caused a terrible rift in the family. He's gone back to work but the canary's still on strike'

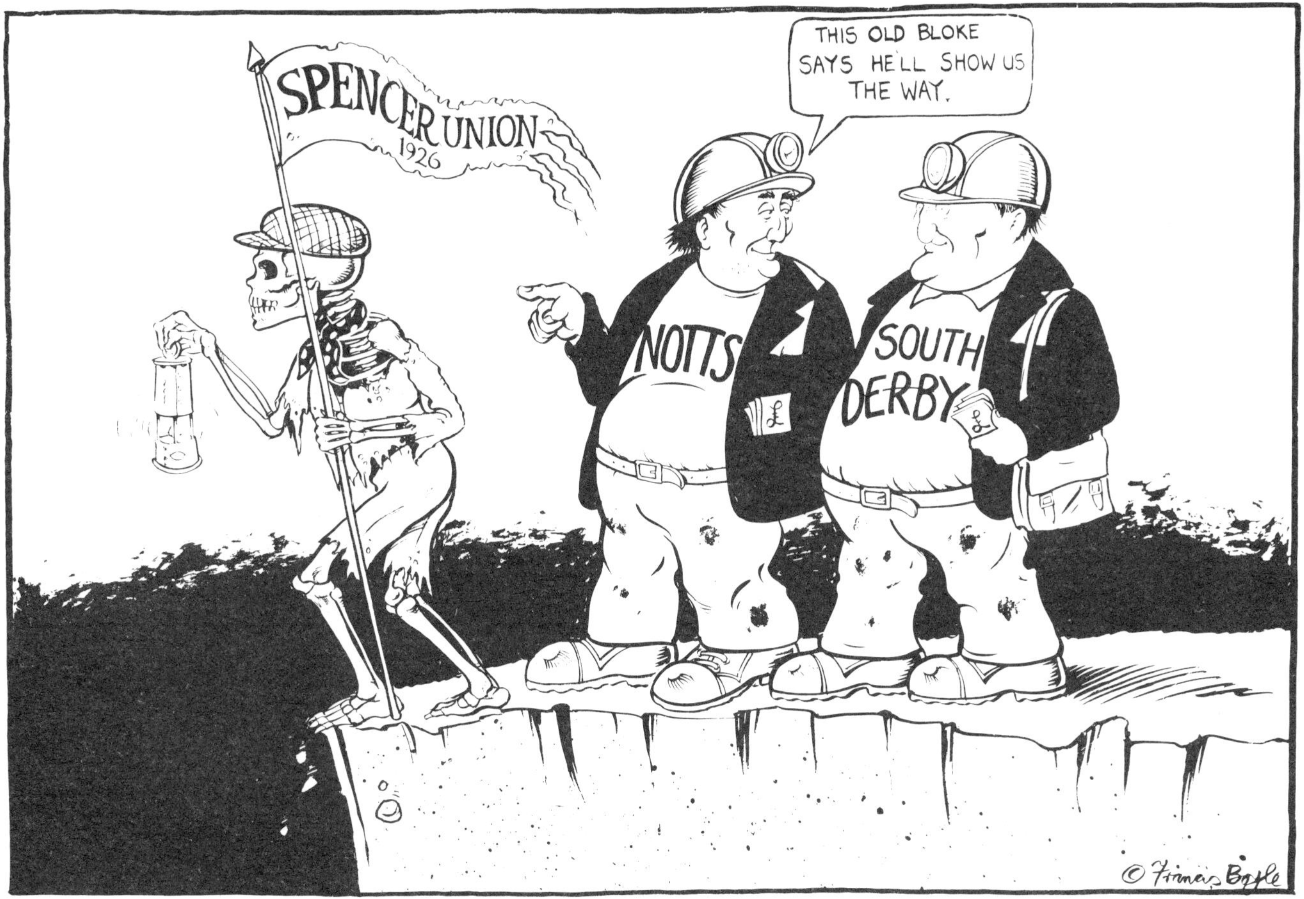
SPENCER UNION
1926
THIS OLD BLOKE SAYS HE'LL SHOW US THE WAY.
NOTTS
SOUTH DERBY
© Francis Boyle

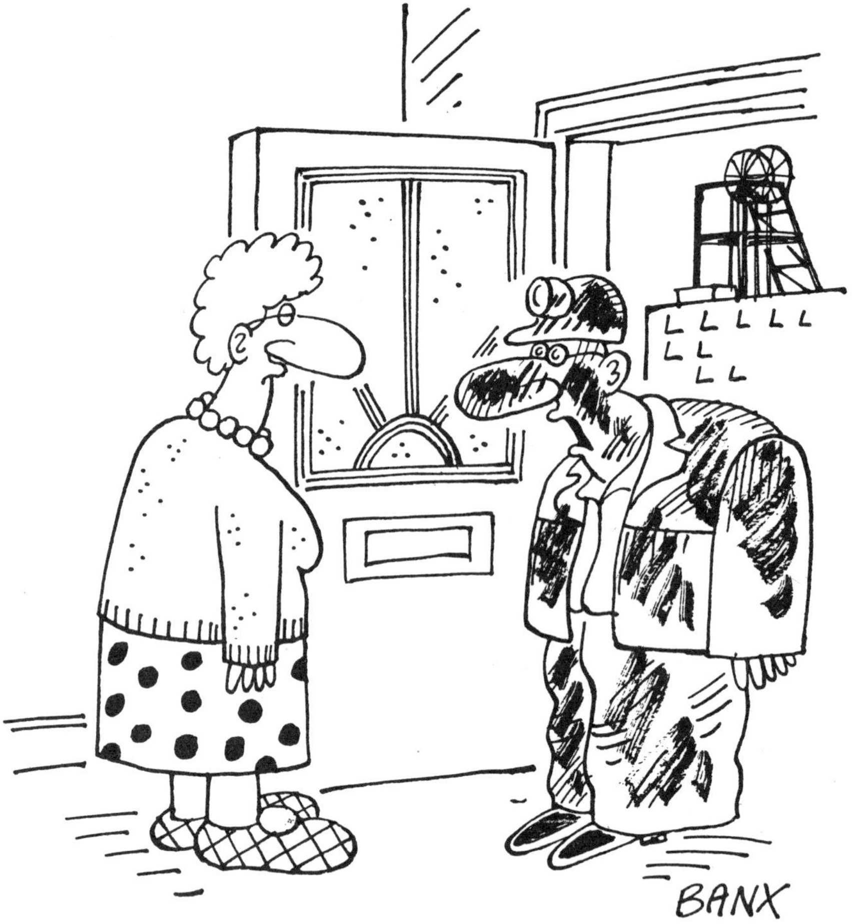
BANX

'I've been replaced by a younger scab'

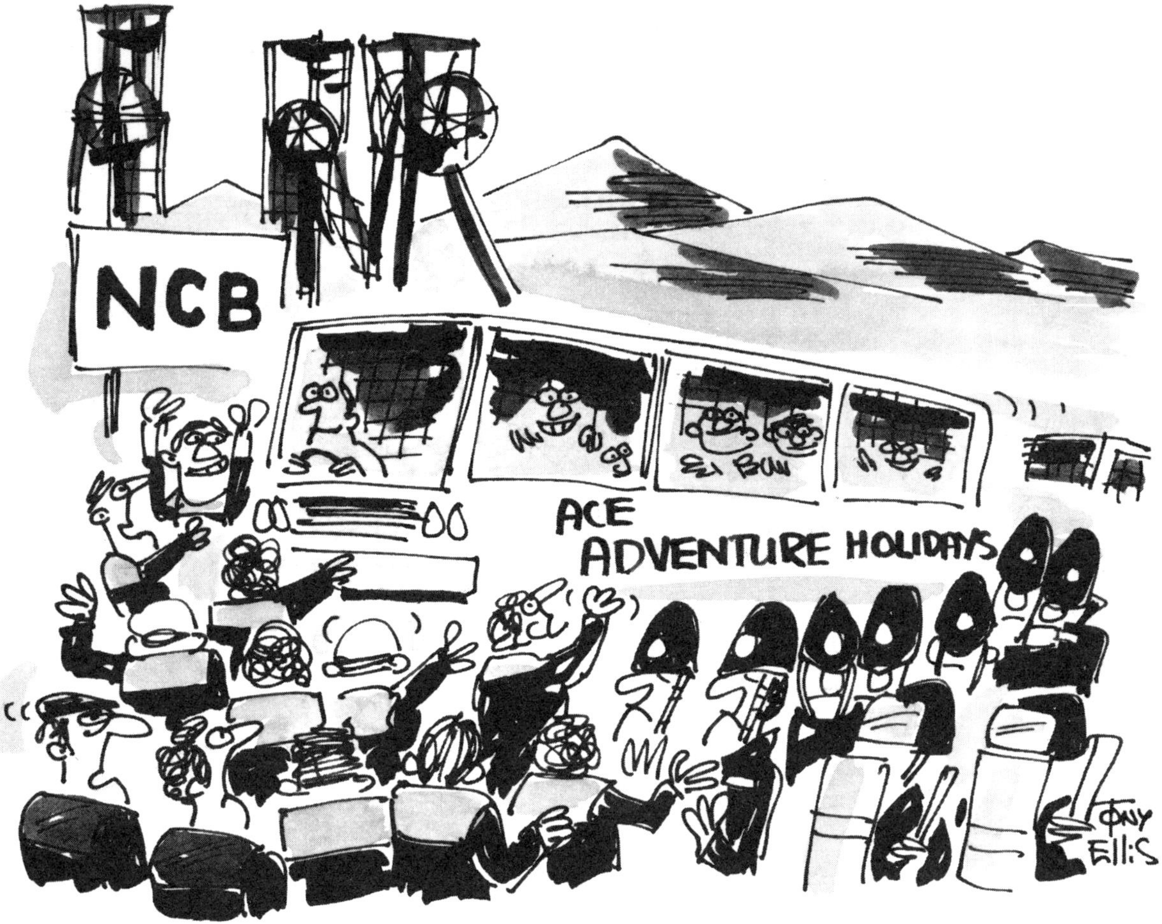
NCB
ACE
ADVENTURE HOLIDAYS
Tony Ellis

'Bloody entrepreneurs!'

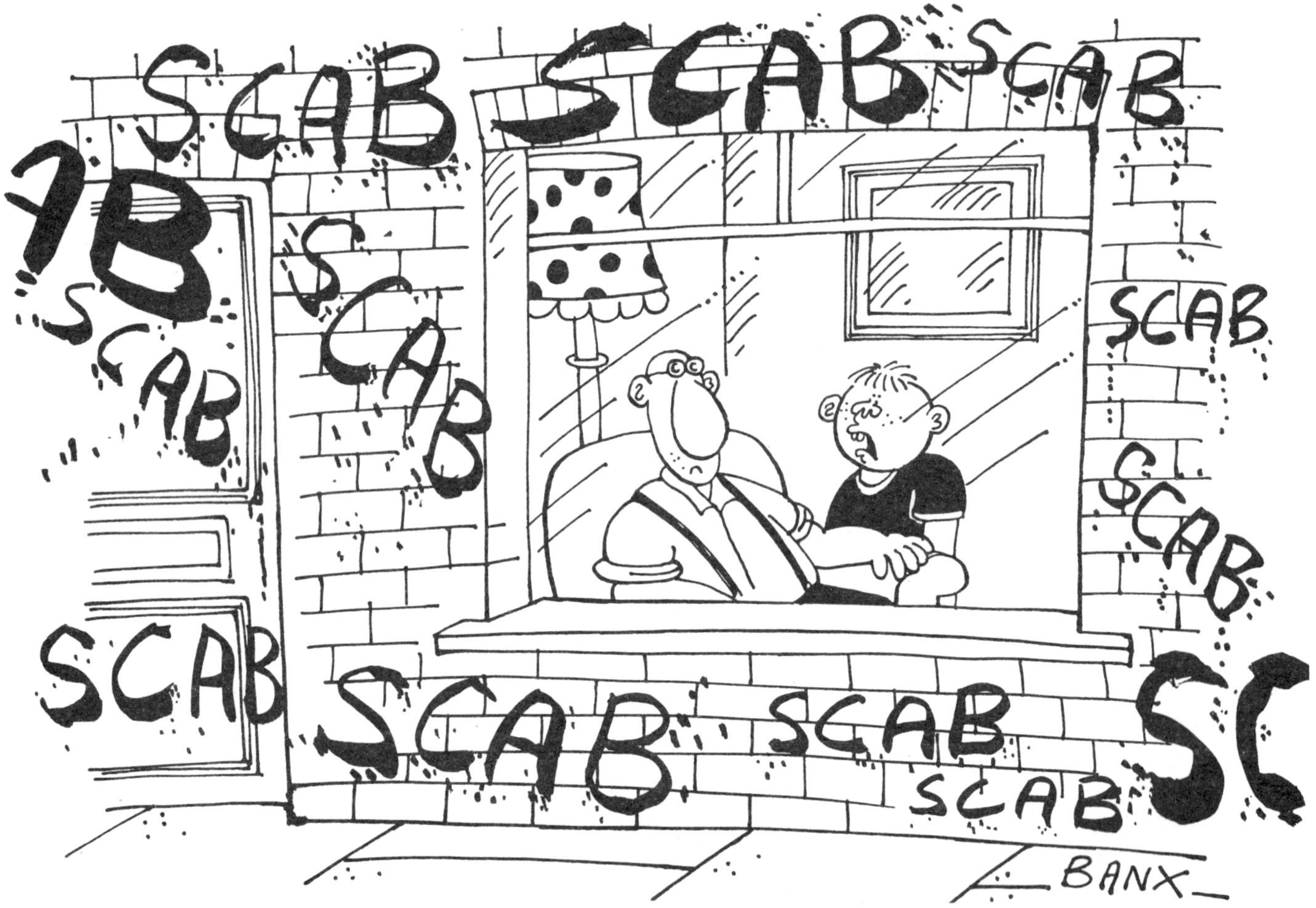
SCAB
SCAB
SCAB
SCAB
SCAB
SCAB
SCAB
SCAB
SCAB
SCAB
SCAB
BANX

'What did *you* do during the great strike of 84–85, Dad?'

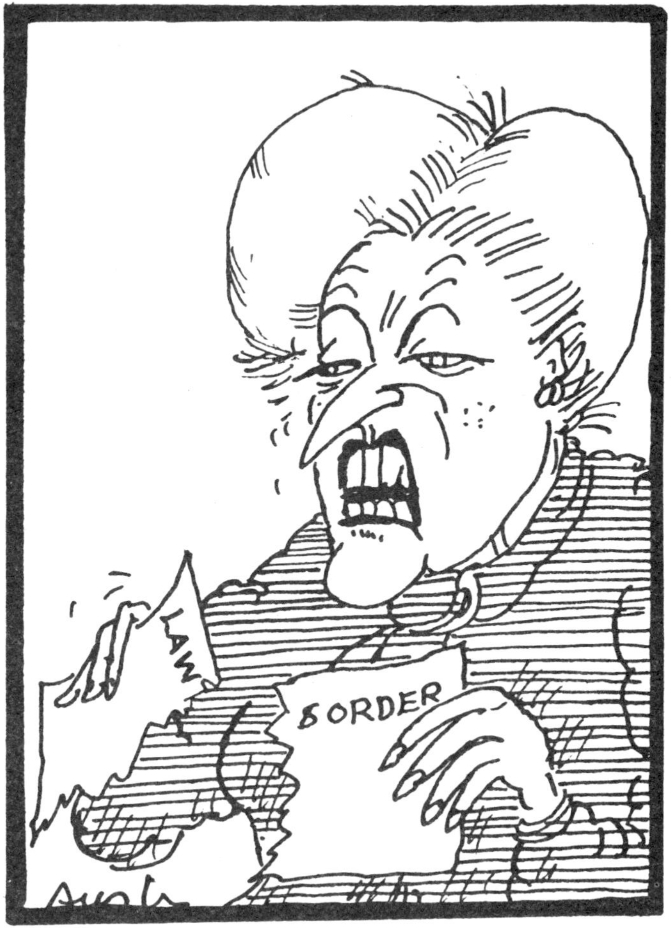
LAW
& ORDER

'To hell with the law, I want *order*'

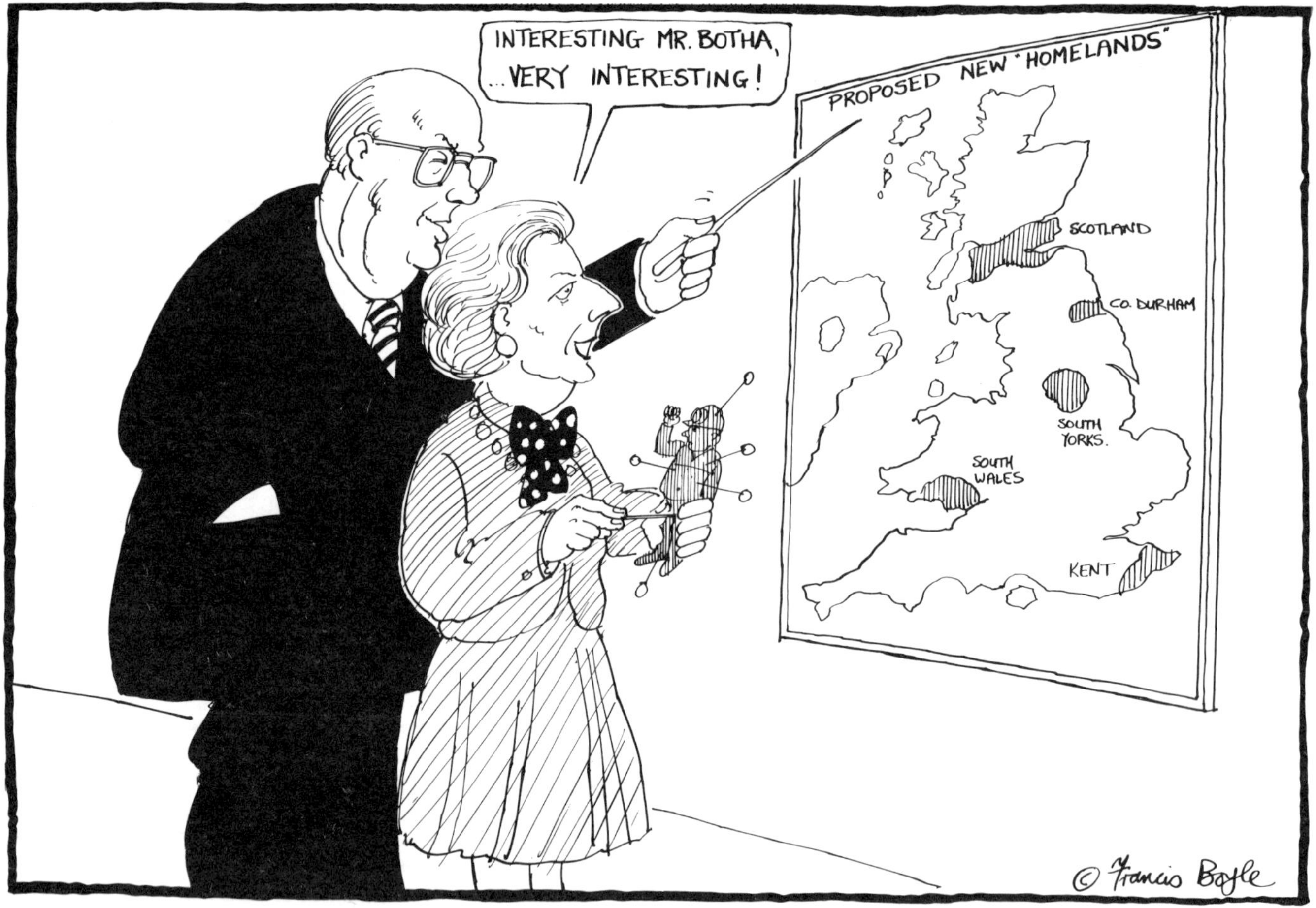
INTERESTING MR. BOTHA, ...VERY INTERESTING!
PROPOSED NEW "HOMELANDS"
SCOTLAND
CO. DURHAM
SOUTH YORKS.
SOUTH WALES
KENT
© Francis Boyle

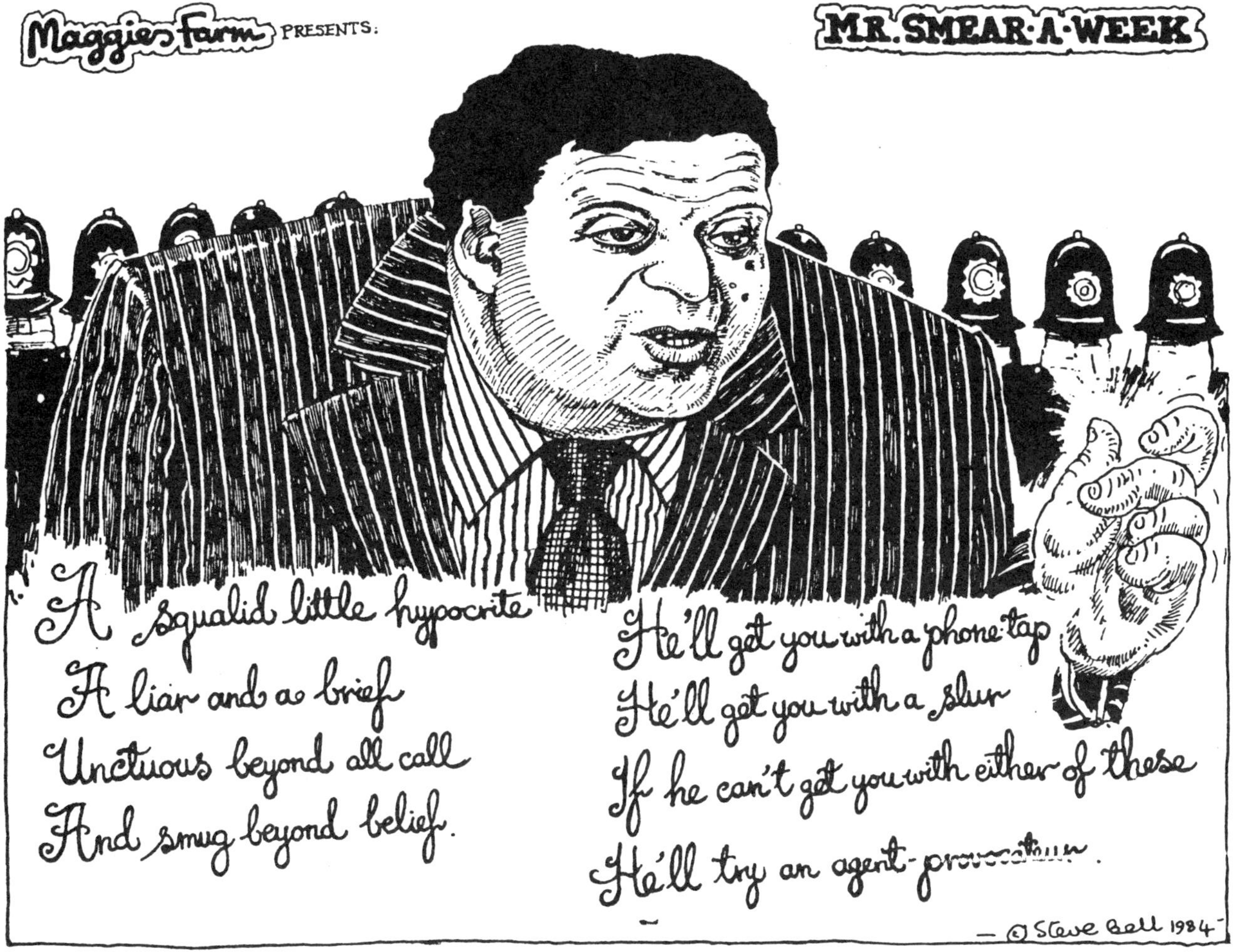
Maggie's Farm PRESENTS:
MR. SMEAR-A-WEEK
A squalid little hypocrite
A liar and a brief
Unctuous beyond all call
And smug beyond belief.
He'll get you with a phone-tap
He'll get you with a slur
If he can't get you with either of these
He'll try an agent-provocateur.
— © Steve Bell 1984

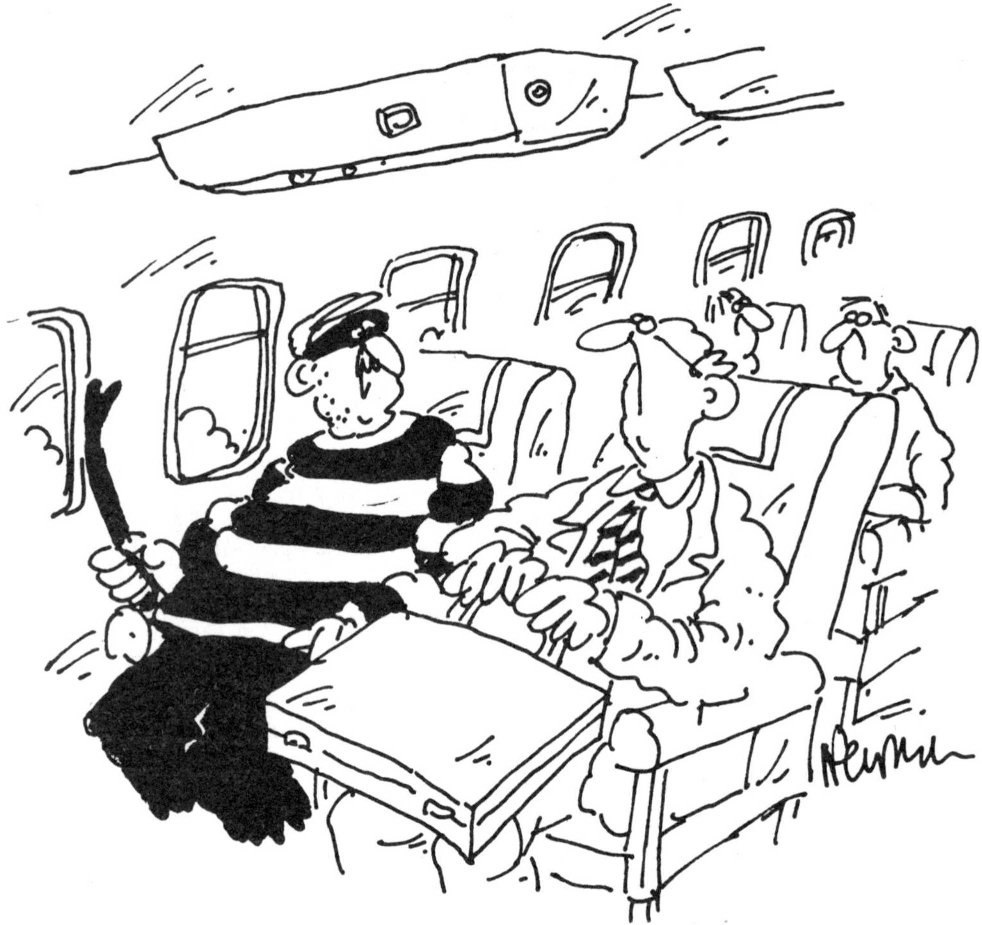

‘To be honest, I haven’t done much sequestrating before’

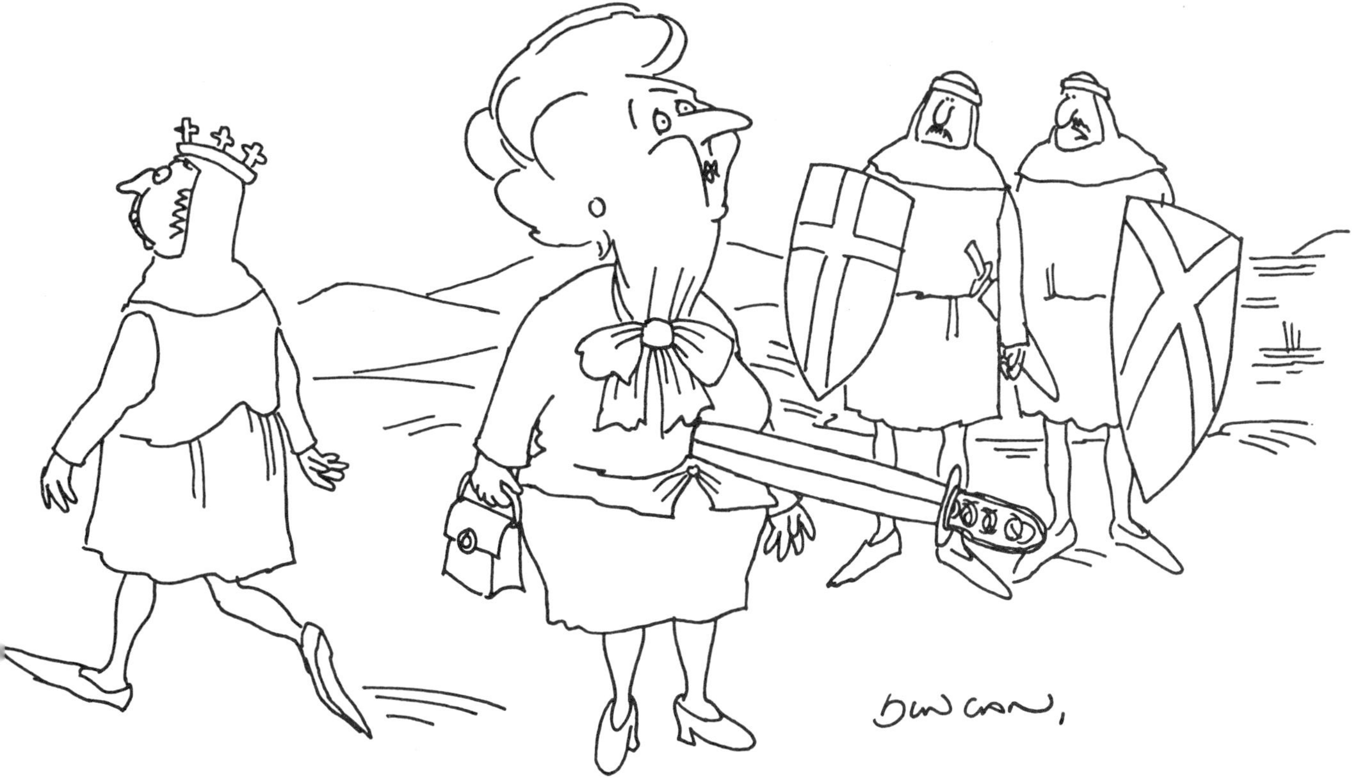
DUNCAN

'I had no idea there was ever any mention of replacing the sword in the stone'

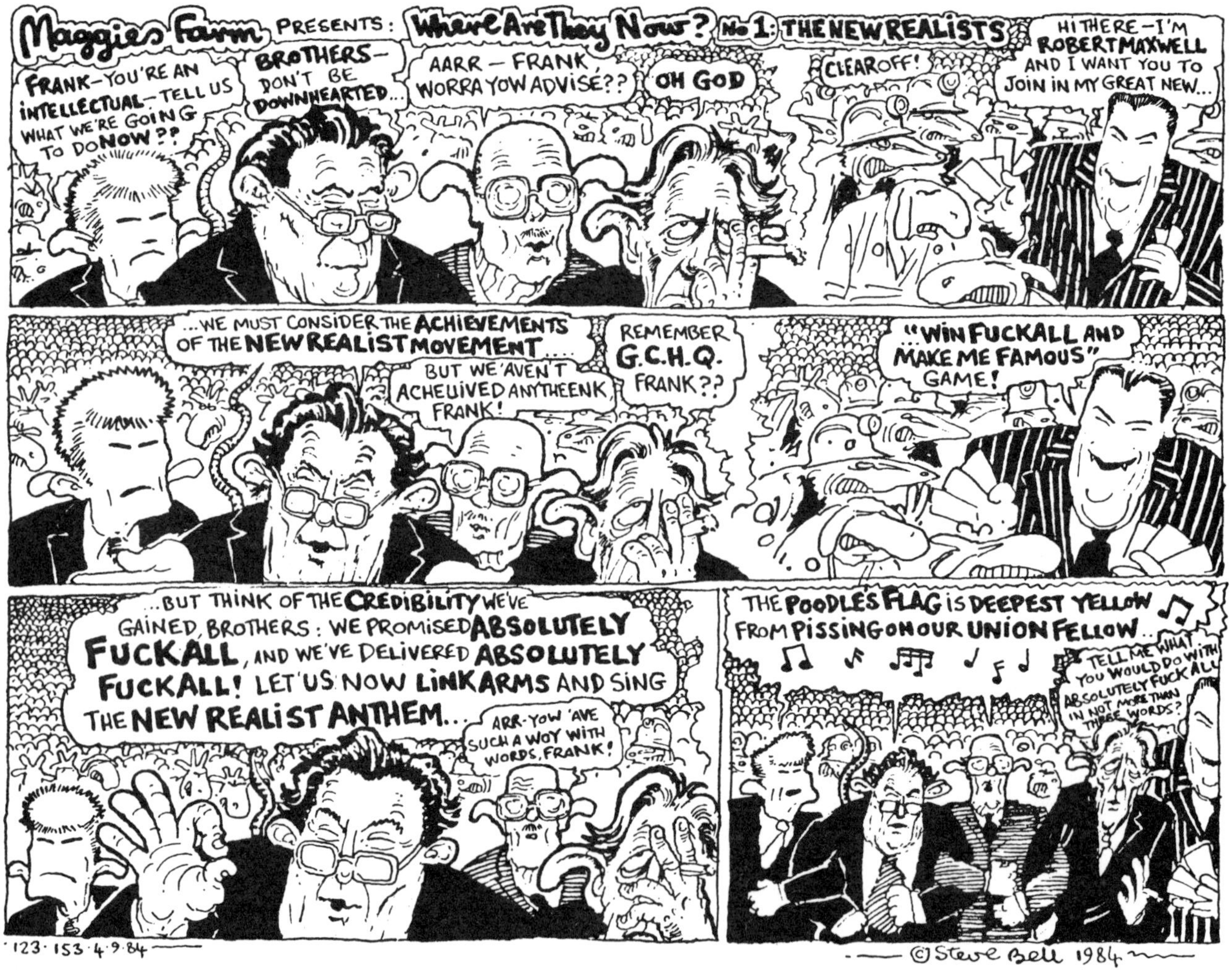

Maggie's Farm PRESENTS: Where Are They Now? No 1: THE NEW REALISTS
FRANK—YOU'RE AN INTELLECTUAL—TELL US WHAT WE'RE GOING TO DO NOW??
BROTHERS—DON'T BE DOWNHEARTED...
AARR—FRANK, WORRA YOW ADVISE??
OH GOD
CLEAR OFF!
HI THERE—I'M ROBERT MAXWELL AND I WANT YOU TO JOIN IN MY GREAT NEW...
...WE MUST CONSIDER THE ACHIEVEMENTS OF THE NEW REALIST MOVEMENT...
BUT WE 'AVEN'T ACHEUIVED ANYTHEENK FRANK!
REMEMBER G.C.H.Q. FRANK??
..."WIN FUCKALL AND MAKE ME FAMOUS" GAME!
...BUT THINK OF THE CREDIBILITY WE'VE GAINED, BROTHERS: WE PROMISED ABSOLUTELY FUCKALL, AND WE'VE DELIVERED ABSOLUTELY FUCKALL! LET US NOW LINK ARMS AND SING THE NEW REALIST ANTHEM...
ARR-YOW 'AVE SUCH A WOY WITH WORDS, FRANK!
THE POODLES FLAG IS DEEPEST YELLOW FROM PISSING ON OUR UNION FELLOW...
TELL ME WHAT YOU WOULD DO WITH ABSOLUTELY FUCK ALL IN NOT MORE THAN THREE WORDS?
123·153·4·9·84
©Steve Bell 1984

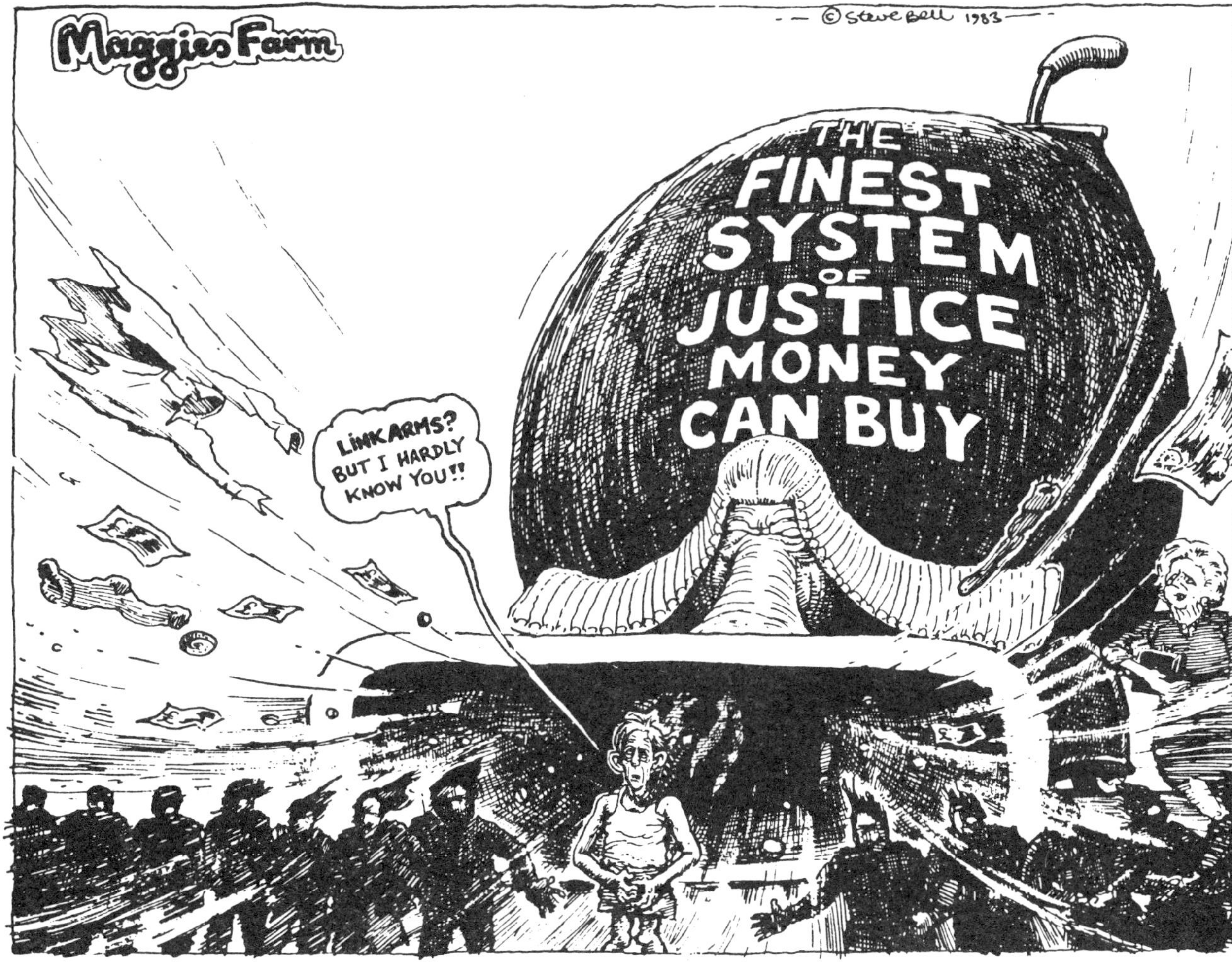
Maggies Farm
© Steve Bell 1983
THE FINEST SYSTEM OF JUSTICE MONEY CAN BUY
LINK ARMS? BUT I HARDLY KNOW YOU!!

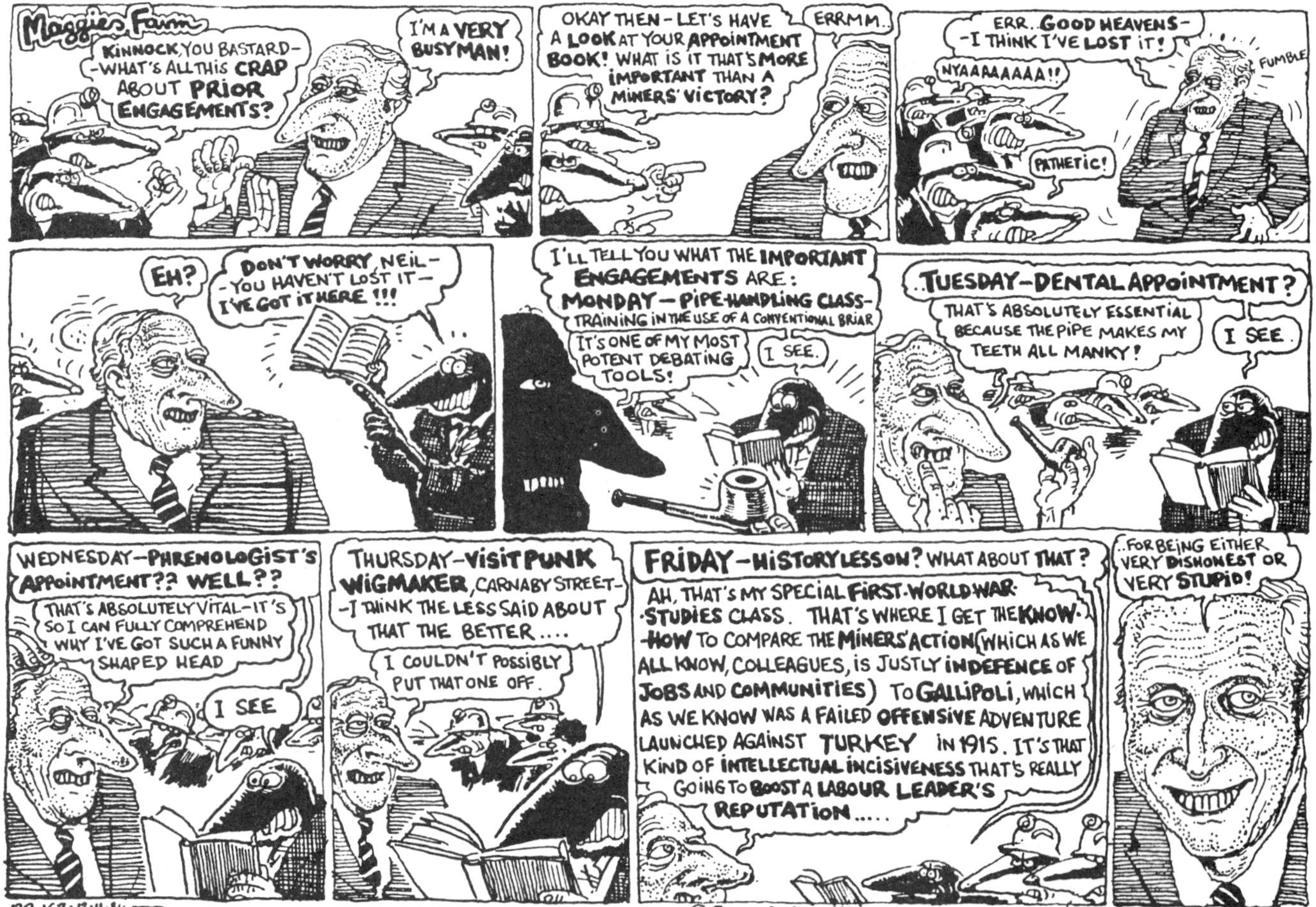
Maggie's Farm
KINNOCK, YOU BASTARD— —WHAT'S ALL THIS CRAP ABOUT PRIOR ENGAGEMENTS?
I'M A VERY BUSY MAN!
OKAY THEN — LET'S HAVE A LOOK AT YOUR APPOINTMENT BOOK! WHAT IS IT THAT'S MORE IMPORTANT THAN A MINERS' VICTORY?
ERRMM..
ERR.. GOOD HEAVENS — I THINK I'VE LOST IT!
NYAAAAAAAA!!
FUMBLE
PATHETIC!
EH?
DON'T WORRY, NEIL — YOU HAVEN'T LOST IT — I'VE GOT IT HERE !!!
I'LL TELL YOU WHAT THE IMPORTANT ENGAGEMENTS ARE: MONDAY — PIPE-HANDLING CLASS — TRAINING IN THE USE OF A CONVENTIONAL BRIAR
IT'S ONE OF MY MOST POTENT DEBATING TOOLS!
I SEE.
..TUESDAY — DENTAL APPOINTMENT?
THAT'S ABSOLUTELY ESSENTIAL BECAUSE THE PIPE MAKES MY TEETH ALL MANKY!
I SEE.
WEDNESDAY — PHRENOLOGIST'S APPOINTMENT?? WELL??
THAT'S ABSOLUTELY VITAL — IT'S SO I CAN FULLY COMPREHEND WHY I'VE GOT SUCH A FUNNY SHAPED HEAD
I SEE
THURSDAY — VISIT PUNK WIGMAKER, CARNABY STREET — —I THINK THE LESS SAID ABOUT THAT THE BETTER....
I COULDN'T POSSIBLY PUT THAT ONE OFF.
FRIDAY — HISTORY LESSON? WHAT ABOUT THAT?
AH, THAT'S MY SPECIAL FIRST-WORLD-WAR-STUDIES CLASS. THAT'S WHERE I GET THE KNOW-HOW TO COMPARE THE MINERS' ACTION (WHICH AS WE ALL KNOW, COLLEAGUES, IS JUSTLY IN DEFENCE OF JOBS AND COMMUNITIES) TO GALLIPOLI, WHICH AS WE KNOW WAS A FAILED OFFENSIVE ADVENTURE LAUNCHED AGAINST TURKEY IN 1915. IT'S THAT KIND OF INTELLECTUAL INCISIVENESS THAT'S REALLY GOING TO BOOST A LABOUR LEADER'S REPUTATION.....
..FOR BEING EITHER VERY DISHONEST OR VERY STUPID!

133-163-12-11-84

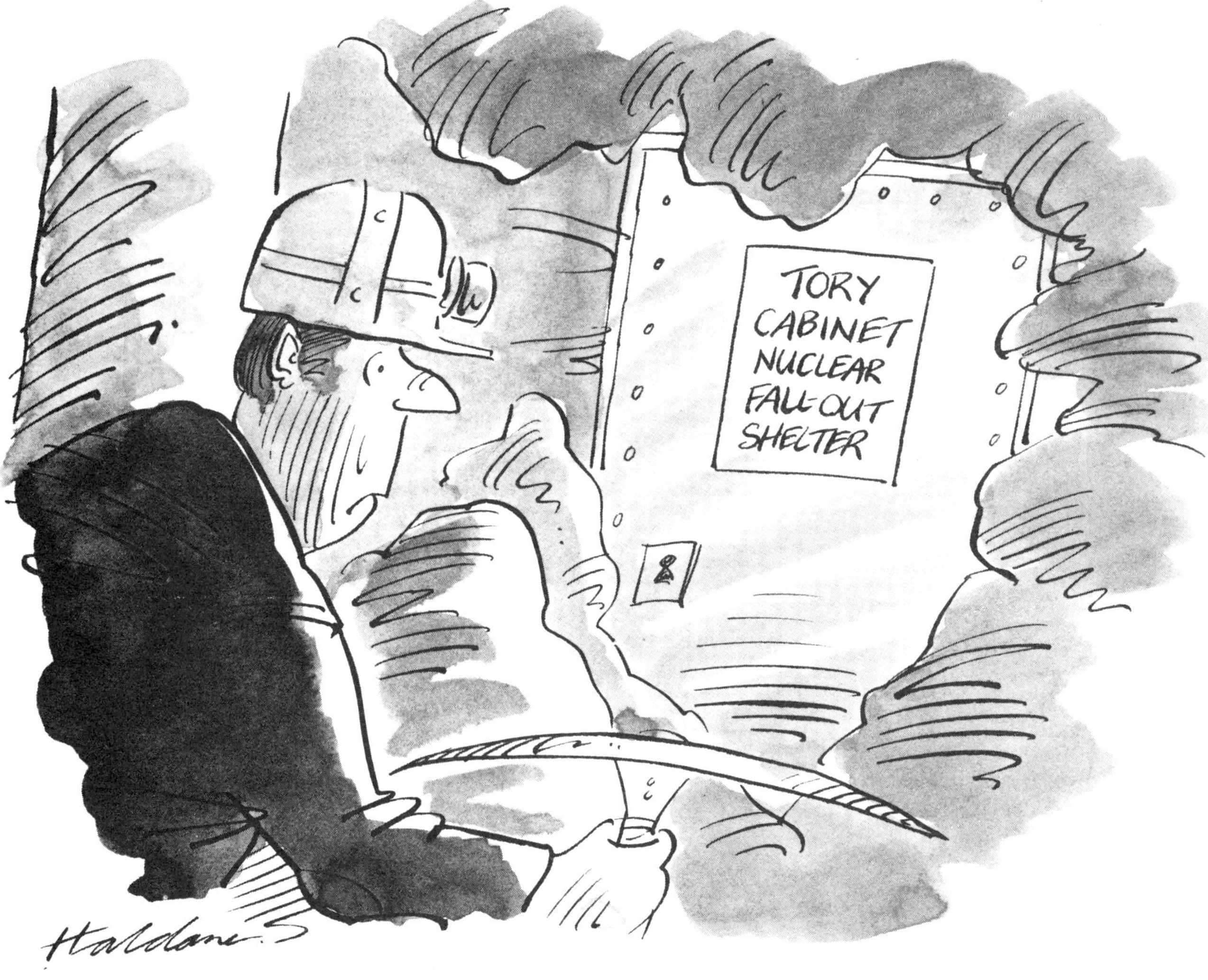
TORY
CABINET
NUCLEAR
FALL-OUT
SHELTER
Haldane

ARTH

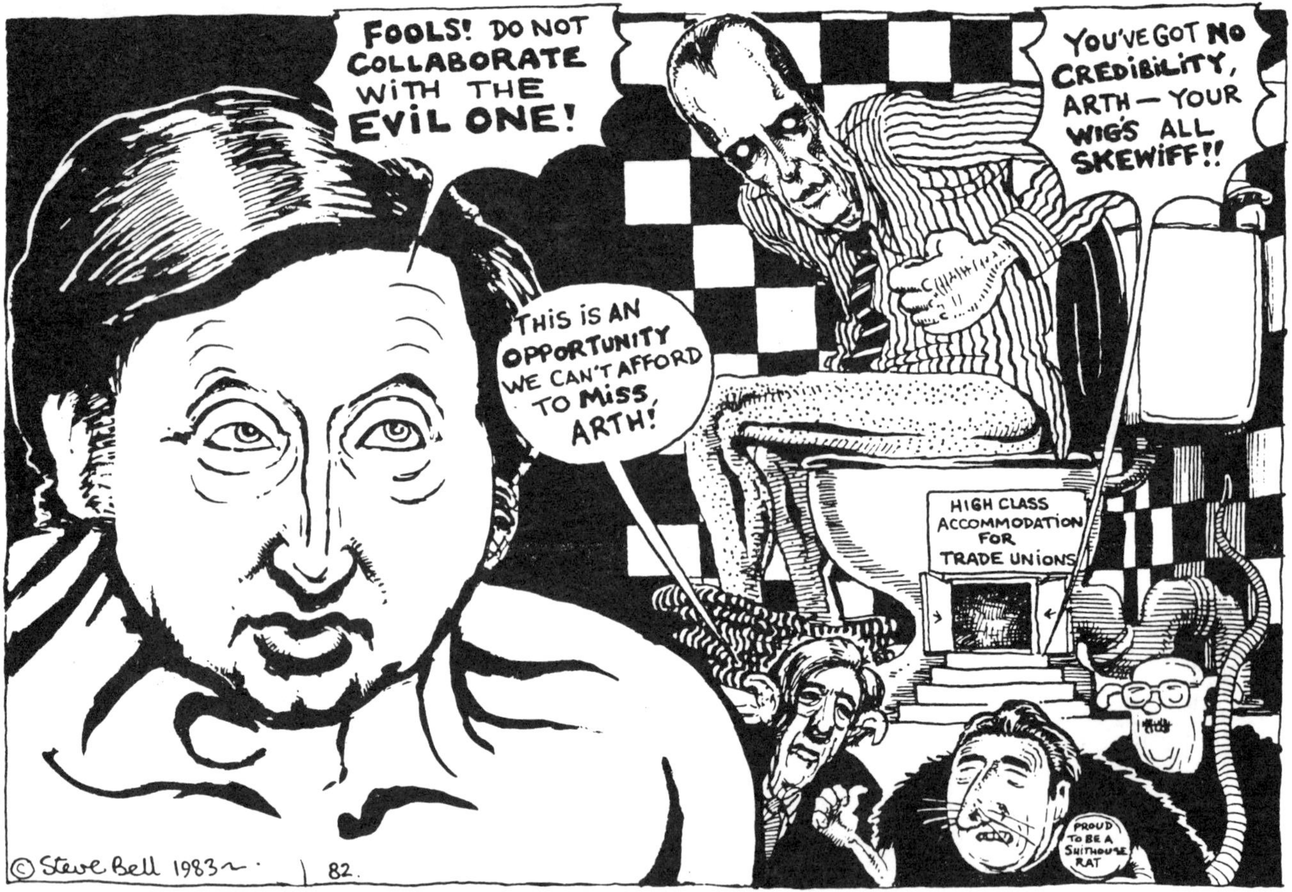

FOOLS! DO NOT COLLABORATE WITH THE EVIL ONE!
YOU'VE GOT NO CREDIBILITY, ARTH — YOUR WIG'S ALL SKEWIFF!!
THIS IS AN OPPORTUNITY WE CAN'T AFFORD TO MISS, ARTH!
HIGH CLASS ACCOMMODATION FOR TRADE UNIONS
PROUD TO BE A SHITHOUSE RAT
© Steve Bell 1983

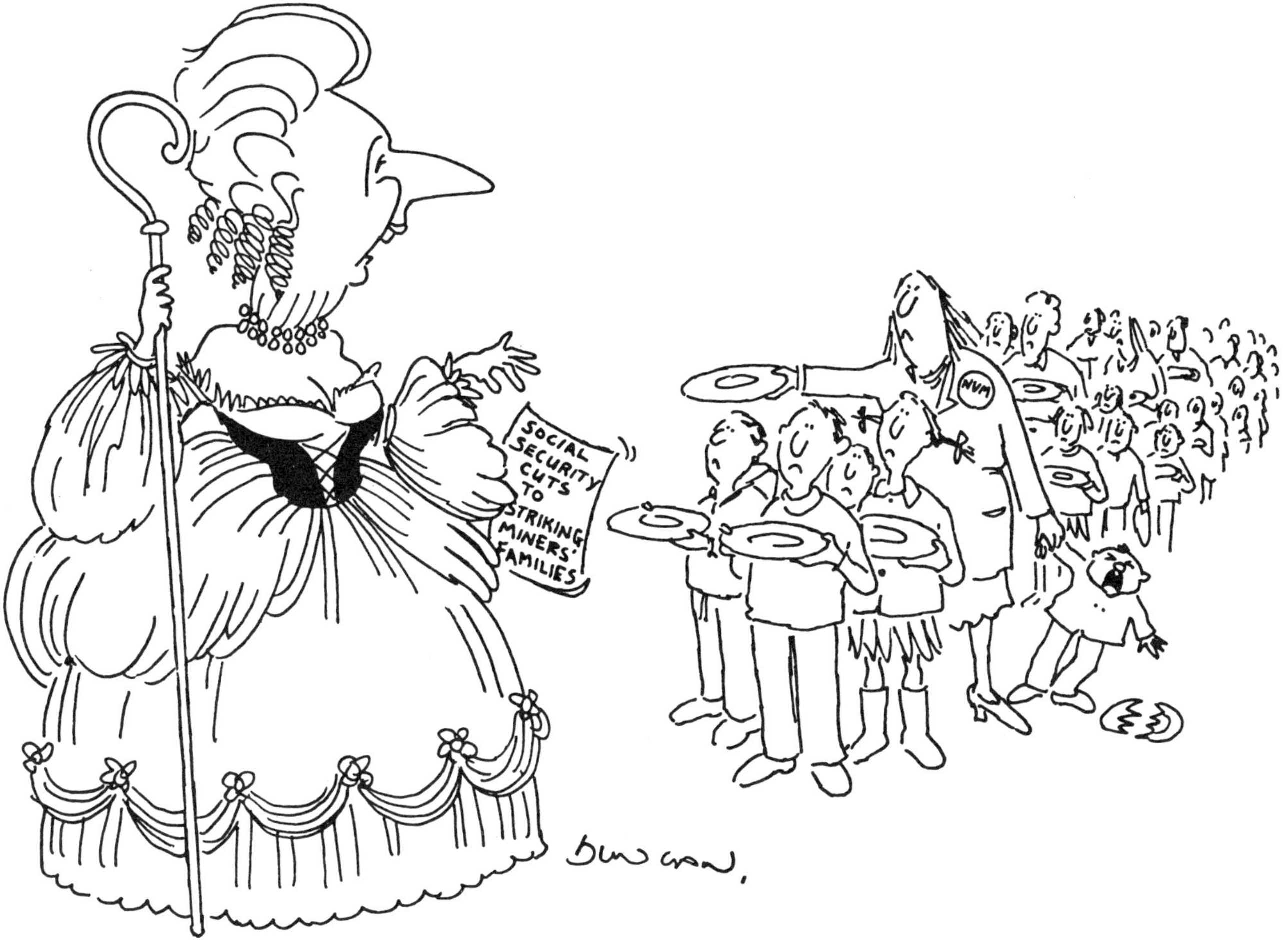
SOCIAL SECURITY CUTS TO STRIKING MINERS' FAMILIES
NUM
DUNCAN.

'Let them eat cake'

AN INTERVIEW WITH MR. KINNOCK.

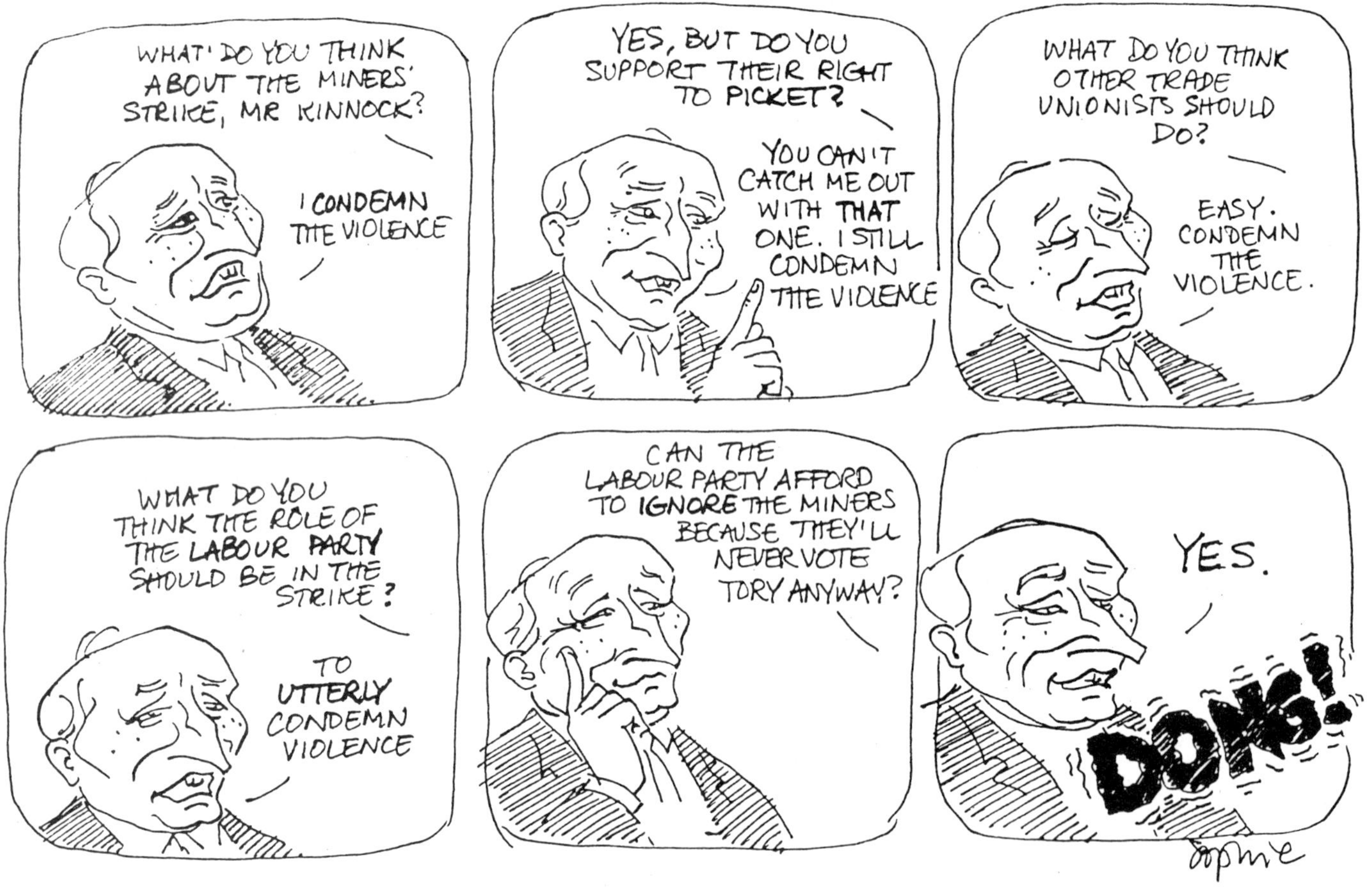

WHAT DO YOU THINK ABOUT THE MINERS' STRIKE, MR KINNOCK?
I CONDEMN THE VIOLENCE
YES, BUT DO YOU SUPPORT THEIR RIGHT TO PICKET?
YOU CAN'T CATCH ME OUT WITH THAT ONE. I STILL CONDEMN THE VIOLENCE
WHAT DO YOU THINK OTHER TRADE UNIONISTS SHOULD DO?
EASY. CONDEMN THE VIOLENCE.
WHAT DO YOU THINK THE ROLE OF THE LABOUR PARTY SHOULD BE IN THE STRIKE?
TO UTTERLY CONDEMN VIOLENCE
CAN THE LABOUR PARTY AFFORD TO IGNORE THE MINERS BECAUSE THEY'LL NEVER VOTE TORY ANYWAY?
YES.
DOING!
Sophie

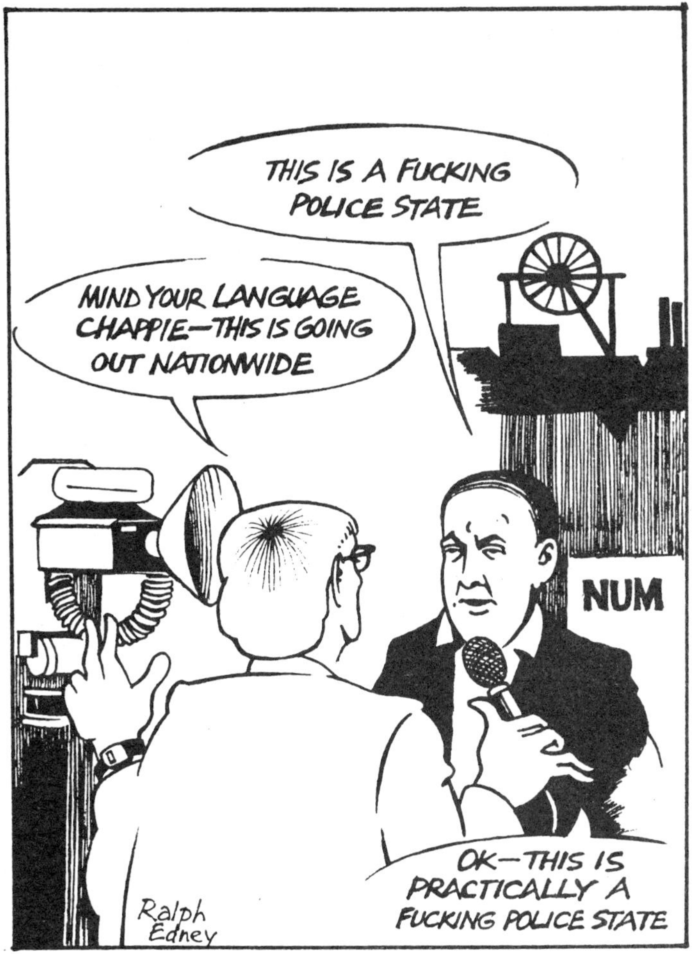
THIS IS A FUCKING POLICE STATE
MIND YOUR LANGUAGE CHAPPIE—THIS IS GOING OUT NATIONWIDE
OK—THIS IS PRACTICALLY A FUCKING POLICE STATE
NUM
Ralph Edney

LADY CALLS THE TUNE

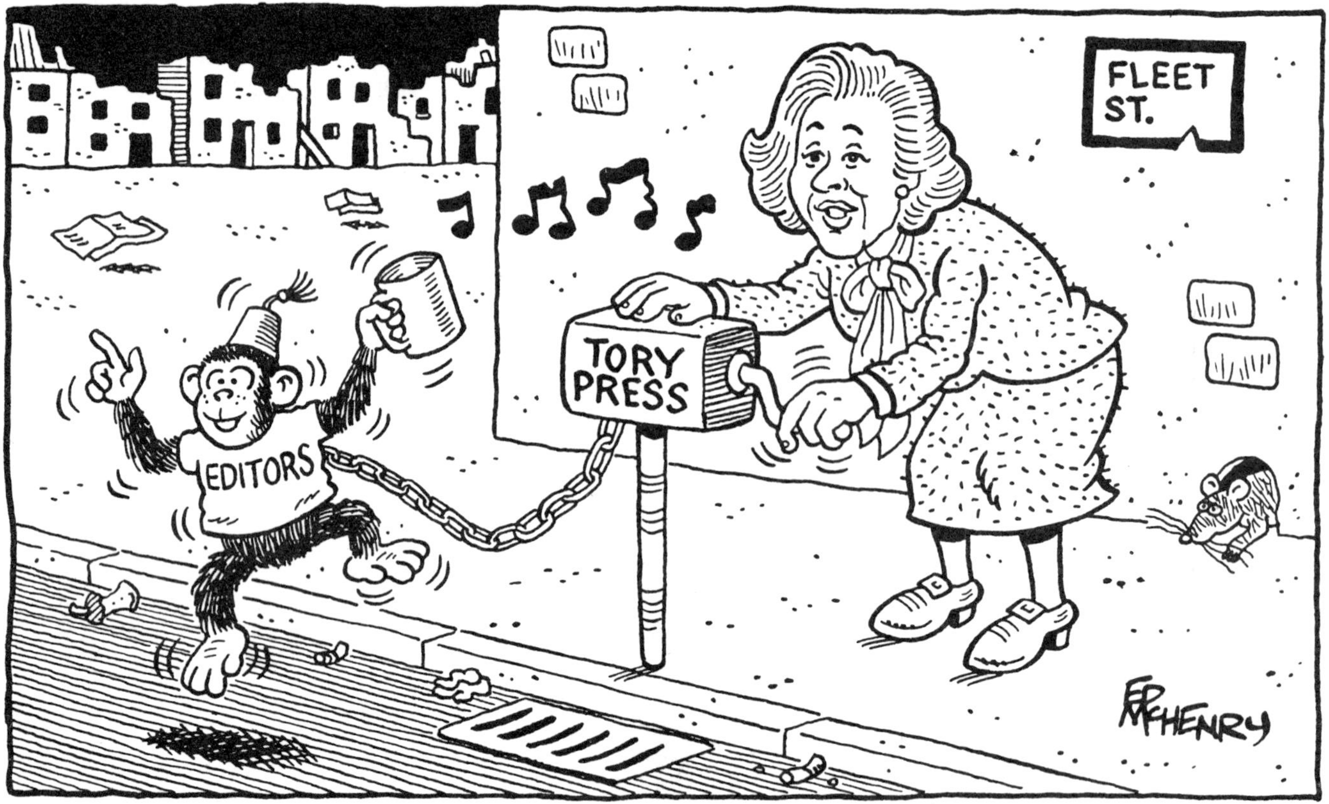
FLEET ST.
TORY PRESS
EDITORS
ED McHENRY

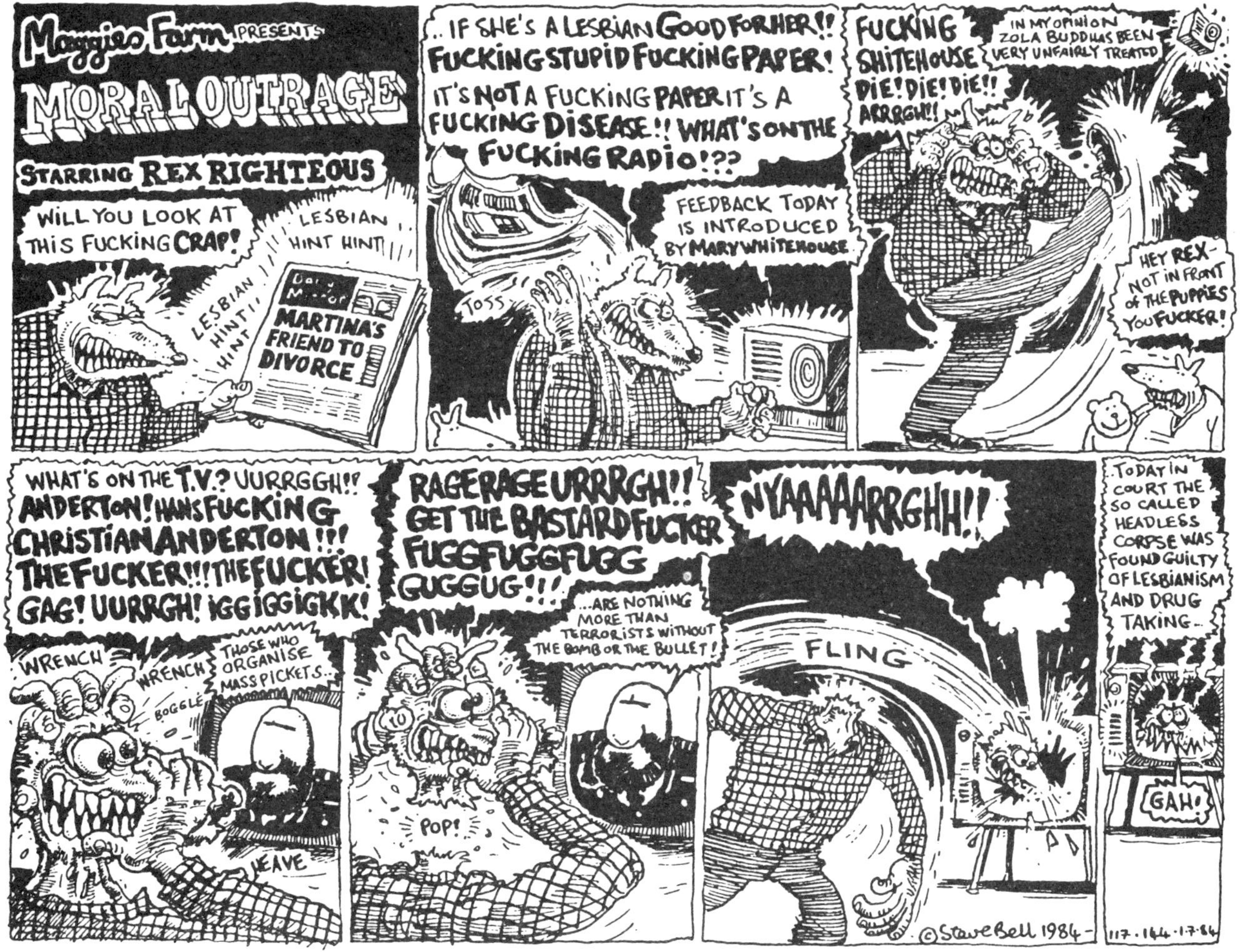
Maggie's Farm PRESENTS
MORAL OUTRAGE
STARRING REX RIGHTEOUS
WILL YOU LOOK AT THIS FUCKING CRAP!
LESBIAN HINT HINT
LESBIAN HINT HINT
Daily Mirror
MARTINA'S FRIEND TO DIVORCE
.. IF SHE'S A LESBIAN GOOD FOR HER!! FUCKING STUPID FUCKING PAPER! IT'S NOT A FUCKING PAPER IT'S A FUCKING DISEASE!! WHAT'S ON THE FUCKING RADIO!??
TOSS
FEEDBACK TODAY IS INTRODUCED BY MARY WHITEHOUSE
FUCKING SHITEHOUSE DIE! DIE! DIE!! ARRRGH!!
IN MY OPINION ZOLA BUDD HAS BEEN VERY UNFAIRLY TREATED
HEY REX - NOT IN FRONT OF THE PUPPIES YOU FUCKER!
WHAT'S ON THE T.V.? UURRGGH!! ANDERTON! HANS FUCKING CHRISTIAN ANDERTON!!! THE FUCKER!!! THE FUCKER! GAG! UURRGH! IGGIGGIGKK!
WRENCH
WRENCH
BOGGLE
THOSE WHO ORGANISE MASS PICKETS...
HEAVE
RAGE RAGE URRRGH!! GET THE BASTARD FUCKER FUGGFUGGFUGG GUGGUG!!!
...ARE NOTHING MORE THAN TERRORISTS WITHOUT THE BOMB OR THE BULLET!
POP!
NYAAAAARRGHH!!
FLING
...TODAY IN COURT THE SO CALLED HEADLESS CORPSE WAS FOUND GUILTY OF LESBIANISM AND DRUG TAKING...
GAH!
© Steve Bell 1984 -
117 · 144 · 1.7.84

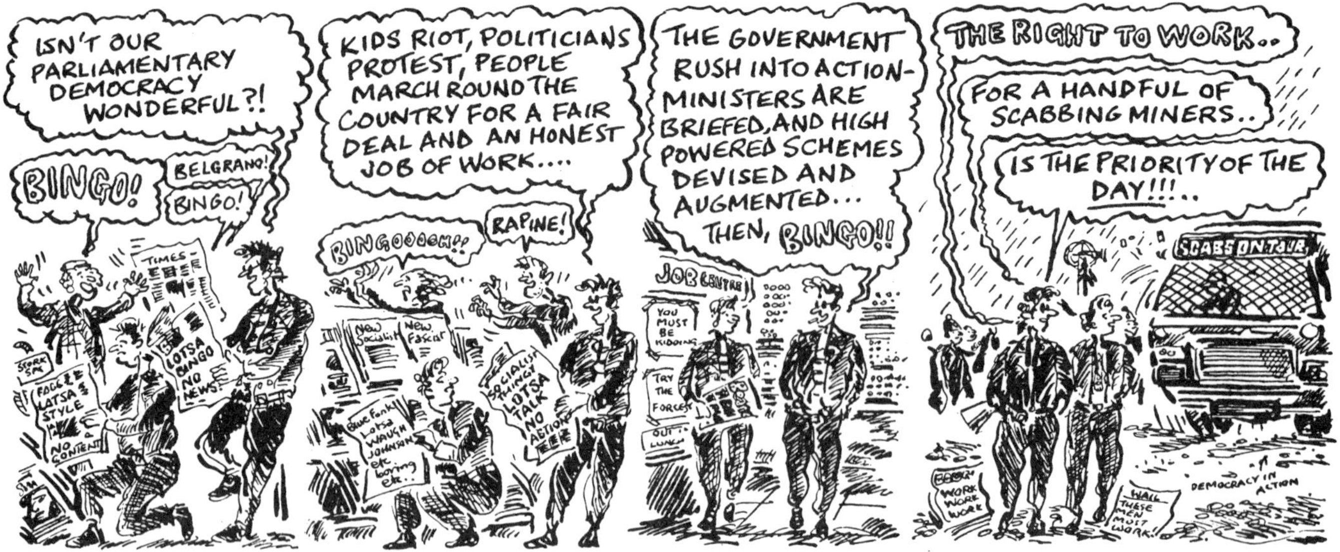
ISN'T OUR PARLIAMENTARY DEMOCRACY WONDERFUL?!
BINGO!
BELGRANO!
BINGO!
TIMES
LOTSA BINGO NO NEWS!
LOTSA STYLE
NO CONTENT
KIDS RIOT, POLITICIANS PROTEST, PEOPLE MARCH ROUND THE COUNTRY FOR A FAIR DEAL AND AN HONEST JOB OF WORK....
BINGOOOOOH!!
RAPINE!
New Socialist
New Fascist
SOCIALIST THINGY LOTSA TALK NO ACTION
THE GOVERNMENT RUSH INTO ACTION-MINISTERS ARE BRIEFED, AND HIGH POWERED SCHEMES DEVISED AND AUGMENTED...
THEN, BINGO!!
JOB CENTRE
YOU MUST BE KIDDING
TRY THE FORCES
OUT TO LUNCH
THE RIGHT TO WORK..
FOR A HANDFUL OF SCABBING MINERS..
IS THE PRIORITY OF THE DAY!!!..
SCABS ON TOUR
WORK WORK WORK
THESE MEN MUST WORK!
DEMOCRACY IN ACTION

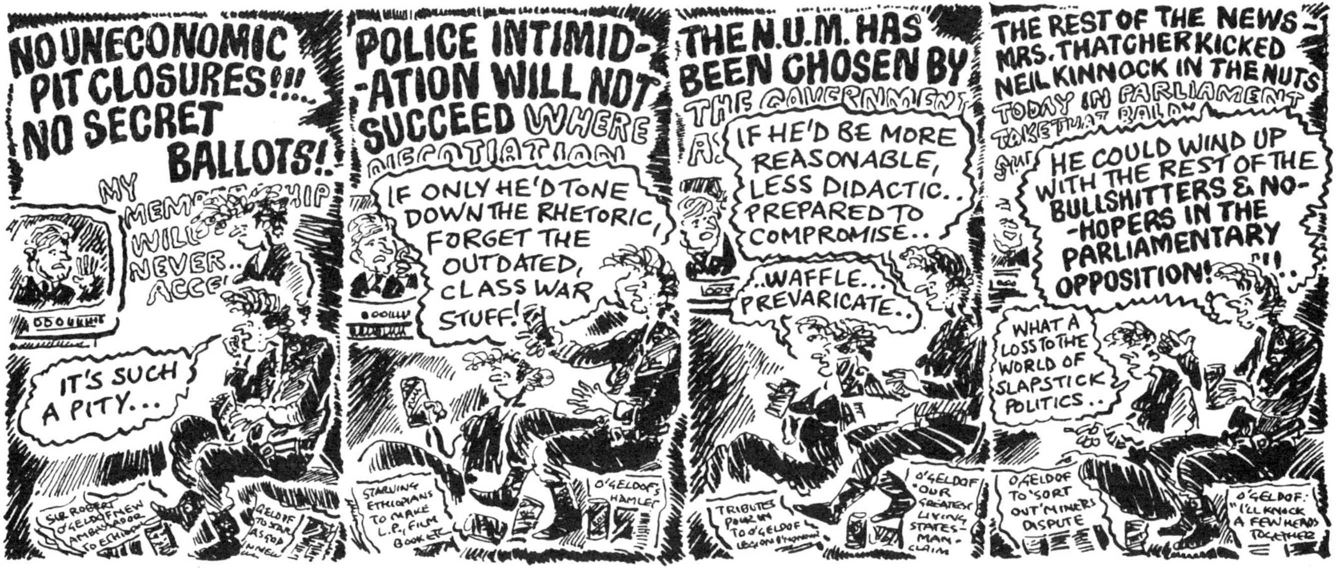
NO UNECONOMIC PIT CLOSURES!!!... NO SECRET BALLOTS!..
MY
NEVER..
IT'S SUCH A PITY...
SIR ROBERT O'GELDOF NEW AMBASSADOR TO ETHIOPIA
GELDOF TO STAR AS GOD IN NEW
POLICE INTIMID-ATION WILL NOT SUCCEED WHERE
IF ONLY HE'D TONE DOWN THE RHETORIC, FORGET THE OUTDATED, CLASS WAR STUFF!
STARVING ETHIOPIANS TO MAKE L.P., FILM BOOK ETC
O'GELDOF'S HAMLET
THE N.U.M. HAS BEEN CHOSEN BY
IF HE'D BE MORE REASONABLE, LESS DIDACTIC.. PREPARED TO COMPROMISE..
..WAFFLE... PREVARICATE..
TRIBUTES POUR IN TO O'GELDOF
O'GELDOF "OUR GREATEST LIVING STATES-MAN" CLAIM
THE REST OF THE NEWS"— MRS. THATCHER KICKED NEIL KINNOCK IN THE NUTS TODAY IN PARLIAMENT
HE COULD WIND UP WITH THE REST OF THE BULLSHITTERS & NO-HOPERS IN THE PARLIAMENTARY OPPOSITION!"!!..
WHAT A LOSS TO THE WORLD OF SLAPSTICK POLITICS..
O'GELDOF TO 'SORT OUT' MINERS DISPUTE
O'GELDOF: "I'LL KNOCK A FEW HEADS TOGETHER

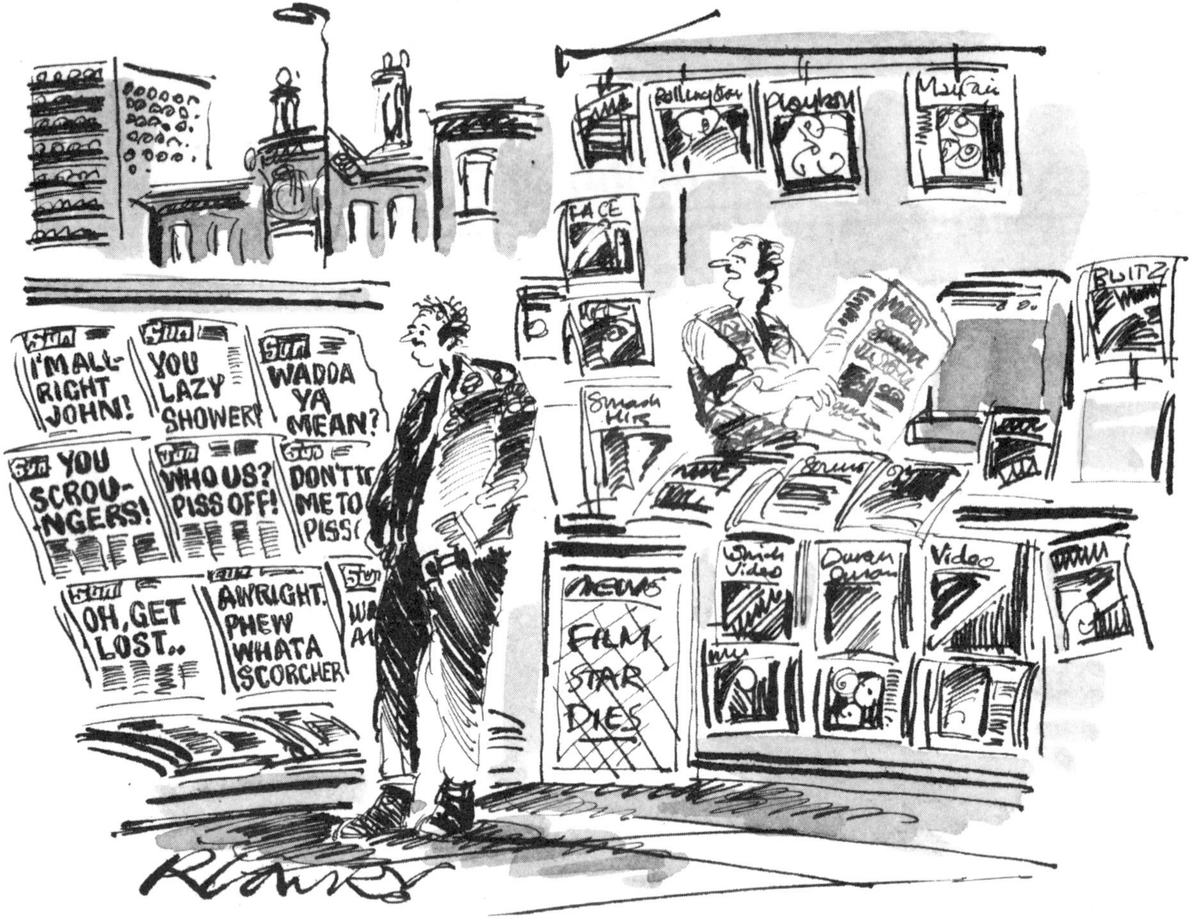
Sun
I'M ALL-RIGHT JOHN!
Sun
YOU LAZY SHOWER!
Sun
WADDA YA MEAN?
YOU SCROUNGERS!
WHO US? PISS OFF!
Sun
OH, GET LOST..
AWRIGHT. PHEW WHATA SCORCHER
NEWS
FILM STAR DIES
FACE
Playboy
Mayfair
BLITZ
Smash Hits
Which Video
Duran Duran
Video

'It's just the *Sun* talking to itself again'

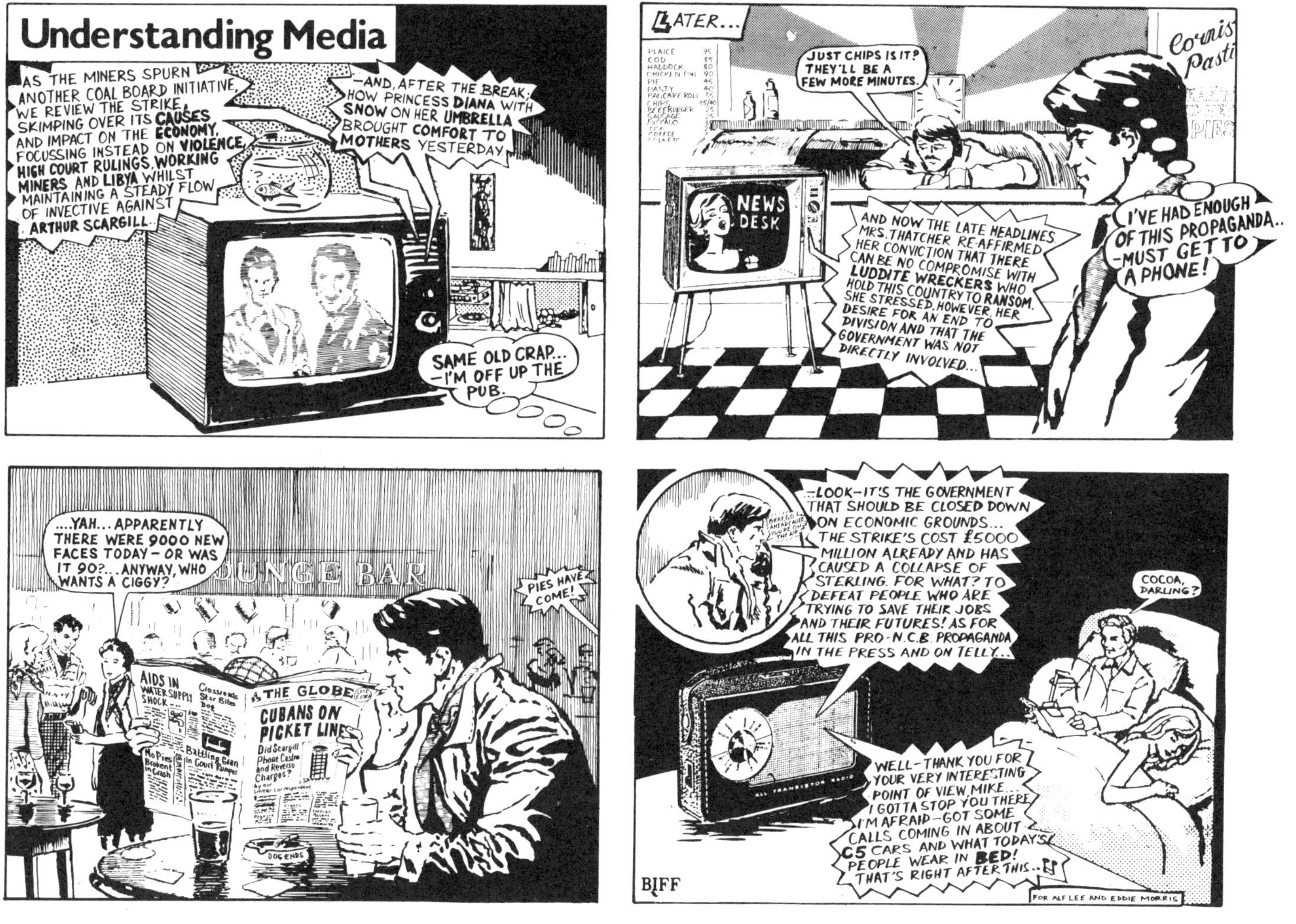
Understanding Media
AS THE MINERS SPURN ANOTHER COAL BOARD INITIATIVE, WE REVIEW THE STRIKE, SKIMPING OVER ITS CAUSES AND IMPACT ON THE ECONOMY, FOCUSSING INSTEAD ON VIOLENCE, HIGH COURT RULINGS, WORKING MINERS AND LIBYA WHILST MAINTAINING A STEADY FLOW OF INVECTIVE AGAINST ARTHUR SCARGILL...
—AND, AFTER THE BREAK; HOW PRINCESS DIANA WITH SNOW ON HER UMBRELLA BROUGHT COMFORT TO MOTHERS YESTERDAY.
SAME OLD CRAP... —I'M OFF UP THE PUB.
LATER...
JUST CHIPS IS IT? THEY'LL BE A FEW MORE MINUTES.
NEWS DESK
AND NOW THE LATE HEADLINES. MRS. THATCHER RE-AFFIRMED HER CONVICTION THAT THERE CAN BE NO COMPROMISE WITH LUDDITE WRECKERS WHO HOLD THIS COUNTRY TO RANSOM. SHE STRESSED, HOWEVER, HER DESIRE FOR AN END TO DIVISION AND THAT THE GOVERNMENT WAS NOT DIRECTLY INVOLVED...
I'VE HAD ENOUGH OF THIS PROPAGANDA.. -MUST GET TO A PHONE!
Cornish Pasties
PIES
....YAH... APPARENTLY THERE WERE 9000 NEW FACES TODAY — OR WAS IT 90?... ANYWAY, WHO WANTS A CIGGY?
LOUNGE BAR
PIES HAVE COME!
AIDS IN WATER SUPPLY SHOCK
Crossroads Star Bites Dog
THE GLOBE
CUBANS ON PICKET LINES
Did Scargill Phone Castro and Reverse Charges?
No Pies Broken in Crash
Battling Bran in Court Rumpus
DOG ENDS
—LOOK—IT'S THE GOVERNMENT THAT SHOULD BE CLOSED DOWN ON ECONOMIC GROUNDS... THE STRIKE'S COST £5000 MILLION ALREADY AND HAS CAUSED A COLLAPSE OF STERLING. FOR WHAT? TO DEFEAT PEOPLE WHO ARE TRYING TO SAVE THEIR JOBS AND THEIR FUTURES! AS FOR ALL THIS PRO-N.C.B. PROPAGANDA IN THE PRESS AND ON TELLY...
COCOA, DARLING?
WELL—THANK YOU FOR YOUR VERY INTERESTING POINT OF VIEW, MIKE... I GOTTA STOP YOU THERE I'M AFRAID—GOT SOME CALLS COMING IN ABOUT C5 CARS AND WHAT TODAY'S PEOPLE WEAR IN BED! THAT'S RIGHT AFTER THIS...
ALL TRANSISTOR RADIO
BIFF
FOR ALF LEE AND EDDIE MORRIS

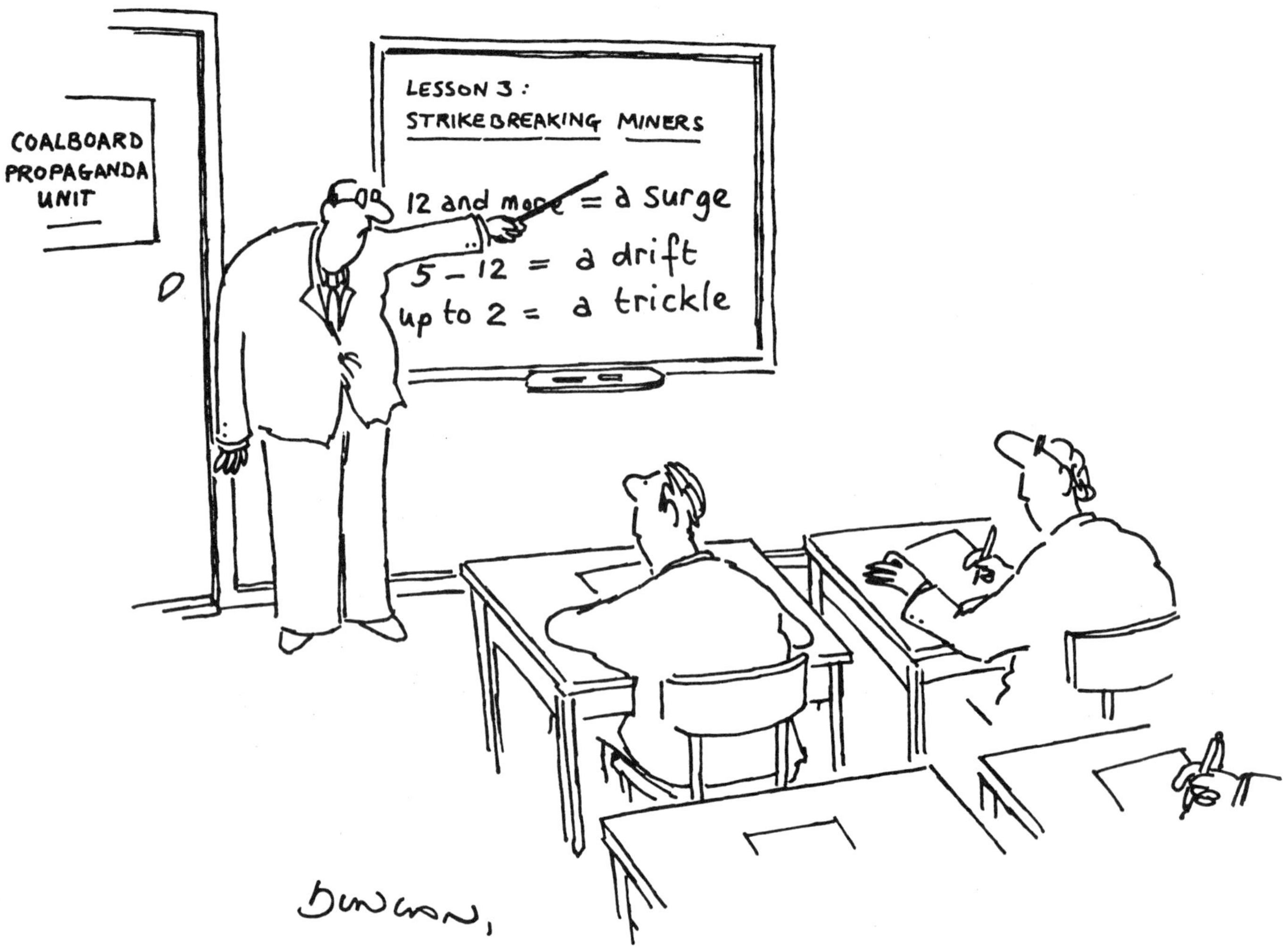
COALBOARD PROPAGANDA UNIT
LESSON 3 :
STRIKEBREAKING MINERS
12 and more = a surge
5 _ 12 = a drift
up to 2 = a trickle
DUNCAN,

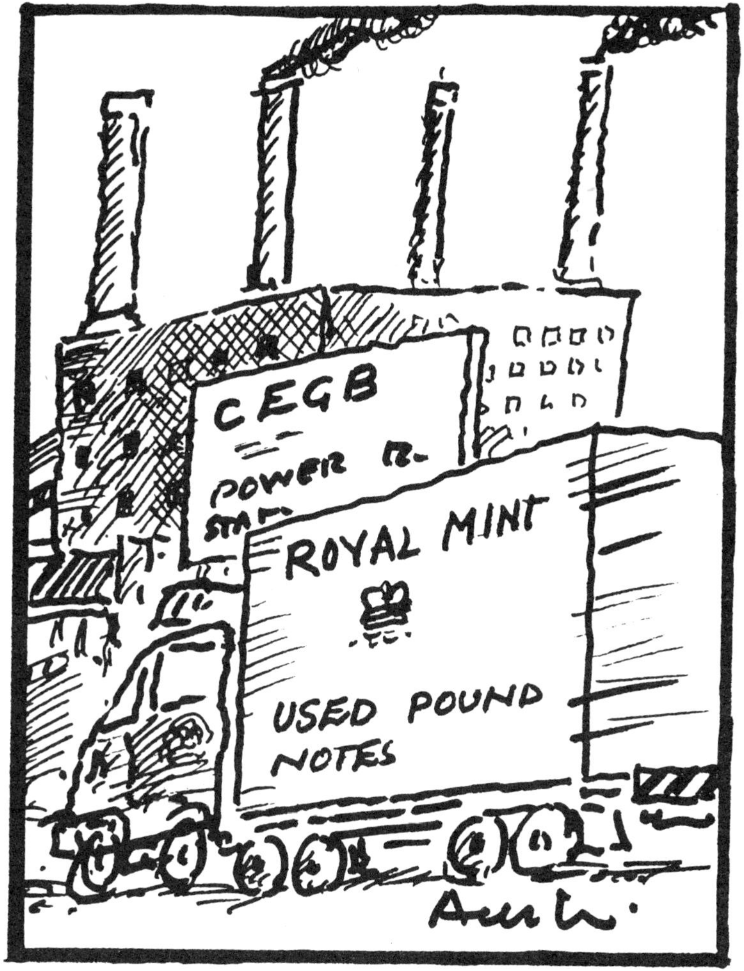
CEGB
POWER
ROYAL MINT
USED POUND
NOTES

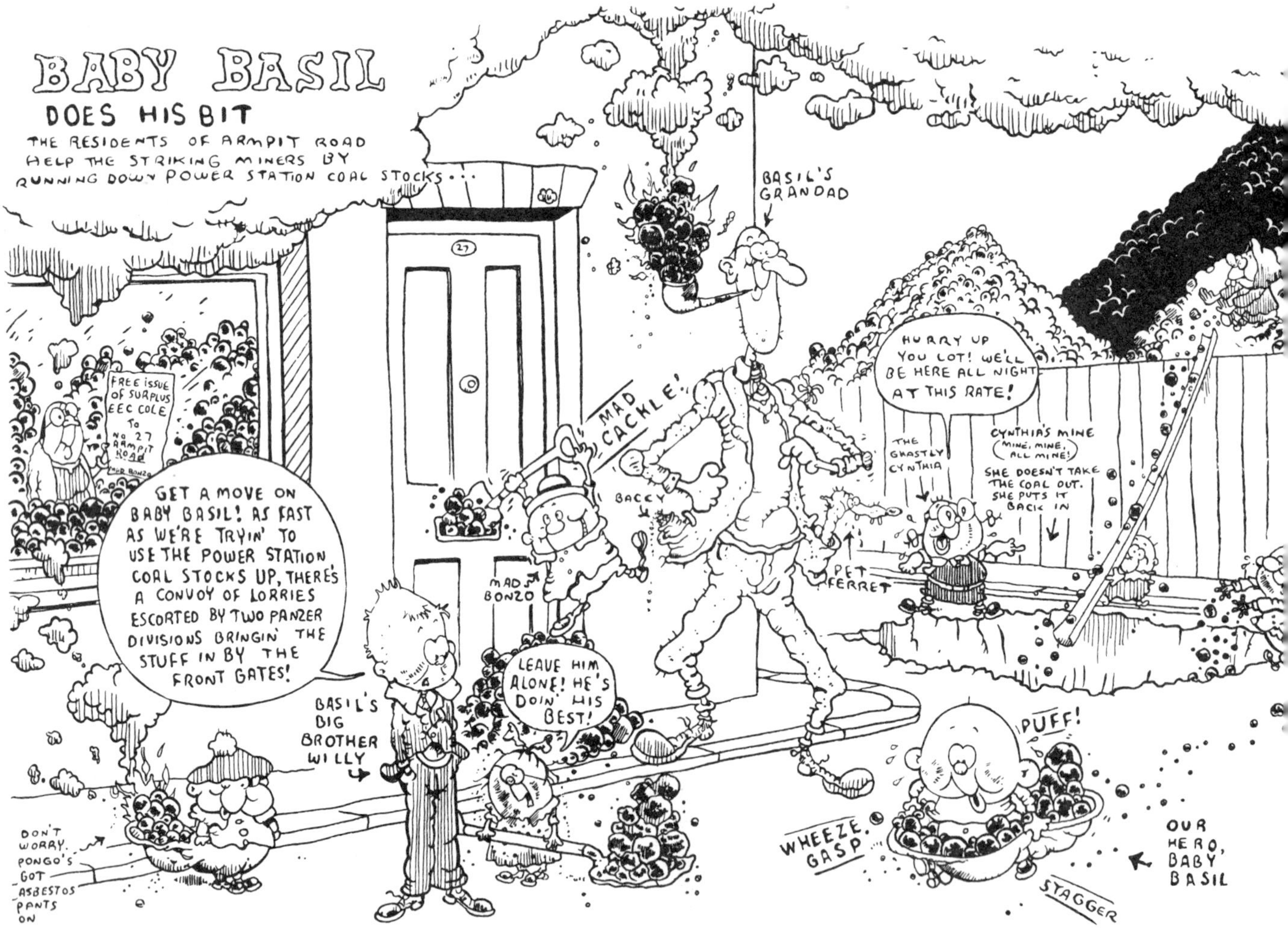
BABY BASIL
DOES HIS BIT
THE RESIDENTS OF ARMPIT ROAD HELP THE STRIKING MINERS BY RUNNING DOWN POWER STATION COAL STOCKS...
BASIL'S GRANDAD
FREE issue OF SURPLUS EEC COLE To No 27 ARMPIT ROAD
MAD BONZO
MAD CACKLE!
BACCY
HURRY UP YOU LOT! WE'LL BE HERE ALL NIGHT AT THIS RATE!
THE GHASTLY CYNTHIA
CYNTHIA'S MINE (MINE, MINE, ALL MINE!)
SHE DOESN'T TAKE THE COAL OUT. SHE PUTS IT BACK IN
PET FERRET
MAD BONZO
GET A MOVE ON BABY BASIL! AS FAST AS WE'RE TRYIN' TO USE THE POWER STATION COAL STOCKS UP, THERE'S A CONVOY OF LORRIES ESCORTED BY TWO PANZER DIVISIONS BRINGIN' THE STUFF IN BY THE FRONT GATES!
LEAVE HIM ALONE! HE'S DOIN' HIS BEST!
BASIL'S BIG BROTHER WILLY
PUFF!
DON'T WORRY. PONGO'S GOT ASBESTOS PANTS ON
WHEEZE. GASP
STAGGER
OUR HERO, BABY BASIL

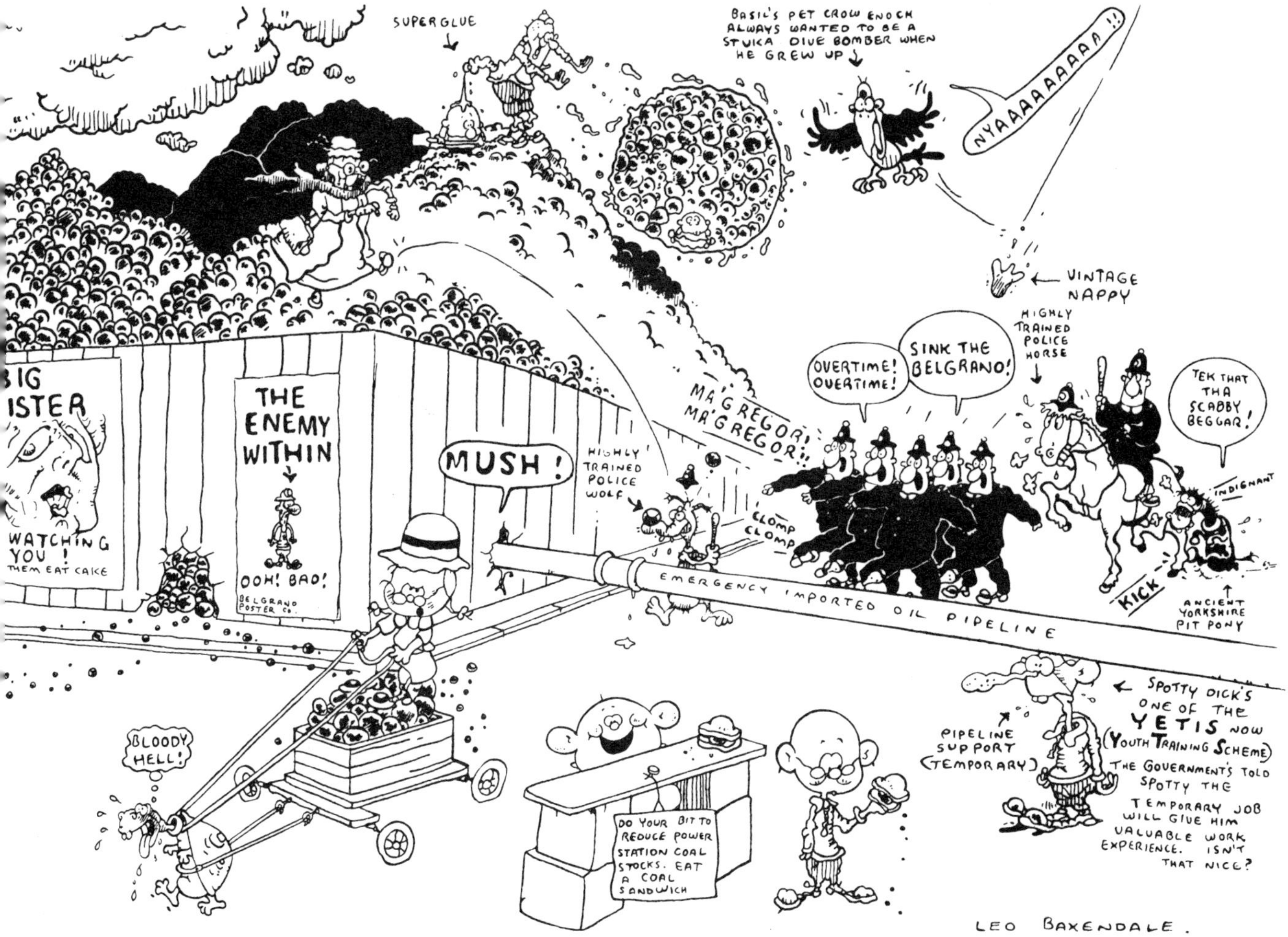
SUPERGLUE
BASIL'S PET CROW ENOCH ALWAYS WANTED TO BE A STUKA DIVE BOMBER WHEN HE GREW UP
NYAAAAAAAAAA!!
VINTAGE NAPPY
BIG SISTER WATCHING YOU! THEM EAT CAKE
THE ENEMY WITHIN
OOH! BAD!
BELGRANO POSTER CO.
MUSH!
HIGHLY TRAINED POLICE WOLF
MA'GREGOR! MA'GREGOR!
OVERTIME! OVERTIME!
SINK THE BELGRANO!
HIGHLY TRAINED POLICE HORSE
TEK THAT THA SCABBY BEGGAR!
CLOMP CLOMP
INDIGNANT
KICK
ANCIENT YORKSHIRE PIT PONY
EMERGENCY IMPORTED OIL PIPELINE
SPOTTY DICK'S ONE OF THE YETIS NOW (YOUTH TRAINING SCHEME) THE GOVERNMENT'S TOLD SPOTTY THE TEMPORARY JOB WILL GIVE HIM VALUABLE WORK EXPERIENCE. ISN'T THAT NICE?
PIPELINE SUPPORT (TEMPORARY)
BLOODY HELL!
DO YOUR BIT TO REDUCE POWER STATION COAL STOCKS. EAT A COAL SANDWICH
LEO BAXENDALE.

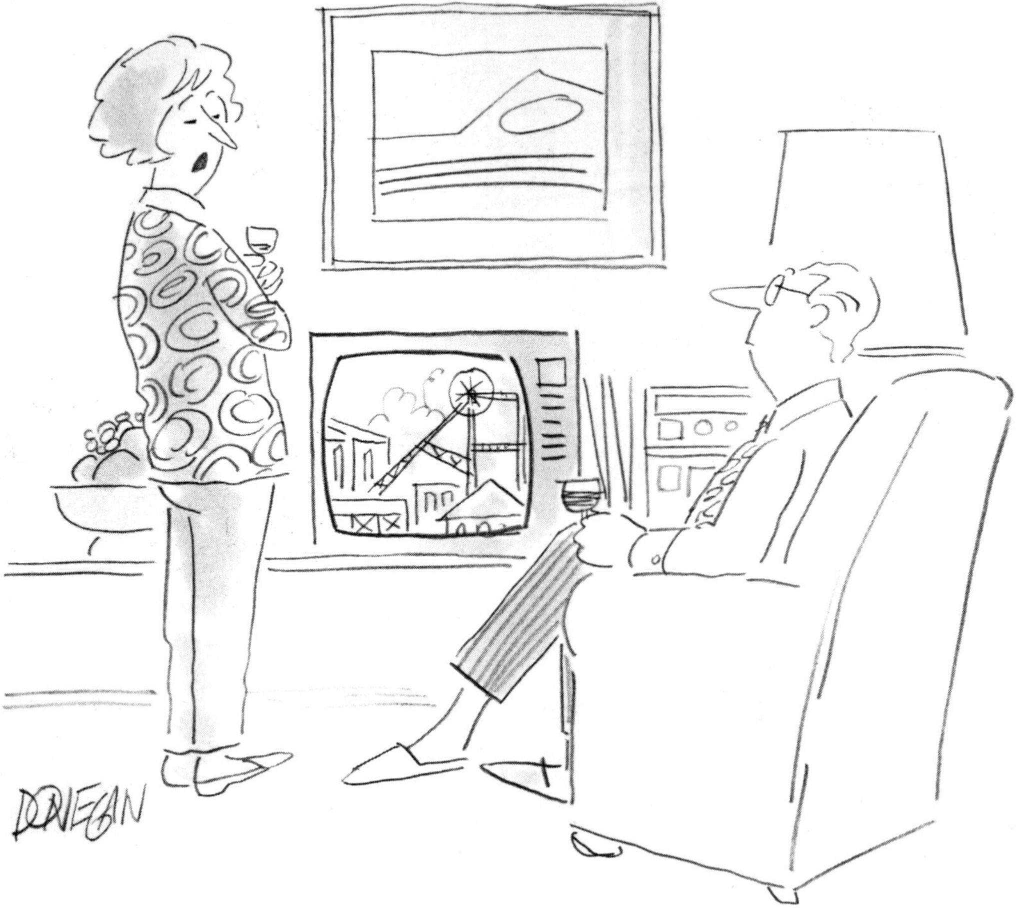
DONEGAN

'Why don't they close them *all* down? I mean, they don't look very nice, do they?'

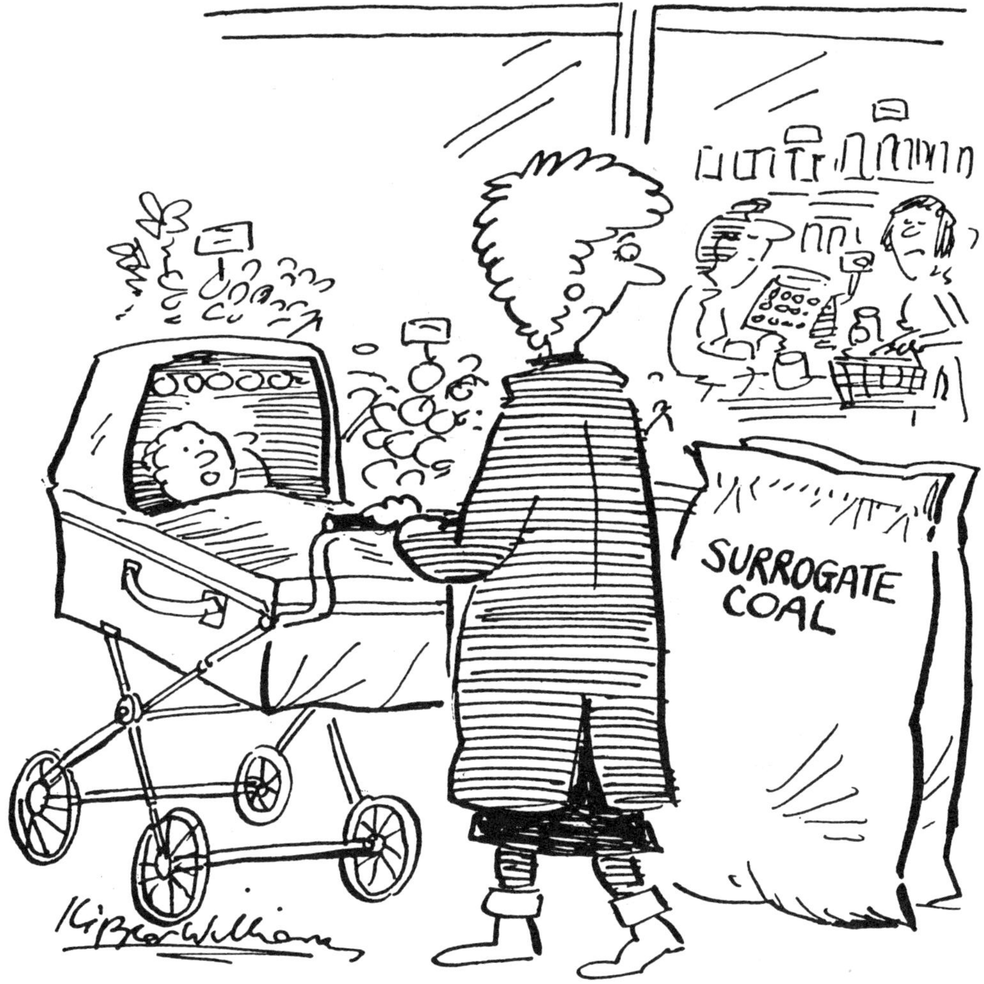
SURROGATE COAL
Kipper Williams

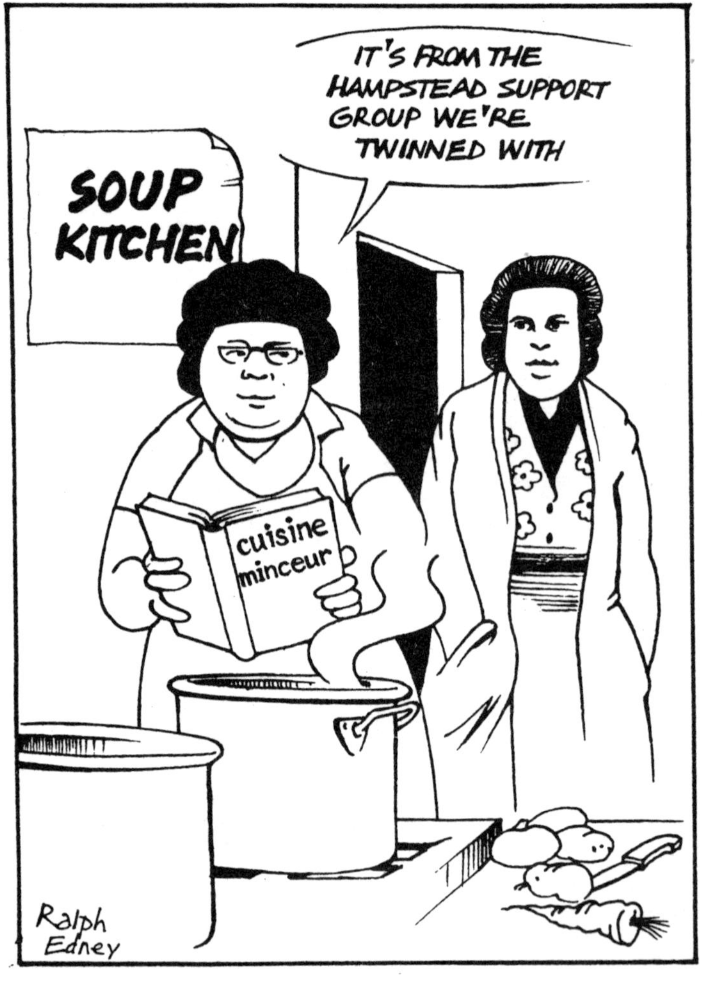
IT'S FROM THE HAMPSTEAD SUPPORT GROUP WE'RE TWINNED WITH
SOUP KITCHEN
cuisine minceur
Ralph Edney

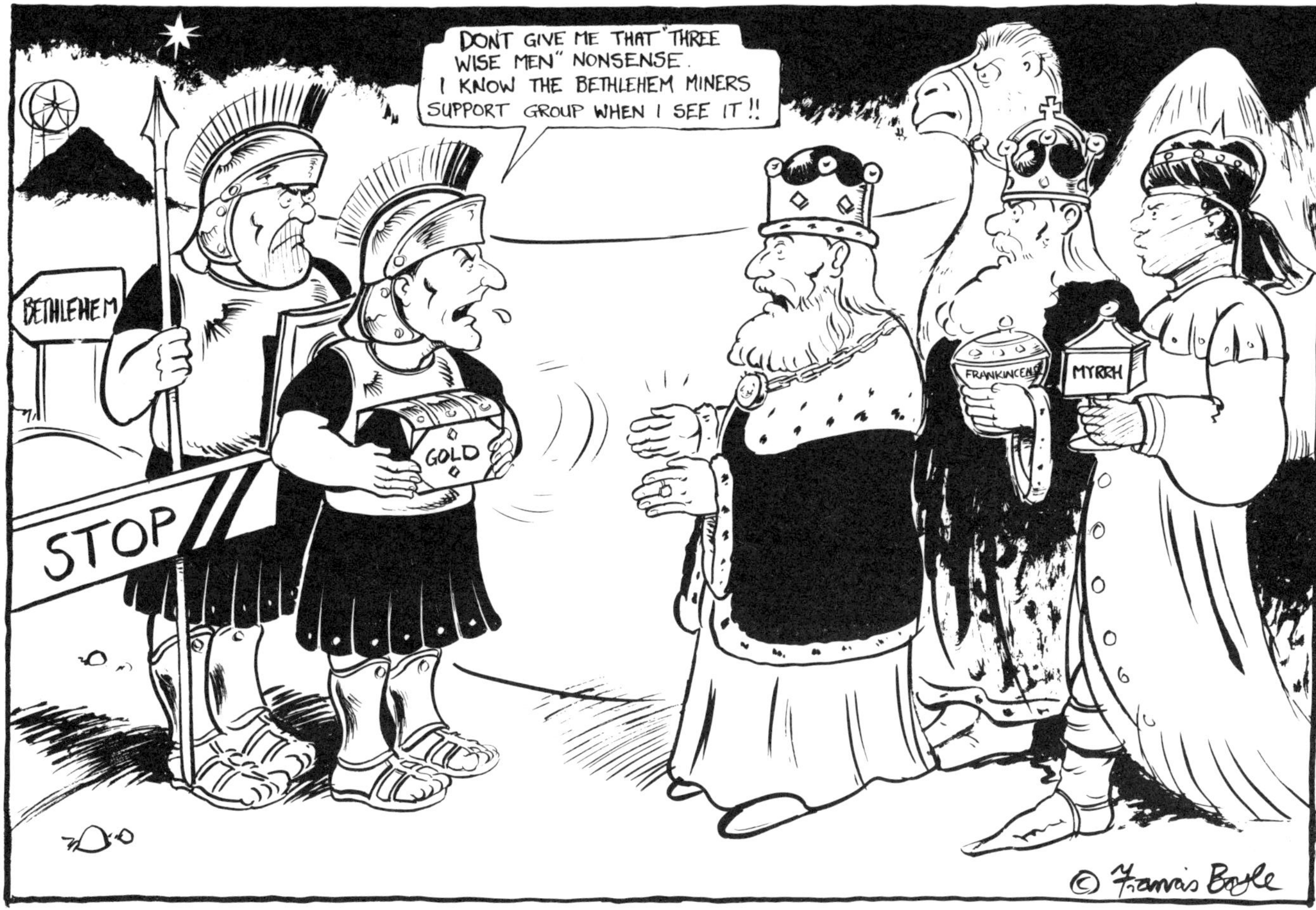
DON'T GIVE ME THAT "THREE WISE MEN" NONSENSE. I KNOW THE BETHLEHEM MINERS SUPPORT GROUP WHEN I SEE IT!!
BETHLEHEM
STOP
GOLD
FRANKINCENSE
MYRRH
© Francis Boyle

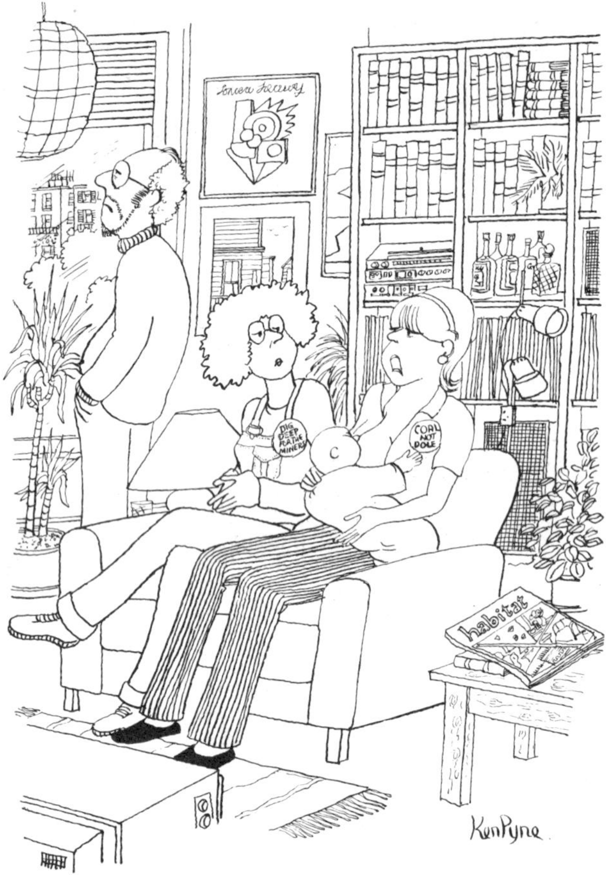
DIG DEEP FOR THE MINERS
COAL NOT DOLE
habitat
KenPyne

'Yes, we've made crippling sacrifices – we've stopped buying The *Guardian* and we're sending the money to the miners instead'

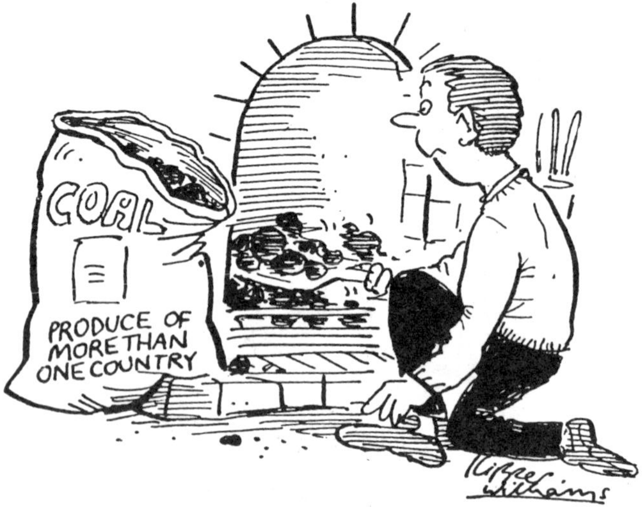
COAL
PRODUCE OF MORE THAN ONE COUNTRY

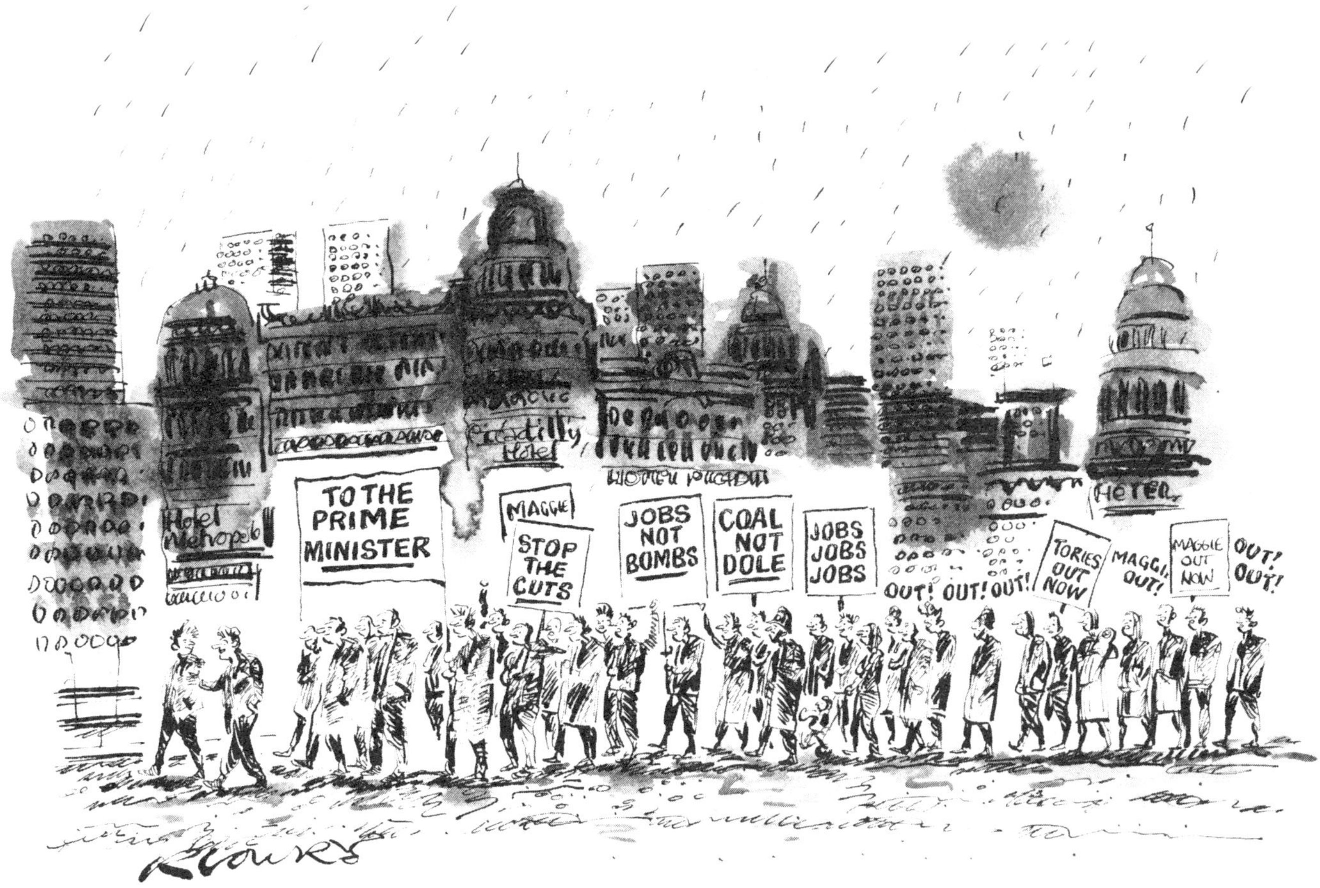
TO THE PRIME MINISTER
MAGGIE
STOP THE CUTS
JOBS NOT BOMBS
COAL NOT DOLE
JOBS JOBS JOBS
OUT! OUT! OUT!
TORIES OUT NOW
MAGGI OUT!
MAGGIE OUT NOW
OUT! OUT!
HOTEL

'It's a small business I started as a result of the government's exhortations – out of workograms'

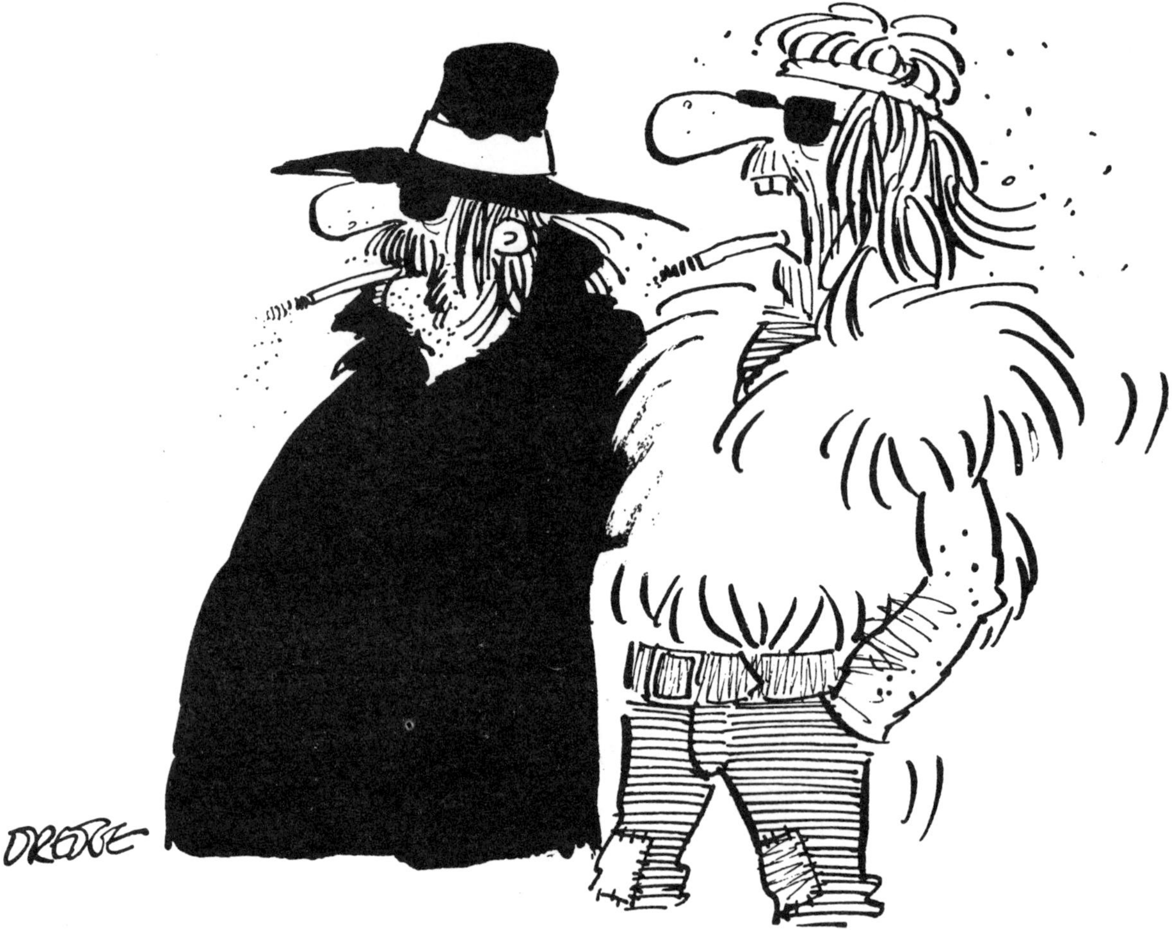
DREDGE

'Bad news man – I hear they're picketing the coke plant'

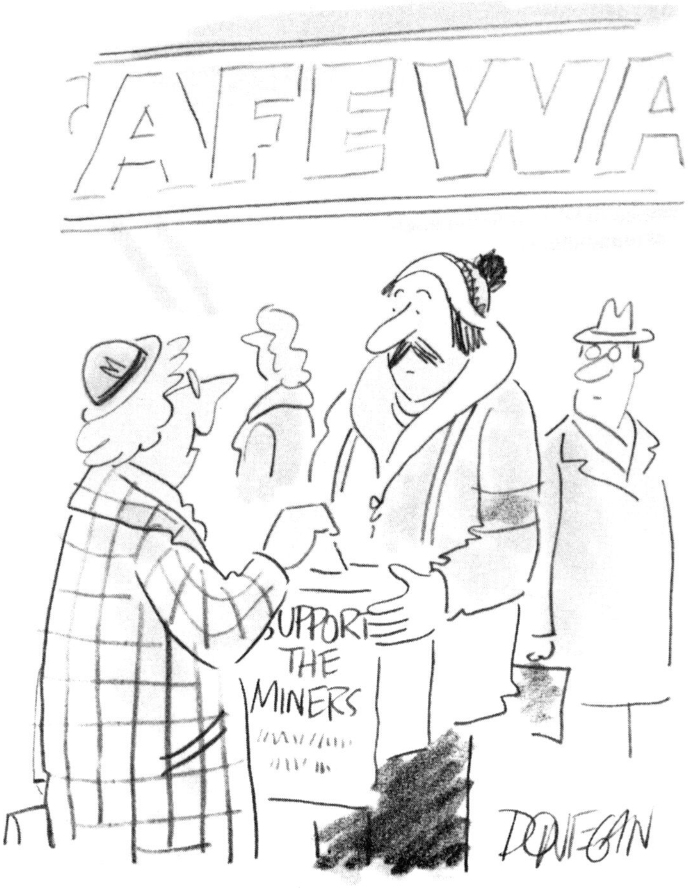
AFEWA
SUPPORT THE MINERS
DONEGAN

'. . . and there's a little something extra for your poor little pit ponies'

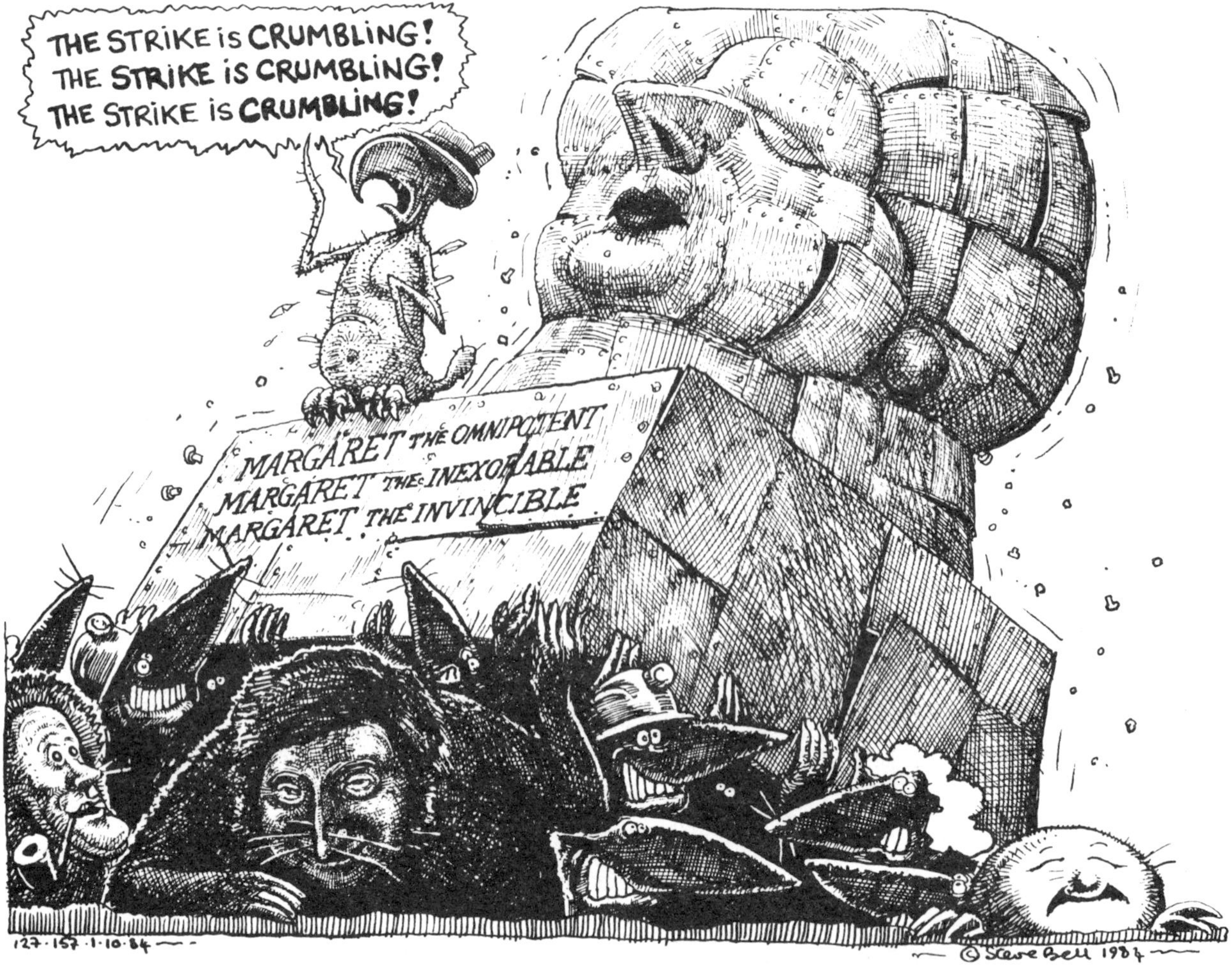
THE STRIKE is CRUMBLING!
THE STRIKE is CRUMBLING!
THE STRIKE is CRUMBLING!
MARGARET THE OMNIPOTENT
MARGARET THE INEXORABLE
MARGARET THE INVINCIBLE
127·157·1·10·84
© Steve Bell 1984

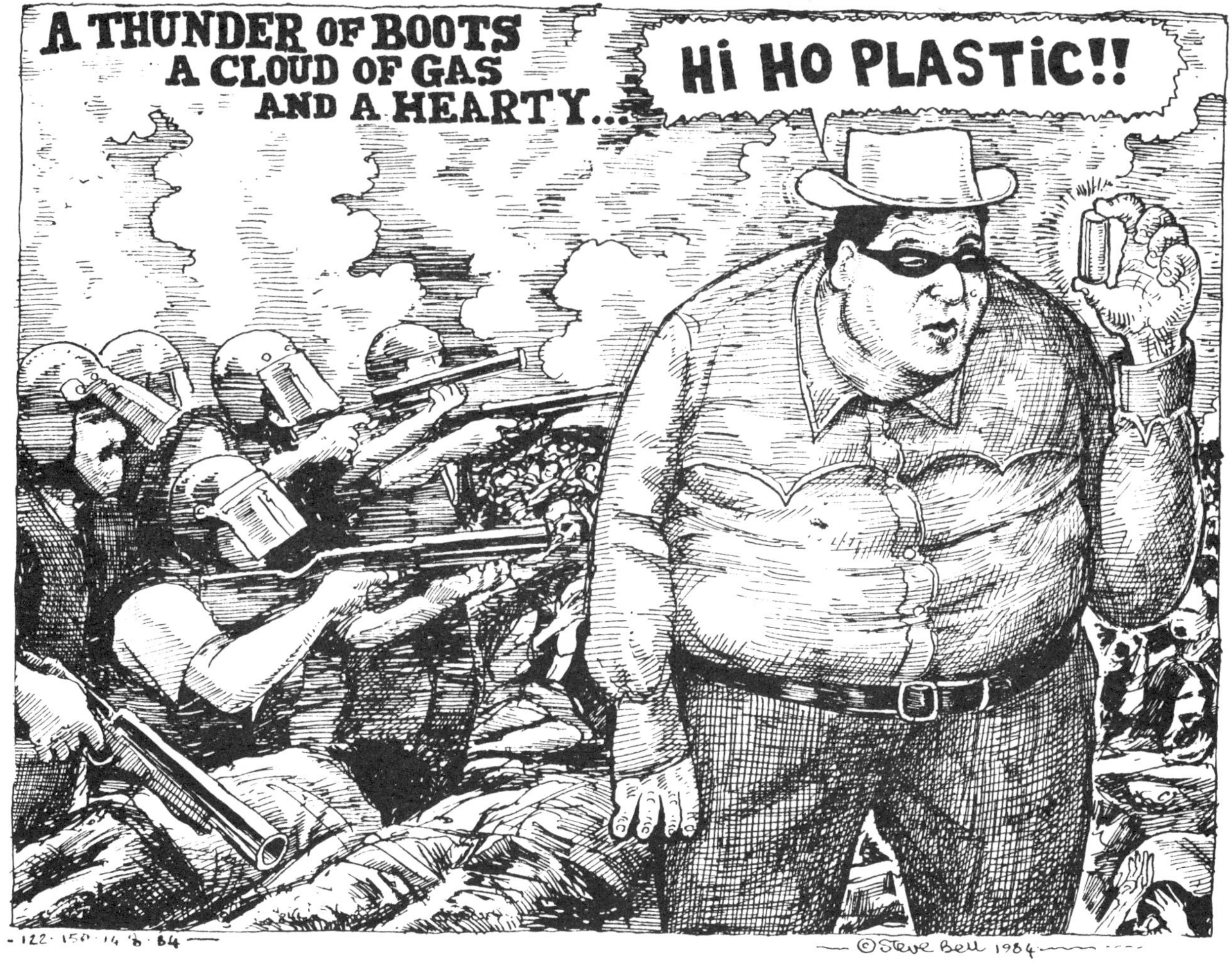
A THUNDER OF BOOTS
A CLOUD OF GAS
AND A HEARTY...
HI HO PLASTIC!!
122·150·14·8·84
©Steve Bell 1984

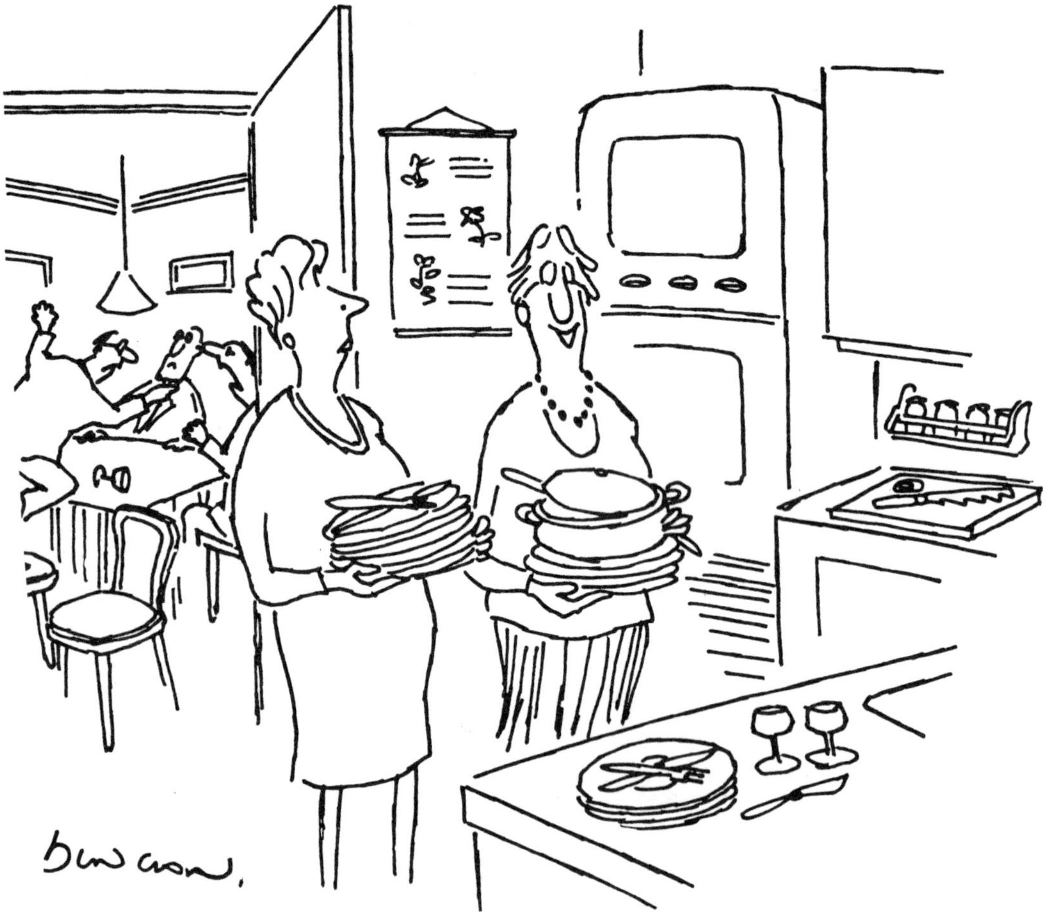

'I can't think what we used to discuss at dinner parties before the miners' strike'

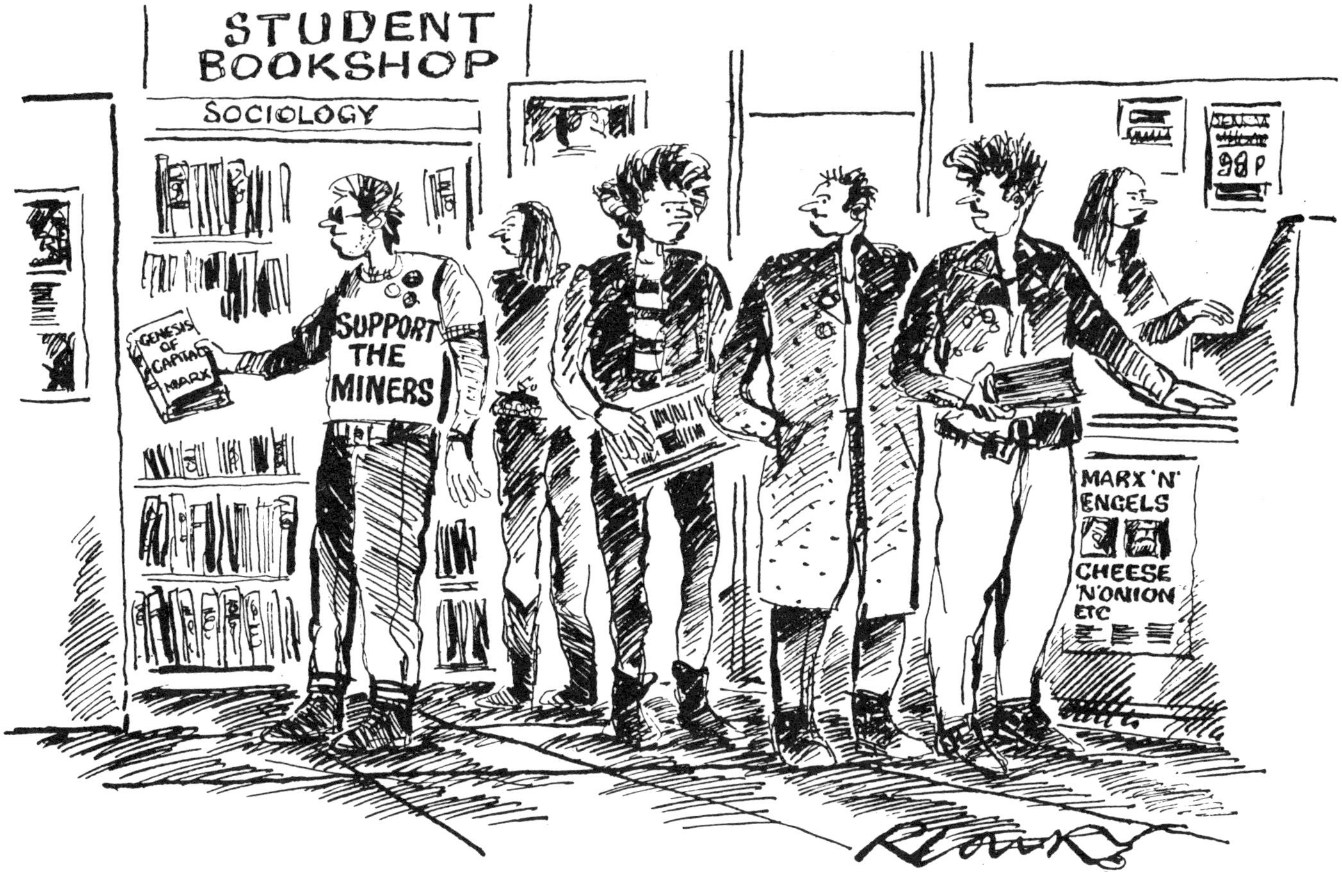
STUDENT BOOKSHOP
SOCIOLOGY
GENESIS OF CAPITAL MARX
SUPPORT THE MINERS
98P
MARX 'N' ENGELS
CHEESE 'N' ONION ETC

'It's his proleier than thou attitude I can't stand'

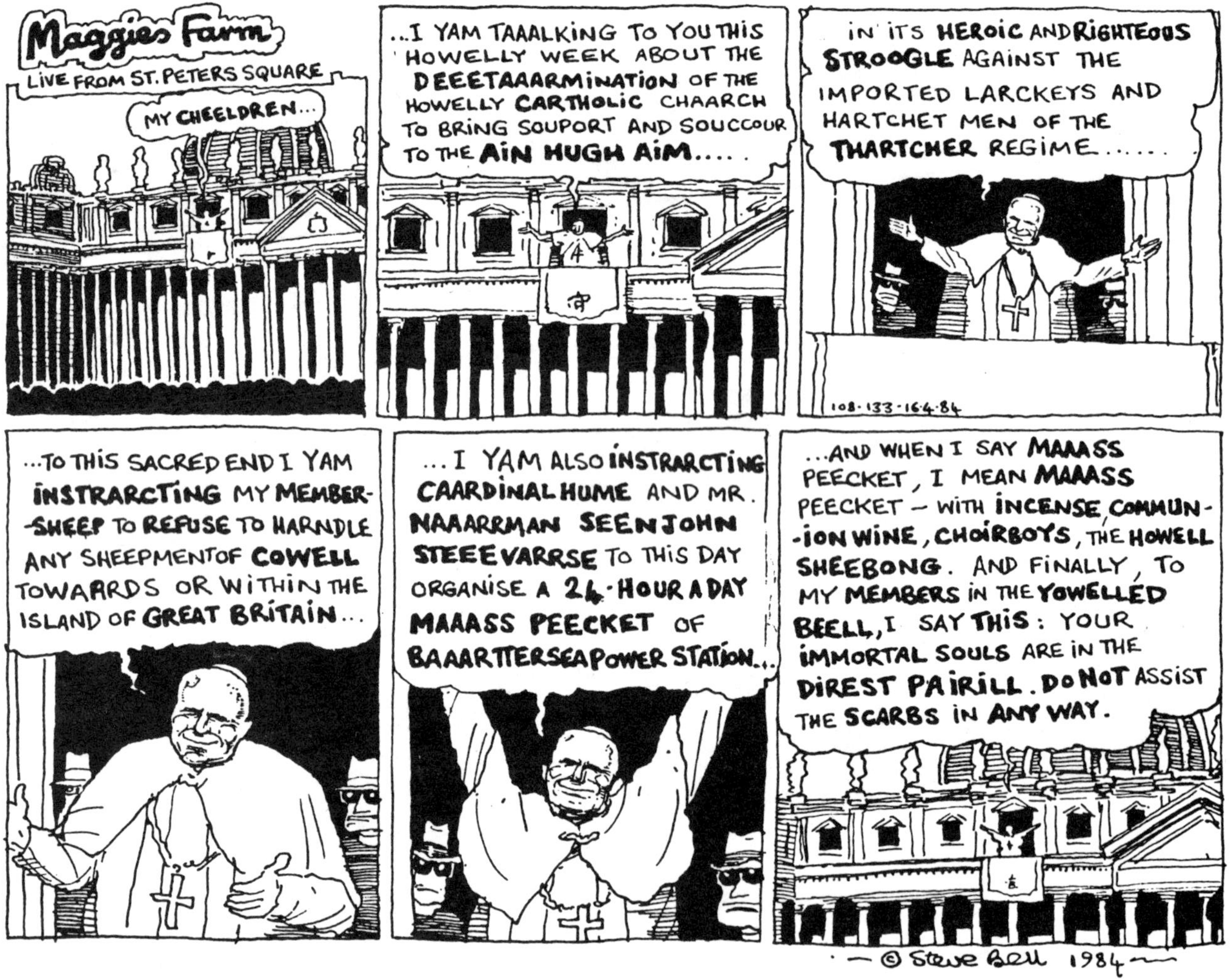
Maggies Farm
LIVE FROM ST. PETERS SQUARE
MY CHEELDREN...
...I YAM TAAALKING TO YOU THIS HOWELLY WEEK ABOUT THE DEEETAAARMINATION OF THE HOWELLY CARTHOLIC CHAARCH TO BRING SOUPORT AND SOUCCOUR TO THE AIN HUGH AIM.....
IN ITS HEROIC AND RIGHTEOUS STROOGLE AGAINST THE IMPORTED LARCKEYS AND HARTCHET MEN OF THE THARTCHER REGIME......
108-133-16-4-84
...TO THIS SACRED END I YAM INSTRARCTING MY MEMBER-SHEEP TO REFUSE TO HARNDLE ANY SHEEPMENT OF COWELL TOWARRDS OR WITHIN THE ISLAND OF GREAT BRITAIN...
...I YAM ALSO INSTRARCTING CAARDINAL HUME AND MR. NAAARRMAN SEEN JOHN STEEEVARRSE TO THIS DAY ORGANISE A 24-HOUR A DAY MAAASS PEECKET OF BAAARTTERSEA POWER STATION...
...AND WHEN I SAY MAAASS PEECKET, I MEAN MAAASS PEECKET - WITH INCENSE, COMMUN-ION WINE, CHOIRBOYS, THE HOWELL SHEEBONG. AND FINALLY, TO MY MEMBERS IN THE YOWELLED BEELL, I SAY THIS: YOUR IMMORTAL SOULS ARE IN THE DIREST PAIRILL. DO NOT ASSIST THE SCARBS IN ANY WAY.
© STEVE BELL 1984

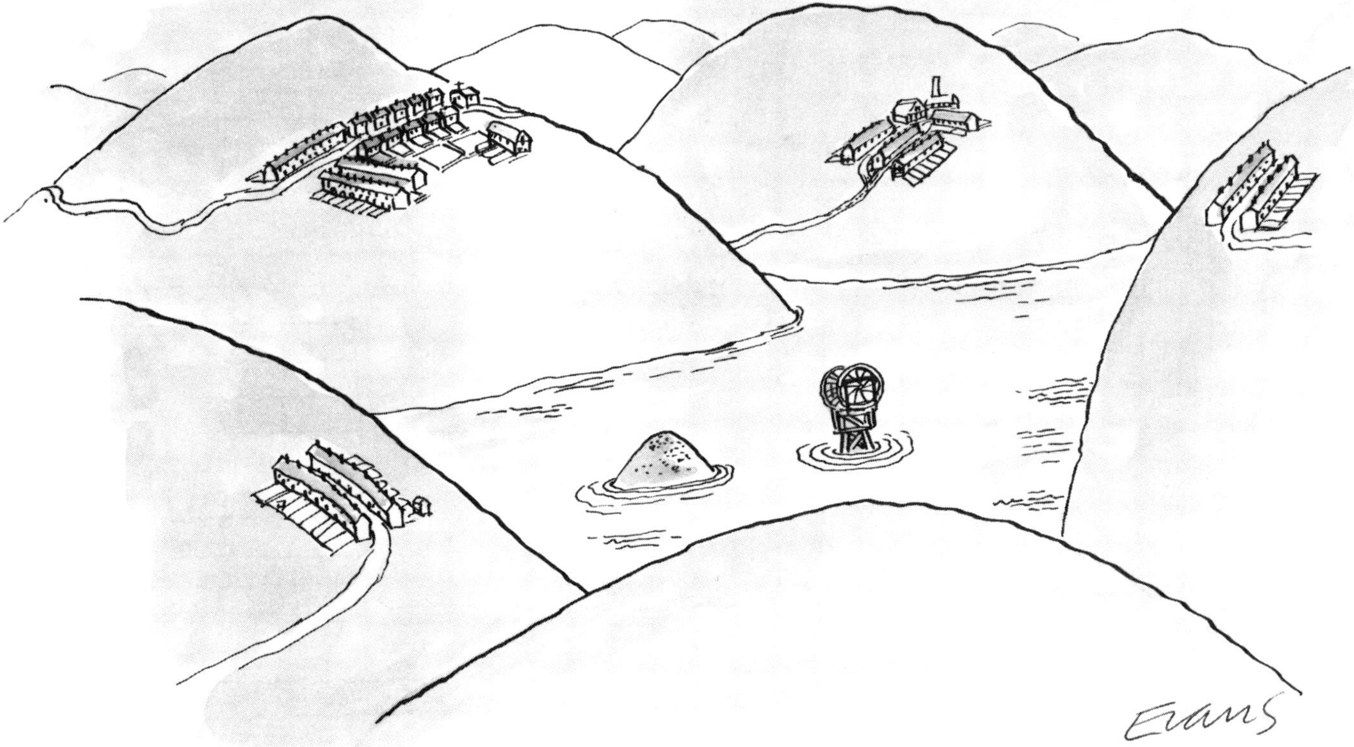
Evans

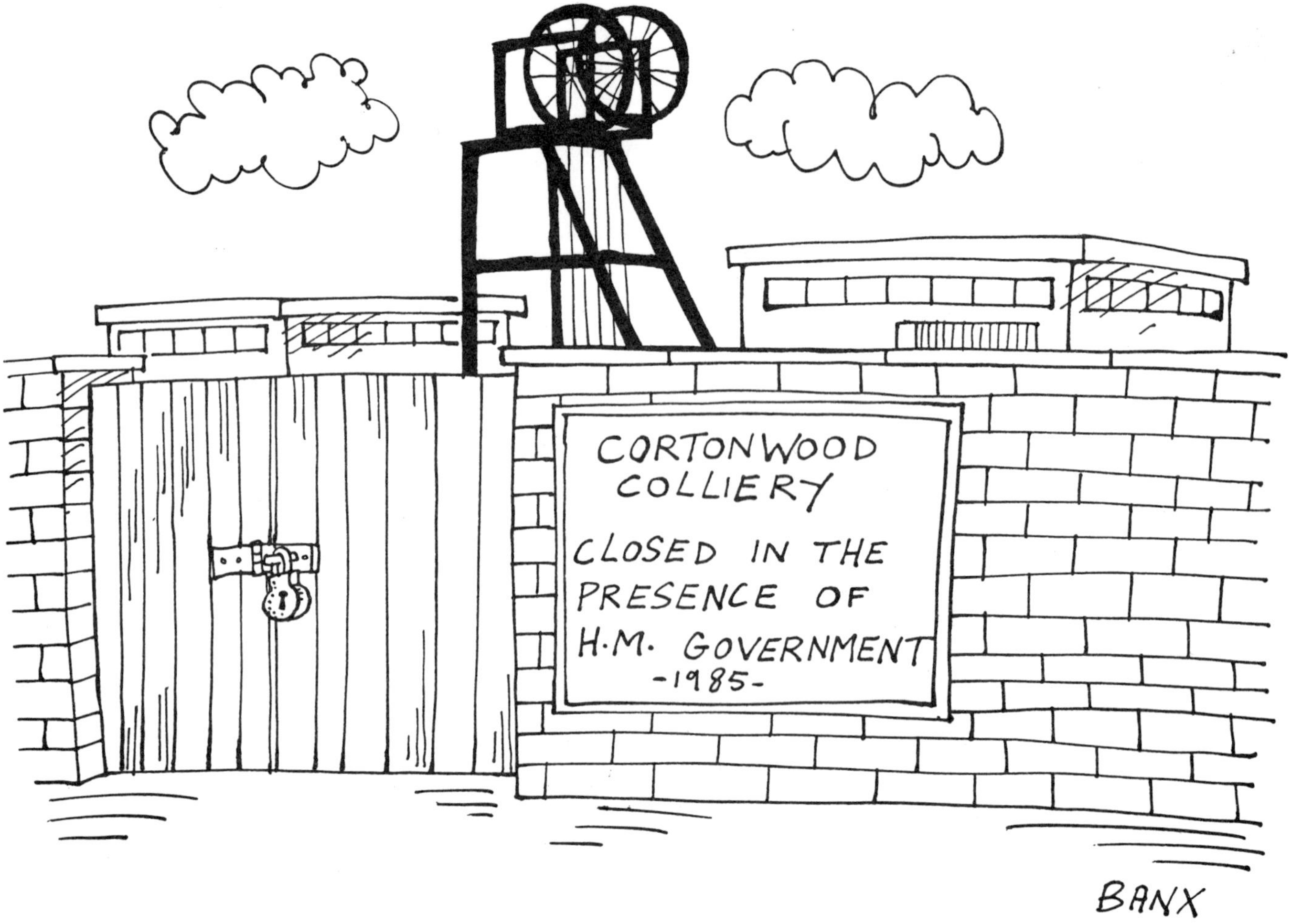
CORTONWOOD
COLLIERY
CLOSED IN THE
PRESENCE OF
H·M· GOVERNMENT
-1985-
BANX